Greenhill Books

FIGHTING THE
BREAKOUT

FIGHTING THE BREAKOUT

THE GERMAN ARMY IN NORMANDY
FROM 'COBRA' TO THE FALAISE GAP

by
Generalmajor Rudolf-Christoph Freiherr von Gersdorff (Chief of
Staff, German Seventh Army) and Generaloberst Paul Hausser
(Commander-in-Chief, German Seventh Army)

with
General der Artillerie Wilhelm Fahrmacher, General der
Panzertruppen Hans Eberbach and General Heinrich
Freiherr von Luettwitz

Edited by David C. Isby

Greenhill Books, London
Stackpole Books, Pennsylvania

Greenhill Books

This edition of
Fighting the Breakout:
The German Army in Normandy from 'Cobra' to the Falaise Gap
first published 2004 by
Greenhill Books, Lionel Leventhal Limited, Park House,
1 Russell Gardens, London NW11 9NN
www.greenhillbooks.com
and
Stackpole Books, 5067 Ritter Road, Mechanicsburg, PA 17055, USA

British Library Cataloguing in Publication Data
Fighting the breakout : the German Army in Normandy
from 'Cobra' to the Falaise Gap
1. Germany. Heer – History – World War, 1939–1945
2. World War, 1939–1945 – Campaigns – France – Normandy
3. World War, 1939–1945 – Personal narratives, German
I. Luettwitz, Freiherr von
II. Isby, David C.
940.5′42142

ISBN 1-85367-584-9

Designed and typeset by Roger Chesneau
Printed and bound in Great Britain by
MPG Books Limited, Bodmin, Cornwall

Contents

List of Illustrations

Introduction

This volume is the narrative, from the viewpoint of some German generals, of the climax of the Normandy campaign, from the US breakout in Operation "Cobra" on 25 July to the near-destruction of the German forces in the Falaise Gap by 20–21 August. Unlike the other collections of translated accounts concerning the German Army in Normandy and published by Greenhill, it is primarily the work of a single individual who had been one of the key participants—Baron von Gersdorff, who was then a colonel on the General Staff (Oberst i.G.), serving as Chief of Staff of the Seventh Army. His background as a thoroughly trained German staff officer is seen in his chapters, starting off with an estimate of the German situation, the Allied (enemy) situation, the terrain, and then a summary of the events.

Yet there is more to von Gersdorff than the summaries suggest. He had, in 1943, decided to act as a suicide bomber to kill Hitler, but had not had the opportunity. He had links to the 20 July conspiracy against Hitler, and throughout the operations described was in danger of arrest, torture, and summary execution. In attempting the break out through the Falaise Gap, he found himself to be a "Panzer leader," in command of a small but extremely well-armed and desperate combined-arms Kampfgruppe.

Each of the chapters by von Gersdorff is paired with one from the man who was his boss throughout most of the events described. General Paul Hausser was Commander-in-Chief of the Seventh Army from 29 July. Different politically and personally from von Gersdorff, Hausser was considered the "father of the Waffen SS," and his perceptions provide a contrast to the main narrative. Eberbach's chapter is included, in part, to provide greater depth regarding the activities of Fifth Panzer Army, on the British-Canadian front, whereas the focus of von Gersdorff and Hausser is primarily on the Seventh Army opposite the US forces.

While these documents are of great value, they must also be used with some care. They were written by participants—many of whom never wrote their memoirs or other accounts in any language—whose memories were still fresh, and their immediacy is not matched by attention to detail or their impartiality; for example, dates and locations are sometimes wrong or inconsistent. They were the first draft, not the last word, of the German assessment of the Normandy campaign. However, when compared with the German memoirs of the 1950s and 1960s that were translated into English—works which shaped the overall view of the war for many years, and which remain in print—these documents are no worse, and may be better.

These documents have been used as source material in all subsequent writing on Normandy, especially that in the English language. The potential value of a selection of these documents is suggested by their presence in the bibliographies of almost all the books that have appeared dealing with Normandy. They represent, together, a necessary source, but not a sufficient source.

The bottom line reached by the contributors to this book is not new or original. Because these accounts were the first postwar English language versions, and have been the most accessible to English-speaking historians, they have provided much of the accepted wisdom of the German view of Normandy. The authors had no knowledge of "Ultra," nor that the Allies had become proficient at decrypting their radio communications. The view that the German defeat in Normandy reflected Allied material superiority, air superiority, and the interference by Hitler and his favorite generals at high level became the standard presentation of the German view of their defeat for a generation. The significance of Allied airpower, both in the interdiction mission and over the battlefield, is repeated time and again in these documents. In part, it provides a palatable rationale for their defeat, allowing the authors to point at the absent Luftwaffe. That Allied material superiority should in the end prove decisive should not have come as a surprise to German officers, many of whom came of age at the first invention of the *Materialschlacht*—at Verdun in 1916. Today's readers are unlikely to accept this view at face value. Any general left alone with a typewriter to describe his war—especially a general who has lost his battles—is going to have a powerful impetus to exonerate himself (and those with whom he was associated) and put the blame elsewhere. In recent times, many military leaders have carried out these activities with much less excuse.

One of the values in relying on von Gersdorff and Hausser as providers of the primary narrative is that they provides a consistent view of the decisive battle as seen from Seventh Army Headquarters. Von Gersdorff's job, as Chief of Staff, was to try to make divisions move when and where the Army commander needed them to move. Any reader of his narratives will soon have an appreciation of how difficult this was. The narratives give a guided tour of Clausewitz's definition of friction at the operational level of war, as it appeared in a German Army Headquarters while it was losing a decisive battle. Some sixty years after these events, the tendency is to look on the movement of divisions as the arrows on a map or the shifting of cardboard counters in a wargame. Von Gersdorff shows not only the difficulty of the operational level of war, but the importance of the command and control mechanisms.

The translations vary. There is little attempt at consistency in matters such as grammar and capitalization or in the use of German or English-language terms and abbreviations. Even the efficient staff officer von Gersdorff divides up his chapters in different ways for no compelling reason.

In order to assist the reader, every effort has been made to correct the spellings of the placenames referred to by the authors of the accounts which follow. However, many of the references are ambiguous, and a few defy identification. In these instances, an editorial mark in square brackets has been inserted into the text.

David C. Isby
Washington, DC

The Contributors

General der Panzertruppen Hans Eberbach Commanded Panzer divisions and Corps on the Eastern Front. On Staff of Army Group B on D-Day. Commander Panzer Group West (later Fifth Panzer Army) starting 3 August 1944. On 5 August 1944 was Commander Fifth Panzer Army, and subsequently Commander Panzer Group Eberbach. On 22 August 1944 was given command of Seventh Army (placed under Fifth Panzer Army). Captured by British troops August 1944.

General der Artillerie Wilhelm Fahrmacher Commanding General XXV Corps in Brittany from 1942 until the end of the war (holding out in Festung Lorient). Commanded LXXXIV Corps in Normandy from 12 to 18 June after the death of General Marcks. Previously commanded 5th Infantry Division in Poland and France, and VII Corps in 1940–42. After the war, turned over to the French by the Americans. PoW until 1950 (not prosecuted for war crimes). Military advisor to Egyptian Army 1951–58.

Generalmajor Rudolf-Christoph Freiherr von Gersdorff As an Oberst i.G., von Gersdorff took over as Chief of Staff Seventh Army at end of July 1944, replacing Generalleutnant Max Pemsel. He was previously intelligence chief of Army Group Center on the Eastern Front. In this role, he joined with Oberst Henning von Tresckow in an anti-Hitler conspiracy. On 21 March 1943 he volunteered to act as a suicide bomber to kill Hitler in Berlin. He did not get within lethal range but managed to defuse the grenades before detonation.

Generaloberst Paul Hausser Commander-in-Chief Seventh Army 29 June–20 August 1944, taking over when Generaloberst Friedrich Dollmann died of a heart attack. A Waffen-SS officer (formerly an Army General), instrumental in forming that force. Considered politically reliable by Hitler, unlike von Kluge and von Gersdorff. Extensive combat in the east. Commanded II SS-Panzer Corps before appointment (opposed by both von Rundstedt and Rommel) to Seventh Army.

General der Panzertruppen Heinrich Freiherr von Luettwitz Commanding General 2nd Panzer Division. Wounded in the Falaise Pocket. Escaped, commanded a corps during the Ardennes offensive. Holder of the Knight's Cross with Oakleaves and Swords.

Sources

Photographs
All photographs not otherwise indicated as having other sources have been lent from the collection of Steven Zaloga, who also wrote their captions.

Maps
Unfortunately, few of the maps and sketches included with the original reports are suitable for reproduction. As substitutes, therefore, the maps in this book are from published sources, each being identified below by a bracketed number .

Unpublished maps
German 1:200,000 series, 1941. (Held at Library of Congress, Washington DC: G5830S 200.G41. Source of map pp. 234–5.)
German 1:80,000 series, 1941. (Held at Library of Congress, Washington DC: G5830S 80.G41. Source of map p. 240.)
US Army Mapping Service, M661 series, 1944 . (Held at: Library of Congress, Washington DC: G5830S 100.U5. Source of maps pp. 50–1, 92–3.)

Published maps
Martin Blumenson, *Breakout and Pursuit*, US Army Center for Military History, Washington, 1961, GPO. (Source of maps pp. 26, 28, 32, 40, 111, 127, 130, 152, 164, 188, 208.)
William M. Hammond, *Normandy. Vol. 18:The US Army Campaigns of World War II*, US Army Center for Military History, Washington, 1992, GPO. (Source of maps pp. 22, 40.)
David W. Hogan, *Northern France. Vol. 30: The US Army Campaigns of World War II*, US Army Center for Military History, Washington, 1992, GPO. (Source of map p. 168.)
T. Dodson Stamps and Vincent J. Esposito (eds.), *A Military History of World War II*, US Military Academy, West Point, 1953. (Source of map p. 106.)
US Army Twelth Army Group/First Army, *An Operational Report: After Action Reports, Vols 1–14*, n.d. (Source of maps pp. 58, 60.)
US Army XX Corps, *An Operational Report.Vol.1: The Campaigns of Normandy and France, 1 August – 1 September 1944*, n.d. (Source of map p. 138.)

Text
All the essays are from Foreign Military Studies, RG 338, US National Archives. The reports that were the original sources of the essays are identified in the chapter bylines, and are listed on pp.251–2 of this book.

PART ONE

Despite the fall of St-Lô—the exit point from the dense and highly defensible terrain of the Normandy bocage—to US forces on 18 July, the bulk of the German Army's Panzer divisions were still opposite the British sector, south of Caen. Caen had fallen on 10 July, in Operation "Charnwood," but the next major British thrust, Operation "Goodwood," on 18 July, was met with superb defensive fighting by the outnumbered German forces. The decisive breakout from Normandy would not start south of Caen. However, that was where the German attention remained concentrated.

In many ways, Normandy had, since D-Day, become a battle of attrition, in which Allied material superiority was brought to bear. It was also a meeting engagement, and the Allies' control of the sea, and their ability to bring supplies across the beaches as well as through the repaired port of Cherbourg, meant that they were able to get more troops and resources to the battlefield than the Germans. Much of the German Army still remained in coastal defense positions, concerned about another Allied amphibious invasion. The Allied airborne forces that had airdropped on D-Day had been withdrawn to Britain, and the Germans also had to guard against them.

On 20 July, Hitler had survived an assassination attempt by German officers at the "Wolf's Lair," the forward command post in East Prussia. The conspiracy was brutally surpressed. Hitler's suspicion of the military leadership—especially in the Army—and faith in his own invincibility were both increased by the events of that day.

The Germans had, since D-Day, a copy of US pre-invasion plans in their possession. They knew that Patton's Third Army—not yet operational—was to go westward from Avranches to take the Brittany ports, protected by Hodges' First Army. They would then wheel on the right of the British and Canadian armies south of Caen, and then advance jointly to the Seine.

15

Chapter 1

The Situation Prior to 25 July

by Generalmajor Rudolf-Christoph Freiherr von Gersdorff
Translated by H. Wollner (B-722)

The campaign in northern France began on 25 July 1944 with the start of the American offensive in the St-Lô area, which changed a war of position for the Normandy bridgehead into a war of movement for France, and ended on 14 September 1944 when the Allied major offensive came to a temporary standstill in Holland/Belgium, before the West Wall, and in the larger Metz area.

The Normandy battle, which had preceded the campaign in northern France, had achieved the first objective which the Allied command had set for itself in the invasion of the European mainland, namely, the establishment of a bridgehead large enough to permit the concentration and supply of the troops necessary for the European campaign. Though the attainment of this objective had taken considerably longer than had originally been estimated, the battles in Normandy had nevertheless given the Allied command the advantage of exposing the weak points of the German command and troops, of pinning down the bulk of the available German reserves, of greatly weakening the German forces, which were handicapped by personnel and matériel shortages, and, finally, of providing combat experience for the Allied troops.

I

During the battle in Normandy, the German Supreme Command was compelled to let the enemy determine the pace of action. The chance which offered itself during the battle to Supreme Command—to daringly put everything on one card and to conduct a decisive counteroffensive without regard for flanks or possible frontal gaps, in accordance with tested German principles of command—had irredeemably been missed. Because of the fear of additional Allied landing operations along other coastal sectors, and also because the enemy had been underrated, the German reserves had, at first, been brought forward only in a dilatory manner and, consequently, too slowly, as well as in numbers which were too small, and at intervals which were too far apart, so that it was impossible either to achieve a superiority in defense, or to assemble sufficient forces for the purpose of conducting any promising counterdrives. Our sole aim was to establish a connected front of the World War I type without employing the methods of modern mobile warfare which had brought the great successes in World War II.

When all scattered attempts at offensive action—undertaken, as they had been, with forces which were too weak and inadequately supported—had been shattered by the Allied superiority in the air and on the ground, the German Command allowed itself to be forced

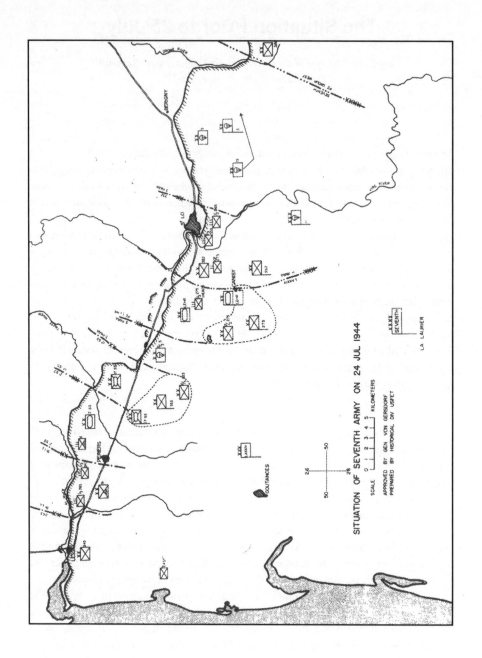

SITUATION OF SEVENTH ARMY ON 24 JUL. 1944

SCALE 0 1 2 3 4 5 KILOMETERS

APPROVED BY GEN VON GERSDORF
PREPARED BY HISTORICAL DIV USFET

onto the defensive and confined itself to "filling the holes" with the new forces (which were approaching only at a dragging pace) and preventing strategic enemy penetrations. During this immobile defensive combat in a battle of attrition, the German troops, who were inferior with regard to material, became more and more exhausted. The inadequate replacement of troops and material at the front which blocked the Allied bridgehead brought about a constant thinning of the front, so that it became purely a matter of arithmetic to figure out when this front would break up. Therefore, without the possibility of bringing forward strong reserves and strong air force units, only the decision to abandon the largest part of France and to withdraw beyond the Seine and Yonne could still have averted an otherwise certain catastrophe, and, in view of the shorter fronts, could have made it possible to release sufficient forces for offensive and flexible countermeasures. Inasmuch as it was impossible for the German Supreme Command to come to such a difficult decision because of inner political and foreign policy reasons, it was obvious to the local command that a strategic Allied breakthrough, and, with it, the destruction of the bulk of the German forces in the west, had to be expected. Despite a frank and lucid estimate of the situation by the High Command of the German forces in the west, Supreme Command did not alter its decisions, though the overall situation was so obvious that no realistically thinking person could entertain any doubts. However, Supreme Command deceived itself and the German people with its belief in Providence. The overriding principle of command remained: "We'll manage somehow."

II

The bulk of the German forces in the west had been no match for the demands made in every aspect of the decisive battle against the most modern opponent in World War II. As an explanation, the following reasons are cited:

1. The operations staffs (Army, Corps, and Division) consisted in part of over-age officers who were not accustomed to combat. The personnel requirements of the Eastern and Southern Fronts had used up the best personnel, so that the best choice of officers was often no longer represented at the Western Front. The following will serve as a glaring example: The Staff of Seventh Army, which, in matters of command, was to bear the entire burden of the defense against the invasion, had no war or combat experience of any kind, except for the crossing of the Rhine in 1940. The rejuvenation and reformation of the staffs, which was undertaken in the beginning of 1944, could not take sufficient effect in the short period before the invasion.

2. The overwhelming majority of the German infantry divisions were so-called static divisions, formed from training units and coast defense units. Aside from the inferior quality of the personnel (men who were sick, personnel unable to perform field duties on the Eastern Front, older age groups, fathers of large families, unreliable foreign nationals), the matériel and equipment were so inadequate that these units were unfit for mobile warfare. The following illustration will also serve as a particularly glaring example: The artillery regiments of the static divisions did not have available a full complement of draft horses, but were only able to move one battalion at a time with the aid of horse-team units. Some of the units were equipped

only with the obsolete MG 08/15 and with various mixed weapons of foreign manufacture, and had a correspondingly inadequate supply of ammunition and spare parts. Most importantly, however, the antitank and antiaircraft equipment was utterly inadequate, obsolete and unsuited to large-scale combat. When these units were forced out of the fortified installations of the Atlantic Wall and had to fight in open terrain, their actual combat value proved to be very limited.

In some cases, the German units whose personnel and matériel were good (Panzer, Panzer Grenadier, and Fallschirm Jaeger divisions) had the disadvantage of having only very recently been organized or reformed. On the whole, all these units were wasted one by one in unfeasible missions because of their inappropriate commitment by Supreme Command.

3. The German Air Force was out of the picture from the very start, and, during the entire battle in the west, was never able to play even a modest defensive role. The consequent mastery of the air on the Allied side created such unequal combat conditions for the ground forces that it must be considered the main reason for the steadily increasing, decided superiority of the Allied forces. Since all tactical movements and supply activities could take place only during the hours of darkness, all German measures were characterized by the fact that they were "too late." Being without sufficient active and passive air defense, the German troops were faced with an additional burden, which, considering the other disadvantages mentioned above, had a decisive effect.

4. The Atlantic Wall, which had, of course, been particularly neglected at the actual invasion front, proved incapable of standing up to modern Allied attack weapons. Because of its inadequate construction and insufficient depth, it did not develop into the important obstacle it had been expected to become. However, in view of the Atlantic Wall, and the decision to make a determined defense there, the German command had omitted to construct and prepare positions in the rear and lines of resistance in the depth of the German defense of the continent.

5. Aside from the severe damage inflicted on the entire German supply [system] as a result of Allied air superiority, the system did not measure up to the requirements of modern large-scale combat. Supplies were stored in too centralized and concentrated a manner, on account of lack of space and transportation facilities, and, for the same reasons, could not be decentralized or shifted in accordance with the demands of the situation. The German armed forces in the west, therefore, suffered supply difficulties during the entire battle in France, which more or less affected almost every field, primarily in regard to ammunition, fuel, and spare parts. Of course, in this connection, too, the general effects of the shortages which troubled Germany during the fifth year of the war played a decisive role. The supply of tanks, antitank weapons, and all other weapons could never—not even approximately— cover the requirements or replace the losses incurred in action.

7. OB West, the highest military command at the Western Front, had no authority over all the armed forces (Wehrmachtbefugnisse), so that collaboration between the Army, the Luftwaffe, and the Navy necessarily remained inadequate.

III

Besides the three infantry divisions (716, 352, 709) which had originally been employed at the invasion front during the battle in Normandy, an additional eight infantry divisions, two Fallschirm Jaeger divisions, combat groups drawn from three infantry and one Fallschirm Jaeger division, as well as nine Panzer divisions and one Panzer Grenadier division, were also involved. A large part of all the available reserves had thus already been committed. As a result, the German forces in southern France and Brittany had been weakened to such a degree that Army Group Blaskowitz and XXV Infantry Corps could not possibly give up any additional forces without stripping their coastal sectors and ports to such an extent as to be unable to conduct a successful defense. On the other hand, the forces of the Fifteenth Army and of the military district of Holland had, thus far, been drained comparatively little: on the contrary, Supreme Command, in anticipation of a new invasion between the Somme and the Seine, transferred two additional infantry divisions (271 and 272) from southern France to the Rouen area, in order to assemble strong reserves in the rear of the left wing of the Fifteenth Army. 9 and 11 Pz. Divs, which had completed their rehabilitation in southern France, were the only mobile units still available. The removal of these units to the invasion front naturally implied that the weak forces occupying the Mediterranean coast would not be able to conduct a successful defense against the invasion from North Africa, which was expected with certainty. (After the American breakthrough at St. Lô, 9 Pz. Div. and 708 Inf. Div. were, nevertheless, removed from southern France). Two additional divisions (89 and 363) were, at the time, in the process of approaching the invasion front from other theaters of operation. The reorganization of 6 Fallsch. Jg. Div. was completed in central France. In view of the development of the situation, the command decided, after all, to remove at first five additional infantry divisions (84, 85, 331, 344, and 17 Lw. Field) from northern France and Belgium, and order, or plan, their departure to the invasion front. These forces, however, because of a lack of transportation facilities and because of enemy air superiority, were not expected to arrive at the scene of battle before the beginning or middle of August.

Apart from the eight or nine divisions already mentioned, the German command was able to resort to five additional infantry divisions (47th, 49th, 348th, 347th, and 18th Luftwaffe Field) by almost entirely stripping the coasts of northern France, Belgium, and Holland. However, in this connection, it must again be emphasized that the majority of these units were static coastal divisions that had been made mobile by improvised measures. The local command at the invasion front had available only the following strategic reserves on 24 July, which were all located in the rear of the center of the Panzer Gruppe West: 2nd, 116th and 9th SS-Panzer Divisions. However, the command, with great difficulties, had been able to procure local tactical reserves (for instance, the 275th and 353rd Infantry Divisions).

IV

The condition of the German units fighting at the invasion front had grown steadily worse during the severe battles in Normandy. Four infantry divisions (16 Lw. Field, 77, 709, 716) had to be considered annihilated. Five additional units (5 FS Jg. Division, and 91, 243, 352,

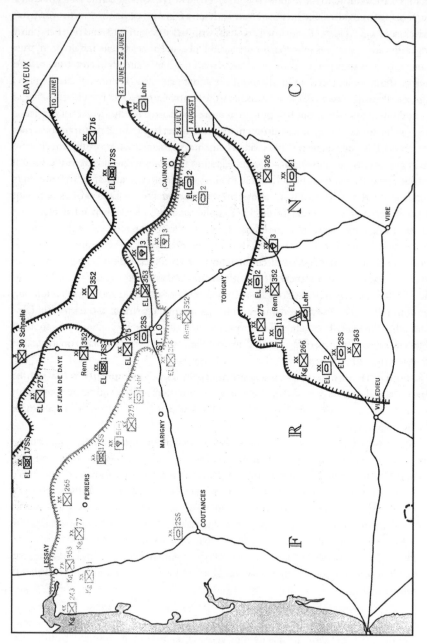

Seventh Army front, 10 June–1 August.

and 353 Inf. Divs) as well as 17 SS-Pz. Gren. Div., were so badly worn out that their fighting qualities were reduced to those of weak combat groups. The same was true concerning the regiments from the Brittany divisions that had been committed on the Normandy front (265, 266, 343, 2 FS Jg.). All the other units had suffered so severely in regard to personnel and equipment that the incurred losses could not even nearly be replaced. In this connection, it is important to note that almost all the annihilated and seriously mauled German units had been committed against the American invasion army.

Apart from the symptoms of exhaustion displayed by the troops as a result of weeks and months of uninterrupted commitment along the front, the inferiority in matériel and, most of all, the enemy's air superiority, brought about a decline of the fighting spirit here and there. In any case, considering the described combat conditions, it is impossible to compare these troops with the German attack units of 1939 to 1942, or even with the divisions still committed on the Eastern Front in 1944. This does not preclude the fact that the units employed on the Western Front, above all the Pz. and FS. Jg. Divs, in view of their composition in respect of personnel, accomplished most excellent combat feats and displayed a maximum devotion to duty and readiness for combat.

The Tactical Situation in the St-Lô Area
Prior to the American Offensive
a. Estimation of the Enemy's Tactical Situation

On 24 July 1944, the 21 German units at full strength (nine infantry, two FS Jg., nine Pz., and one Pz. Gren. division) which were committed at the blocking front, were facing a total of 30 Allied units (13 American and 11 British infantry divisions, as well as 3 American and 3 British armored divisions).

However, apart from the fact that six of the German divisions could only be regarded as weak combat groups, it should be pointed out that the Allied units were not only quantitatively far superior with regard to personnel and matériel, but were generally also far superior with regard to quality, so that the ratio of strength, aside from the purely numerical factor, continued to develop to our disadvantage. The enemy had an overwhelming superiority, especially with regard to all supporting forces (air force, GHQ troops). Furthermore, it should be mentioned that the Allies were able to rely on a safe supply service that was unhampered by enemy activity, while the German supply service was utterly inadequate, because of the general shortcomings and enemy air activity. All in all, therefore, there was such an overwhelming superiority on the Allied side, that, for that reason alone, the German forces were finally capable only of defensive combat.

The difference between the numbers of known American and British units already indicated that the point of main effort of the Allied command was unmistakably located in the American invasion sector. This was still more evident from the formation of the Allied forces. On both sides of St-Lô, along a relatively narrow width, eight American infantry and two American armored divisions—amounting to two-thirds of the American, and one-third of the entire invasion army—were assembled, so it became clearly evident that the point of main effort was definitely developing there. The expected employment of the US Third Army (Gen. Patton), detected by German reconnaissance, also gave rise to the conclusion that the Allied command planned special operations in that area. Finally, the enemy's intentions were also known from documents—orders for the US V and VII Corps—captured at the beginning of the invasion. Even though the enemy's timetable had been thoroughly frustrated, the overall operations had generally proceeded according to plan. Consequently, there was no reason to assume that the Supreme Allied Command would make any basic changes in the strategic plans. On the contrary, all indications pointed to the fact that, after the mopping-up operations in the Cotentin peninsula, and after the completed assembly of sufficient forces, the second phase of the Allied operations, namely, the breakthrough from the western section of the Normandy bridgehead toward the south into the interior of France, or the penetration, at first, of some elements into Brittany, would begin at any moment. Increased enemy sea and air reconnaissance at the western coast of the Cotentin peninsula, the northern coast of Brittany, and the Channel Islands, led to the expectation that the enemy might possibly attempt new landing operations simultaneously with the breakthrough attempt, and that the US 82nd and 101st Airborne Divs, which had previously been withdrawn, might be employed at the same time in direct support of the planned breakthrough operation. On the other hand, in view of the development of the overall situation, the possibility of further strategic landing attempts at other coastal sectors—with the exception of the Mediterranean coast—became more and more doubtful. It was, of course, expected that the American offensive on a narrow front would be accompanied by a simultaneous strong British offensive operation with the objective of at least pinning down German forces. We had to reckon with the fact that these British attacks would concentrate at the previous point of main pressure, namely south of Caen.

It seemed obvious, however, that the decisive breakthrough attempt would be conducted in the American sector. The area between Vire and La Taute because more and more clearly defined as the focal point; this was particularly indicated by the presence of strong armored forces in this area (US 2nd and 3rd Armored Divs). During the week preceding the American offensive, the German reconnaissance also noted the following indications which pointed to the time, locality and strength of the enemy attacks:

1. PW interrogations indicated the employment of Gen. Patton's army in the near future, and, therewith, the employment of a new Staff for the purposes of conducting an operation with mobile forces.
2. Increased enemy air activity, consisting of attacks against supply lines, but, foremost, air reconnaissance, over the entire Seventh Army area.
3. The employment of supporting artillery, first of all on both sides of the Vire, and, during the very last days, also in the Lessay area, at the extreme western wing. Artillery adjustment fire; sudden concentrations of fire against road crossings, artillery positions and command posts; firing on the Vire bridges, in order to disrupt the cross traffic behind the German front; the advancing of artillery positions.
4. The removal of mines by the enemy in the area west of the Vire.
5. Increased enemy air reconnaissance.

In view of all those indications, there could be no doubt about the enemy's intentions in regard to space and time. Only the appearance of very strong artillery (53 light and 8 medium batteries) in the Lessay area, during the last few days prior to the American offensive, made the situation obscure, and indicated the possible employment of the new American army. The Commander-in-Chief of Seventh Army, Oberstgruppenfuehrer Hausser, gave an estimate of the situation to OB West, General Field Marshal von Kluge, on 20 July, in which he stated that the German command expected the start of a strong American offensive at any moment, with the point of main effort in the Vire – La Taute area, and that they calculated that additional attacks would be launched at other frontal sectors (for instance, southwest of Caen, east of the Vire, between La Taute and the coast), in order to tie down German forces.

An entry in the War Diary of the Seventh Army, dated 23 July, reads as follows: "Sudden concentrations of enemy fire against road crossings, artillery positions and command posts, with the point of main effort in the Vire – La Taute sector and the center of the northern front, north of Périers, have noticeably increased during the night. This has been the most significant observation made during the last 24 hours." The events of 24 July, primarily in the Pz. Lehr Div. sector, left no doubt as to the enemy's intentions.

b. Situation in Sector of Panzer Group West

The point of main effort of the German defense against the invasion was concentrated, as before, in the center of the sector of Panzer Group West, in the Caen area. In the course of the reorganization, all 7 Panzer divisions of Panzer Group West were assembled there. For the time being, however, only three divisions (2, 116, 9 SS-Pz.) were held as reserves behind the front, while the other four divisions (21, 12 SS, 1 SS, 10 SS-Pz.) were still committed along the front. 2 Pz. Div. and 9 SS-Pz. Div. also had been pulled out from the front only during the last few days, while 116 Pz. Div. had only just completed its reorganization.

Since Army Group and Army were constantly striving to relieve additional Panzer units from the war of position on the defensive front, they had brought pressure to bear upon Supreme Command to permit the bringing up of the two infantry divisions (271 and 272) which had arrived behind the left wing of the Fifteenth Army. Both infantry divisions were in the process of moving to the front, but were greatly delayed because of the critical situation in the air, and, above all, at the crossing points along the Seine. 272 Inf. Div. (Commander: Gen. Lt. Schack) was supposed to relieve 21 Pz. Div. situated along the left wing of LXXXVI Inf. Corps, while 271 Inf. Div. (Commander: Gen. Dannhauser) was supposed to relieve 10 SS-Pz. Div., which was attached to II SS-Pz. Corps. Only the forward elements of these units had reached their designated sectors on 24 July 1944. These forward elements, however, were immediately committed, and, in matters of command, subordinated for the time being to the Panzer divisions.

The entire process of relieving the Panzer divisions took until the end of the month. Furthermore, 89 Inf. Div. was in the process of transfer to the Panzer Group, in order to relieve an additional Panzer division. XLVII and II SS-Pz. Corps—two of the three employed Corps headquarters staffs (I SS, II SS, XLVII Pz. Corps)—were to be relieved of command by LXXIV Inf. Corps, which on 25 July had been recalled from Brittany. After this reorganization, the Panzer Group would have had two Panzer corps, with 5 and 6 Pz. Divs, as strategic reserves at its disposal.

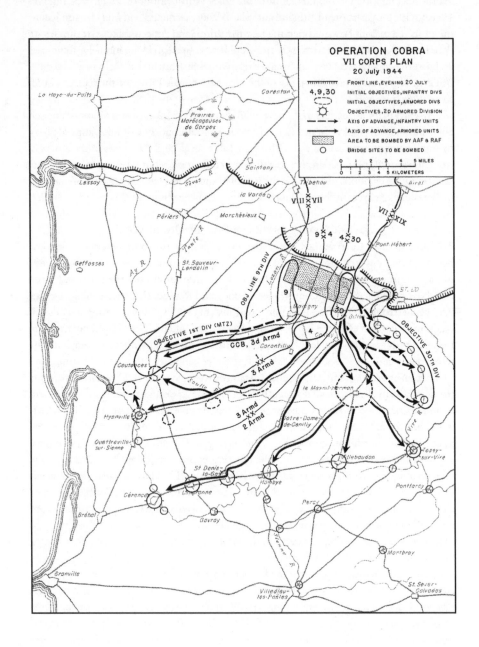

Even though Supreme Command intended to use these forces for strategic purposes, in order to attempt anew the elimination of the Allies' Normandy bridgehead, these reserves were, for the local command, primarily of value because of their being ready for use against the expected major offensive operations by the British and American invading armies. In this connection, OB West, Army Group B, and Panzer Group West continued to consider as the main danger a breakthrough by the British from the Caen area in the general direction of Paris. Moreover, maintaining the German point of main effort of the Panzer Group sector—in spite of the critical situation at Seventh Army—may also have been connected with the fact that the possibility of a new enemy landing operation between the Somme and Seine was still reckoned with, and that, in such an event too, it was, therefore, desired to have the mobile units available for action.

The Panzer Group had been engaged in heavy defensive combat along the front, and, in most cases, had been able only with great difficulty to prevent strategic breakthroughs by the British. In spite of the fact that 8 out of the 10 Panzer units in action at the invasion front were made available—although in a piecemeal manner—it was never possible to score more than local offensive successes. Five additional infantry divisions (16 Lw. Field, 276, 277, 326, 346 Inf. Divs) had, in the meantime, been attached to the Panzer Group, the combat value of which was still fairly good on 24 July (except for the almost completely destroyed 16 Lw. Field Div.), since most of these divisions had only recently been committed. As far as the Panzer units were concerned, 116 Pz. Div. was quite fresh; 1 SS, 9 SS, and 10 SS-Pz. Divs, and 2 Pz. Div., had suffered losses, but were still in possession of about 75 percent of their fighting power. On the other hand, 21 Pz. Div. and 12 SS-Pz. Div. had been seriously mauled while in action for almost two months. On the whole, the fighting power of the Panzer Group on 24 July can be estimated at 4 infantry divisions and 5 or 6 Panzer divisions. By adding the 3 infantry divisions (89, 271, 272) that were in the process of transfer, the ratio of strength, as against the 13 British units, would have been approximately equal; however, in view of the strength and superior weapons of the enemy units, and the far greater supply of GHQ troops (artillery, engineers, etc.) the Germans would be found at a disadvantage.

However, the situation in the air remained the decisive factor for the inferiority of the German conduct of offensive combat. The almost complete absence of the German Air Force had brought about such an overwhelming enemy air superiority that not only were all movements confined to the night hours, but also all large-scale offensive operations by mobile forces were necessarily doomed from the start. Consequently, the mission of the Panzer Group was a purely defensive one, with the purpose of preventing an enemy breakthrough in the direction of Falaise/Paris at all costs. In compliance with this mission, and also because of the entire enemy formation, the German point of main effort automatically developed on both sides of the Caen–Falaise road. The two wings of the Panzer Group were the less endangered points at the front. While, at the left wing, there was the danger that the enemy might endeavor to enlarge his bridgehead by rolling up the Atlantic Wall, and might try to reach the important supply port of Le Havre, the danger at the left wing was in the Caumont area, where a weak spot in the German front (army boundary line) always offered the enemy the chance to attempt a breakthrough into the

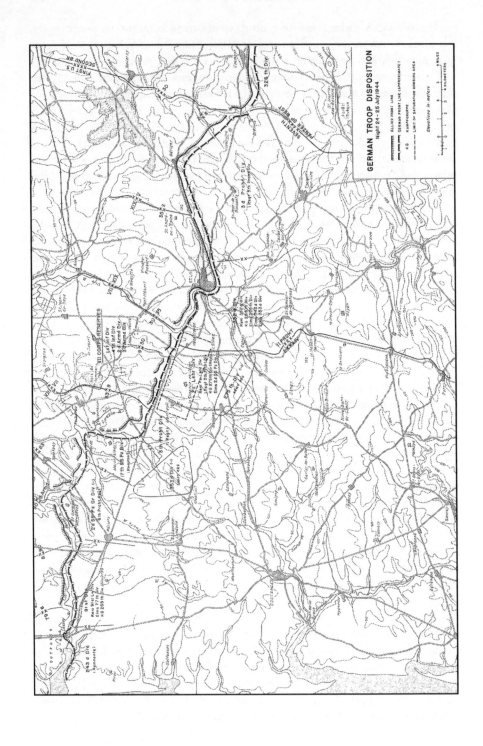

GERMAN TROOP DISPOSITION
Night 24 - 25 July 1944

━━━━━━━ ALLIED FRONT LINE
━ ━ ━ ━ GERMAN FRONT LINE (APPROXIMATE)
KG KAMPFGRUPPE
━━━━━━━ LIMIT OF SATURATION BOMBING AREA

Elevations in meters

interior of France. However, for the time being, there was no serious danger at the left wing, in view of the known enemy formation. It had also been a known fact for quite some time that the boundary line between the British and American invasion forces was located there. The Panzer Group, consequently, definitely reckoned with a strong offensive enemy operation in the direction of Falaise, the start of which had to be expected at any day.

Evaluation of the Terrain

While, at the left wing of the Panzer Group, the typical Normandy hedgerow terrain was predominant, the terrain east of the Orne, in the Caen–Falaise area, was generally open, and as such especially suited to large-scale tank operations. The rivers (Dives, Laize, Orne) ran generally in a south–north direction, so that the generally flat terrain did not offer any sectors suitable for frontal defense. On the other hand, at the Laison–Laize as well as the Dives and Orne, conditions were favorable for flanking positions. The road net at the rear of the front was excellent, but, because of its almost complete lack of cover, offered the Allied air forces particularly good opportunities for attack. This brief evaluation of the terrain was, therefore, also influential in prompting the Panzer Group to establish the point of main effort on both sides of the Caen–Falaise road.

On 24 July, it was comparatively quiet on the entire front, so the Panzer Group hoped still to be able to complete its reorganization prior to the start of the expected enemy offensive.

c. Situation in Sector of Seventh Army

Computing the combat value of the entire Seventh Army on the basis of the combat efficiencies of the individual units, the value arrived at was about 3 full-strength infantry divisions and 2 full-strength Panzer divisions, as against the 13 infantry divisions and 3 Panzer [armored] divisions of the US First Army (ratio 16:5). In this connection, the substantial differences in regard to the quantity and quality of the units, and in respect of the allotting of supporting GHQ troops (artillery, antitank, antiaircraft, etc.) were not taken into consideration.

During July, the Army had repeatedly called attention to its constantly dwindling fighting power, and had requested the bringing up of new and fresh units, as well as a continual flow of replacements. However, hardly any attention was paid to these requests, because Supreme Command still believed the point of main effort to be in Panzer Group West's zone.

Evaluation of the Situation and Terrain

In the course of the preceding heavy battles, the Army—repeatedly offering stubborn resistance, and gaining room by means of local counterattacks—had withdrawn into the line generally running via [La Lande-sur-] Drôme–Bérigny along the road St-Lô–Bérigny south of St-Lô–Périers–north of Périers–Lessay. A strategic breakthrough by the enemy had so far always been prevented at the last minute, though only at the price of heavy losses, which had weakened the fighting power of the Army correspondingly.

The front could, therefore, not be occupied along a continuous line, or in sufficient depth—somewhat like the position [trench] warfare of 1917 to 1918—but consisted of a checkerboard-type system of strongpoints, which, according to the tactical situation and the terrain, were arranged on the "focal point" principle. For the most part, this involved combat groups, composed of various branches of the service, which secured the roads, byways, crossing points and open terrain. Because of the limited fighting power, endeavors were made to take extensive advantage of the terrain and to rely on natural barriers. As the majority of the rivers (Drôme, Elle, Vire, Taute) crossed the front generally in the direction south to north, it was only possible to do this here and there and by intentionally refraining from shortening the front. Whereas, east of the Vire, the front line followed the course of the road to Bayeux in low-lying terrain, and was open to view from the heights north of the road, west of the Vire it was based on the elevated terrain raising in a southerly direction. At the extreme right wing of the Army, the heights of Caumont played a decisive role. On the extreme left wing, the front adjoined the Ay sector. This was the only place which could be said to be secure against mechanized attacks. Generally, the terrain was typical Normandy hedgerow terrain. The terrain influenced the battles of the period immediately following, owing to the fact that the course of all ridges ran from the front in a general southwesterly direction, so that, for purposes of defense, they took the course of the American breakthrough drive, and were not diagonal to the direction of the enemy attack. The terrain was thus not favorable for the defense.

The Army had established a distinct point of main effort in the center of its front, in view of the estimation of the enemy's situation. The point of main effort was signified by the following:

a. The employment of the most combat-fit units in the front. (Pz. Lehr Div., 2 and 17 SS-Pz. Divs);

b. Narrower combat sectors;

c. Artillery concentration;

d. The concentration of the combat groups of 275 and 353 Inf. Divs as tactical reserves.

The provision of these absolutely essential reserves had been made possible only through the ruthless stripping of the Army's left wing, though the weakening of that wing seemed rather foolhardy in view of the strong enemy artillery concentrations which had been observed in that sector. In this connection, the combat group from 353 Inf. Div. (commanded by Gen. Mahlmann) had been pulled out from the front, and placed as tactical reserves in the area southeast of Périers.*

275 Inf. Div. (commanded by Gen. Schmidt), which had come from Brittany, had just arrived in the Army zone. The elements which had already previously been committed at

---

* According to a report by Gen. Mahlmann dated 1 March 1946, the fighting power of this combat group consisted of two infantry regiments totaling five battalions (each battalion about 100 to 120 men strong) and regimental units, including one engineer company, half of one artillery regiment with two battalions (totaling 15 to 18 guns; the other two battalions of the regiment had been left in their previous sector, at the left wing of the Army), one tank destroyer battalion with two assault guns, four to six antitank guns and six to eight antiaircraft machine guns, a signals battalion and supply services.

the invasion front (Combat Group Heinz) remained subordinated to the Pz. Lehr Div. The other, newly arrived elements of the division were assembled as Army reserves in the Canisy–Marigny area.* Of these elements, one infantry battalion was subordinated to 352 Inf. Div., on 24 July, in compliance with orders from Army HQ. Although this measure was undesirable, it was, nevertheless, necessary, in the face of the inadequate fighting power of 352 Inf. Div.

The intentions of Seventh Army were to relieve, with the aid of these infantry units, as many as possible of the Panzer divisions that were committed along the front, and then to assemble same as tactical reserves. During this process of reorganization, it would also have been possible to readjust these units and to reunite dispersed divisions. However, the assembly of 275 and 353 Inf. Divs was only completed on 24 July, so that—because of the enemy's preparations for the offensive, which began on the same day—no time was left for the planned reorganization.

The mission of Seventh Army was confined to the repelling of the expected enemy offensive by a determined defense of positions presently held by the Army. The employment of delaying tactics, or possibly a voluntary withdrawal into the line Caumont–Coutances, which would shorten the front, was completely out of the question, in view of Supreme Command's ideas, so that it was useless to make suggestions in this respect. Conflicts of opinion even arose between the higher headquarters concerning the course of positions north or south of the St Lô–Périers road. The intentions of Pz. Lehr Div., Corps and Army were to have the course of the main line of resistance run along the heights south of the road. However, even the abandonment of such insignificant portions of terrain was forbidden, so that elements of Pz. Lehr Div. and of 5 FS Jg. Div. had to remain in positions made unfavorable by the nature of the terrain, north of the road. The proximity of the road was also a disadvantage, insofar as it presented a perfect secondary target to the enemy air force. In view of the expected enemy preparations for an attack by superior artillery and air force activity, the Army had ordered that, generally, the main line of resistance be occupied only by reduced forces, and that strong local reserves be held in positions of readiness for tactical purposes. In spite of these measures, which were taken in order to create a front line with as much depth as possible, and for the purpose of drafting reserves, it was obvious to the Army that the available forces were inadequate in regard to both quality and quantity, and, consequently, would be unable to prevent an enemy breakthrough for any length of time. Therefore, on 20 July, the Commander-in-Chief personally presented the following estimation† of the situation to OB West, Field Marshal von Kluge:

"The course of the main line of resistance is unfavorable because the left wing is considerably echeloned to the front. The terrain is only favorable on the northern front [north of Périers–Lessay]. In the combat zone of western Normandy, the

---

* According to statements made by Gen. Schmidt on 3 May 1946, the fighting power of 275 Inf. Div. (not counting those elements that had been attached to other units) consisted of: two infantry regimental staffs with three battalions at full strength; one artillery regiment with three battalions; one engineer company; one antitank company (motorized); and the bulk of the signal battalion and supply services.
† Extract from the War Diary of Seventh Army, dated 20 July 1944.

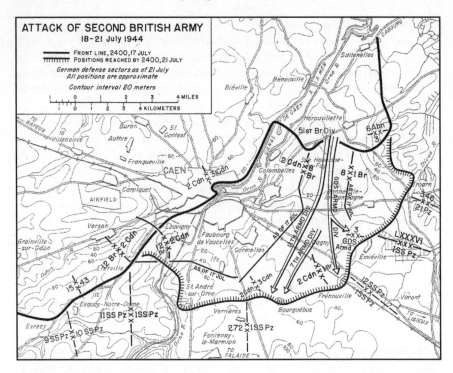

enemy, at present, commands sufficient forces to start a new, large-scale offensive at any time. The indications that the enemy will soon start a drive toward the south and southwest, with the point of main effort west of the Vire, are, among others, reported assemblies of enemy troops before the northern front, the appearance of new divisions (US 5 Inf. Div. and 4 Armored Div.), and renewed enemy air attacks against our supply lines behind the front and in the rear area.

"It seems possible that the enemy might extend his attacks to the area on both sides of the boundary line to Panzer Group West. In the event of a new, large-scale offensive, it must also be assumed that airborne operations, which might possibly be coupled with landing operations from the sea, might take place on the western coast [of the Cotentin peninsula].

"Because of our losses suffered during previous actions, the fighting quality of our units has been, in places, lowered to such an extent that, in the event of enemy attacks supported by strong artillery, penetrations by the enemy cannot be prevented. . . . The employment of 275 Inf. Div. and of 5 FS Jg. Div., which has recently been brought forward, cannot improve the tense situation within the Army. These troops are devoid of any combat experience . . .

"The supply situation will ease only when several trains loaded with fuel and ammunition have arrived . . .

"Therefore, as a prerequisite for the execution of its missions, the Army proposes that the following measures be taken:

"1. The assignment of a fully combat-fit mobile unit as Army reserve in the area west of the Vire, or for the purpose of occupying the boundary line to Panzer Group West. These reserves were, furthermore, to be employed in the event of an enemy air and seaborne landing operation.

"2. A continuous flow of replacements. The combat strength can be maintained only if every division receives at least two replacement battalions each month.

"3. Augmentation of firepower by means of one or two additional rocket projector brigades, more medium artillery, and the replacement of guns, rocket projectors and machine guns lost in action.

"4. A guaranteed increase in the supply of ammunition and fuel, the transportation of which must be rendered secure by fighter planes and antiaircraft artillery protection. This is of particular importance to the Army in the case of the Loire bridges.

"5. Combatting of enemy air artillery observers, heavy bombers and low-flying aircraft by our own fighter planes."

In some cases, the fulfillment of these minimum requests, which had the full support of OB West, depended upon decisions made by Supreme Command. These decisions, however, were only made after the start of the American offensive, so that the transfer of XLVII Pz. Corps (with 2 and 116 Pz. Divs) took place at too late a date, and consequently resulted in the piecemeal employment of these forces.

In respect of strength, the German Air Force was not in a position, even approximately, to fulfill the demands placed upon it. The events of 24 July revealed the intentions of the enemy to a large degree:

a. In II FS Jg. Corps' area of operations, heavy artillery fire nightly, active reconnaissance on both sides, and increased enemy air activity, among other objectives, also against the Vire bridges and roads in the rear area.

b. In LXXXIV Corps' area of operations, heavy artillery fire against the entire front, pattern bombing by several waves of a few hundred two- and four-motored bombers, heavy artillery barrages against the front of Pz. Lehr Div. and against the right wing of 5 FS Jg. Div., and enemy reconnaissance thrusts, which were repelled.

Enemy air and artillery preparations were directed against the area between the main line of resistance and the artillery positions, with points of main effort north of La Chapelle and the Marigny-Montreuil area. Since our troops had reported enemy attacks against II FS Jg. Corps' front as well as LXXXIV Inf. Corps' right wing, the Army was under the impression, on the evening of 24 July, that the enemy offensive had already begun. It was not realized on the German side that American bombers had, in some cases, dropped bombs on their own troops, and that the actual large-scale enemy attack had not yet been launched.

However, the Army's tense situation had not altered, especially since it was the day's final estimate of the situation that, for the time being, it had only been a matter of minor enemy attacks, and that considerably stronger attacks on a broader basis would have to be expected during the next few days. It was, now as before, assumed that the enemy's main objective was to reach the St-Lô–Coutances road west of St-Lô.

The German Supreme Command must have clearly perceived the seriousness of the situation from Army reports; however, it decided only on 27 July to take energetic countermeasures*. This clearly indicates that Supreme Command believed the main danger still to be located in the Caen sector.

d. The Situation in Brittany

Five divisions (3 and 5 FS Jg., 77, 275, and 353 Inf.) had been transferred from Brittany to Normandy during the course of the invasion battles. From all the other units employed in Brittany (2 FS Jg. Div., 265, 266, and 343 Inf. Divs), combat groups—generally reinforced regimental groups—had also been transferred to Normandy.

The two infantry corps committed in Brittany (XXV and LXXIV) were so weakened as a result of this great decrease in strength that the original mission, namely, the defense of the Brittany coast, could no longer be carried out with the forces still available. Aside from the fact that the number of troops was not sufficient for the purpose of occupying the long front, strong elements were also constantly being tied up through the necessary supervision and combatting of the French Resistance movement, which was particularly active in Brittany. Furthermore, the "fortresses" at the Atlantic were not permitted to be reduced in strength, by order of Supreme Command. These fortresses were manned by occupation troops, whose number was exactly specified, belonging to all branches of the service; these were not permitted to be employed in other tasks.

Seventh Army had, consequently, ordered that the defense in Brittany be based only on these fortresses, and that the coastal sectors between the fortresses be observed. The bulk of the weapons which, up to then, had been employed outside of the fortress zones (coast artillery, antilandingcraft guns, antiaircraft guns, etc.) were now committed within the defensive zones of the fortresses.

Seventh Army no longer reckoned with an enemy landing operation in Brittany. This became less likely, the more the tactical situation of the Allied forces in the Normandy bridgehead improved and continued to develop favorably. A new landing operation from the sea or from the air would, in view of the difficult coastal situation in Brittany, amount to a serious risk for the enemy, which he no longer needed to take upon himself. The increased enemy activity on the sea and in the air during the period before 24 July was evaluated by the Seventh Army as [consituting] enemy reconnaissance and deception.

The Allied air attacks on 19 July against the Loire bridges, and during the night of 23 July against the St-Nazaire area, could be connected with the enemy's intentions for an offensive drive from Normandy. Every night there was very active air traffic in Brittany, for the purposes of supplying the French Resistance movement with weapons, ammunition, explosives, means of sabotage, etc. During the month of July, the French Resistance had assumed such proportions that the weakened occupation forces were no longer in full control of all sections of the Brittany peninsula. We succeeded in limiting French sabotage and combat activity by continuously combatting the various groups of French partisans;

---

* *Note:* The 2nd and 116th Panzer Divisions received their orders to start the march only during the noon hours of 27 July.

however, we did not succeed in mopping up the entire area. Therefore, the French Resistance in Brittany, as in southern France, had very unpleasant effects on the occupation forces—though it never played a decisive role.

Since OB West had been given authority over all the German armed forces (Wehrmachtbefugnisse) only on 3 August, the inadequate coordination between the Army, Navy, and Luftwaffe had very detrimental effects in Brittany, as everywhere else in France. Constant friction arose between the various branches of the armed services, especially in the fortresses.

319 Inf. Div. (commanded by Gen. Graf Schmettow) was still employed in the Channel Islands. Requests by Seventh Army to employ elements of that division in Normandy were repeatedly rejected by Supreme Command.

PART TWO

The breakout from Normandy was to start on 24 July with the US Army's Operation "Cobra," mounted by the First Army's V and VII Corps. However, it was postponed, and the carpet-bombing that was to have preceded the offensive was called off. Unfortunately, not all the bombers received the recall signal, and this led to a "fratricide" incident, with US forward positions being bombed. Fritz Bayerlein and Panzer Lehr declared victory, unaware of what the next day was to bring.

"Cobra" opened on the morning of 25 January with intensive air attacks, involving 1,800 heavy bombers carpet-bombing an area 7,000 yds by 2,500 yds. The Panzer Lehr Division suffered heavy losses. Some US bombs again fell short on the forward troops. This delayed the advance and resulted in some 600 casualties, including Lieutenant-General Leslie McNair, head of US Army Ground Forces, who was observing the operation. The widespread cratering of the ground and quickly organized pockets of German resistance held up the initial ground assault. Improved air-ground coordination with Allied tactical aircraft was a feature of "Cobra." Although the initial penetrations were disappointing, by the end of the day the town of Hébécrevon had been finally taken.

The blow fell hard on Seventh Army. The Germans were down to two days' worth of fuel and short on ammunition even before the offensive. Moreover, von Kluge, the Commander of Army Group B, had thought that the next blow would fall in the British sector, and had kept the Panzer divisions concentrated there. But more serious than the shortage of supplies and reserves was the shortage of ideas: the Germans had no plan for dealing with "Cobra." Their logistics were already near collapse, while daytime movement of troops and supplies was limited because of Allied airpower.

Chapter 2

The American Breakthrough

by Generalmajor Rudolf-Christoph Freiherr von Gersdorff
Translated by Eva Elkiner (B-723)

A. 25 July

As anticipated, the Americans launched a major attack between Vire and La Taue [?] on 25 July. Apart from continued, increased air activity, the day passed more or less uneventfully before II FS Jg. Corps' front line, east of the Vire. The possibility that the enemy would extend his obviously large-scale offensive to the sector east of St-Lô still had to be considered. It was definitely expected that the enemy, who was attacking LXXXIV Inf. Corps' right wing, would turn east against II FS Jg. Corps' flank, in order to gain full control over the road junction at St-Lô, and to extend his breakthrough to the east. Heavy low-level attacks at the rear of Corps seemed to indicate his intentions to that effect.

Around 0730 hrs the enemy began to prepare for an attack on LXXXIV Inf. Corps by directing his artillery fire against the main line of resistance and the depth of the defense zone. Much more effective were the enemy's air attacks, which started around 1030 hrs. Approximately 1,000 bombers, mostly of the four-engine type, attacked, by pattern bombing in waves, the St-Lô–Le Mesnil-Vigot–Marigny area. These air attacks, combined with heavy artillery fire, managed to break the resistance of the German units concerned, namely, Pz. Lehr Div. and 5 FS Jg. Div. Heavy losses of personnel and material were suffered by all elements of the unit—especially by the local reserves—and made the success of the following enemy infantry possible. The psychological effect of these attacks must not be overlooked. Admittedly, the first attacks of the enemy were repelled, but this was mainly due to the fact that the enemy was compelled to halt and withdraw his attacking spearheads, because of the renewed pattern bombing of his own air force.

Heavy attacks, supported by a considerable number of tanks, against the entire front of the Pz. Lehr Div. and 5 FS Jg. Div., followed this second bombardment. These attacks were combined with the use of formations of twin-engine aircraft, whose points of main effort were the reserve and artillery areas. Judging by the fact that the enemy committed the main body of his tanks in front of the right wing of the Pz. Lehr Div., it seemed that this was his point of main effort.

During the course of the day, the enemy attack extended to the west as far as Remilly-sur-Lozon. The remnants of the troops, having survived air attacks and artillery fire, bravely defended themselves. The defensive front—decimated through the heavy losses—was unable to prevent deep penetrations by the enemy into the defensive system. The enemy, therefore, succeeded in crossing the road between St-Lô and Périers to the south. The enemy broke through the extreme right wing of Corps and took Hébécrevon. Further to

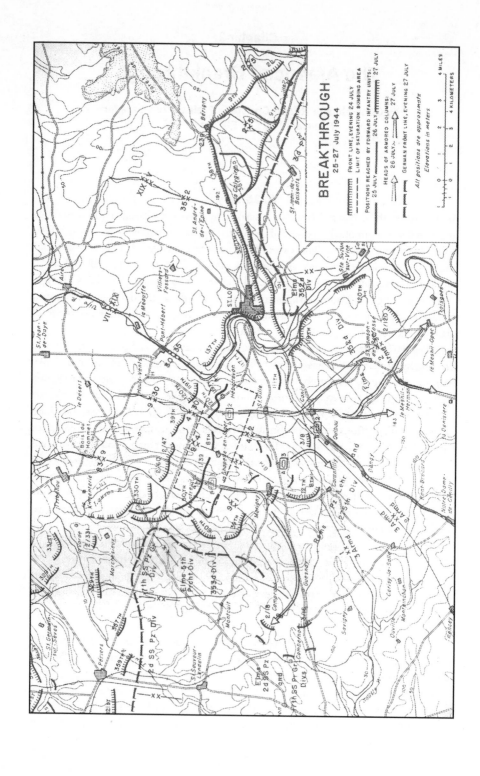

BREAKTHROUGH
25–27 July 1944

the west, we managed to hold La Chapelle-en-Juger, but the enemy was able to penetrate into Montreuil and Le Mesnil-Eury, and to thrust forward to the hills surrounding Lozon. The stability of the German front could no longer be guaranteed.

Therefore, Corps was forced to employ its reserves in order to prevent the threatening penetration. Around noon, 353 Inf. Div.—in reserve, in the rear of 5 FS Jg. Div.—was ordered to recapture the hill southeast of Lozon and to close the gap in the front line between La Duquerie and Lozon. 353 Inf. Div.'s 941 Gren. Regt, to which the remnants of the Panzer Jaeger detachment of the division were assigned, succeeded in reaching the ordered objective in a counterattack from the area of Hauteville-la-Guichard, in spite of being delayed by enemy air activity.

The critical situation in the Pz. Lehr Div. sector also made it necessary to release the weak army reserves—the remnants of 275 Inf. Div.—which were assembled in the Canisy–Marigny area. Prior to this, II Bn of 275 Inf. Div.'s 985 Regt had been assigned to 352 Inf. Div. of II FS Jg. Corps, in order to provide a flank protection at the boundary of LXXXIV Inf. Corps southwest of St-Lô. 984 Gren. Regt was committed in the Pz. Lehr Div. sector within the framework of Kampfgruppe (Battle Group) Heinz and assigned to this division. New Staff and I Bn of 985 Gren. Regt were also released to LXXXIV Inf. Corps, and employed by the latter for the reinforcement of the defense in the Pz. Lehr Div. sector. The divisional artillery regiment was also controlled by the artillery commander of Corps, and was committed to assist the right wing of Corps in the area around Canisy. Only III Bn was assigned to 5 FS Jg. Div. Hence, the main body of the troops was no longer controlled by the division. Around Canisy, only 983 Gren. Regt and elements of the Panzer Jaeger Battalion were still available.

There had been only limited combat activity on LXXXIV Inf. Corps' remaining front. This seemed to clearly indicate the enemy's intention to effect a breakthrough in the sector northeast of St-Lô–Remilly. It had been observed that the enemy concentrated his tanks into assembly areas, particularly south of Remilly, which showed that he would continue his attack with concentrated tank forces on 26 July. A further expansion of the attack by the enemy had to be expected in front of II FS Jg. Corps' II Battalion, and the center and left wing of LXXXIV Inf. Corps.

It had been possible to prevent the enemy's strategic breakthrough on the first day of the battle, but unreasonably high losses were suffered through bombing attacks and artillery fire, and the already weak reserves had been practically annihilated. On the evening of 25 July, LXXXIV Inf. Corps had to commit 353 Inf. Div.'s last regiment—942 Gren. Regt— on the right of 941 Gren. Regt. In order for this regiment to remain successful, the Army was obliged to put 275 Inf. Div.'s reinforced 983 Regt at the disposal of Corps. Corps intended to employ this combat team of the 275 Inf. Div. in a counterattack in the Pz. Lehr Div. sector on 26 July, and to eliminate the enemy's penetration of 25 July. The regiment was ordered to move into a position of readiness for the counterattack via La Chapelle-en-Juger during the night 25/26 July. For this purpose, it was also assigned to Pz. Lehr Div.— which practically eliminated the Commander and Staff of 275 Inf. Div. This was not desirable, but could not be avoided, because, in order to maintain a clear chain of command in the sector in question, the existing circumstances had made it necessary to dissipate the

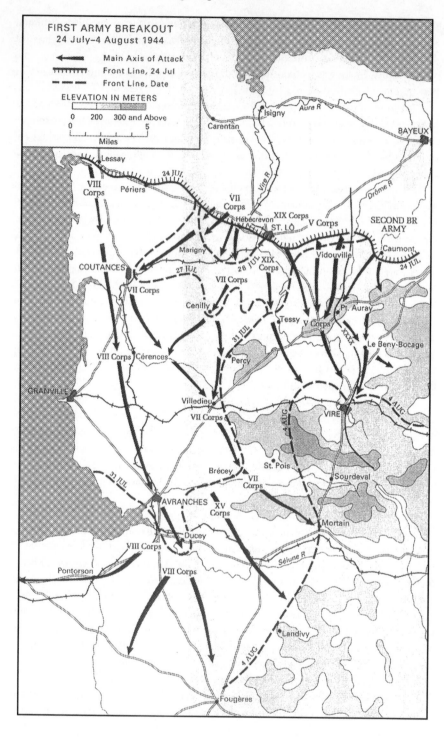

FIRST ARMY BREAKOUT
24 July–4 August 1944

→ Main Axis of Attack
⊓⊓⊓⊓⊓ Front Line, 24 Jul
— — — Front Line, Date

ELEVATION IN METERS

0   200   300 and Above
0   5
Miles

various elements of the division by using them at different points and at different times. Owing to the considerable enemy air activity, 985 Gren. Regt could not reach its operational area in the defensive front of Pz. Lehr Div., and was employed by the division for the purpose of contriving a barrier position northeast of Marigny. On 25 July, all elements of 275 Inf. Div. had suffered considerable losses.

On the evening of 25 July, the Army was ordered to move the Corps Staff of LXXXIV Inf. Corps up to the Caumont sector of Panzer Group West, in order to relieve XLVII Pz. Corps and to transfer the command of the Brittany sector to XXV Inf. Corps. XLVII Pz. Corps was to be relieved of command of 2 and 116 Pz. Divs, which were assembled southeast of Caen. It seems inconceivable that Supreme Command did not consider displacing, on this day, these reserves for the purpose of defending Seventh Army against the American offensive.

B. 26 July

As expected, the enemy's offensive expanded to the sector of II Bn of FS Jg. Corps on 26 July. During the night, strong artillery fire had started along the whole front of Corps, with its main point of effort on the left wing. The enemy had attempted to hinder the supply and bringing up of reserves by a sudden concentration of his long-range artillery on road junctions and assembly areas in the rear. At dawn, the enemy assembled for the attack in the sector to the right of the Army boundaries (at La Lande-sur-Drôme) to south of St-André-de-l'Epine, i.e. the entire sector of 3 FS Jg. Div. These attacks were supported by heavy artillery fire and caused four points of penetration:

1. In the Vidouville–Montrabot area;
2. In the area of St-Germain-d'Elle area;
3. In the Bois de la Billerie [?] area;
4. In the St-Pierre-d'Semilly area.

Of these points of penetration, the following two were the most dangerous: at Vidouville, where the enemy had penetrated up to the road junction, 1 km north of Biéville; and at the Bois de la Billerie, where he had penetrated up to the road junction, 1 km west of Planquais [?].

Corps committed 5 FS Jg. Div.'s 15 FS Jg. Regt, its only reserve, on the right wing for the purpose of the counterattack. The enemy attempted to expand his area of penetration at the Bois de la Billerie to the west and east. At first, the tactical situation at this point did not appear to be threatening, since none of these enemy attacks could be compared in strength with those in his point of main effort, west of St-Lô, and since the combat efficiency of 3 FS Jg. Div. was particularly high. But the tactical development at the LXXXIV Inf. Corps right wing gravely endangered the extreme left wing of II FS Jg. Corps. Supported by tanks, the enemy attacked at first at battalion strength, and succeeded in interrupting the contact between the inner wings of 352 Inf. Div. and Pz. Lehr Div., and, with that, the contact between the two Corps. II FS Jg. Corps, recognizing the very dangerous tactical situation on its left flank, withdrew 12 Reconnaissance Detachment of FS Jg. from the front and committed it as flank protection in the area of Le Mesnil-Herman. Moreover, II Bn of 275 Inf. Div.'s 985 Gren. Regt was released to be employed on the left wing of 352 Inf. Div.

for the purpose of restoring contact. Due to the enemy's air activity, however, the commitment of this battalion was considerably delayed—a fact which made it necessary for 352 Inf. Div. to withdraw its left wing and to build up a defensive flank east of St-Gilles. Thus II FS Jg. Corps was threatened on both flanks of the salient jutting to the northeast.

However, 26 July proved again that the enemy's point of main effort was still in front of the left wing of LXXXIV Inf. Corps. While the Allied air force succeeded in delaying, and even preventing, by uninterrupted activity, German countermeasures—i.e. the bringing up of the reserves, the closing of the gaps in the front line, and the building up of a defensive front in echelons—strong enemy ground forces simultaneously broke through in a direction south-southwest of Hébécrevon and La Chapelle-en-Juger. In spite of the assigned elements of 275 Inf. Div., it was impossible for the considerably weakened Pz. Lehr Div. to prevent the—so far only local—penetrations, on account of the overwhelming superiority of the enemy's equipment, and his complete air superiority.

While the pattern bombing by the American bomber formations and the concentrated artillery fire were the decisive factors on 25 July, 26 July was characterized by low-flying enemy aircraft. Their cooperation with the American ground forces was exemplary. There was not one street or locality within the enemy's area of penetration that was not constantly patrolled by low-flying aircraft. Hence all traffic in the rear of the front line was practically paralyzed or—due to heavy losses—considerably delayed. The use of delayed-action bombs on these occasions was particularly devastating, and inflicted heavy losses. Due to the effect of the enemy's air activity, the commitment of 275 Inf. Div. could not be executed in the prescribed manner and was in fact ineffective.

Admittedly, in the east, the enemy's spearheads—penetrating via Hébécrevon to St-Gilles and via La Chapelle-en-Juger to Marigny—encountered 983 Gren. Regt, which had not yet been able to deploy, and, in the west, 985 Gren. Regt, which was employed in the defense northwest of Marigny. But the fighting qualities of these regiments—as yet inexperienced in battle—had been considerably weakened through the effects of the enemy's air activity. Due to their commitment over a wide area, they fought without cohesion or mutual assistance, which meant that they could only offer local resistance to the enemy, whose equipment was by far superior. Owing to the fact that individual fighting groups were clinging to several points across the terrain, it was possible to delay the strategic breakthrough of the enemy and still, in the evening, hold the hills surrounding Canisy and south of Marigny. However, Pz. Lehr Div. and 275 Inf. Div. had been scattered in such a way, and their losses were of such a serious nature, that no resistance worth mentioning could be offered to the continuation of the enemy's penetration—which had to be expected on 27 July.

353 Inf. Div. was struck on its right wing by the enemy's concentrated attack. During the morning of 26 July this division—in position south of Montreuil and west of Lozon, and facing to the northwest—had established contact between the left wing of Pz. Lehr Div. and 17 SS-Pz. Gren. Regt, and had absorbed the remnants of the 5 FS Jg. Div. At this point it had also been only possible to delay the enemy's advance. The right wing of the division had bent back to the west in the rear of the Montreuil–Marigny road. Marigny had fallen into the hands of the enemy. Only loose contact remained with the adjoining elements of

275 Inf. Div. It was possible to repel weaker enemy attacks against the center and left wing of 353 Inf. Div.; penetrations such as the one on La Tortière [?] were eliminated in counterattacks.

Corresponding to the way it had extended along the II FS Jg. Corps sector, the enemy offensive expanded to the west along the remaining front line of LXXXIV Inf. Corps. Since 0620 hrs, the enemy had been attacking the front of 2 SS-Pz. Div. and 91 Luftlande [Air Landing] Div. more vigorously—supported by armor. These attacks could not be compared in strength, support, or force of penetration with those on the enemy's main point of effort in front of Pz. Lehr Div. However, they succeeded in tying down those forces inserted in the center of Corps, and even led to deeper penetrations. Near Les Milleries we managed to seal off the deepest penetration into the right wing of 2 SS-Pz. Div.; and a penetration in front of 91 Luftlande Div., southwest of St-Patrice-de-Claides, could be stopped near La Panserie [?].

Thereby the strategic position of Seventh Army on the evening of 26 July had become untenable. The enemy had practically broken through the center of the front line, and had only to exploit fully the previously achieved penetrations. From this penetration area, the enemy was able to push forward towards the east and west and to encircle and eliminate II FS Jg. Corps—or the center and left wing of LXXXIV Inf. Corps.

Frontal attacks, which had already led to critical situations, succeeded in pinning down all inserted troops—with the exception of the extreme left wing of the Army. This meant that no considerable forces could be made available for the sealing off, and even less for the elimination, of the enemy's penetration. There were no other reserves available. Even if they could have been made available on account of the situation, they could not get there in less than two or three days—in other words, too late to prevent the collapse of the defense front. Therefore, the only solution left to the Army was to retreat, and to try to make forces available by shortening the front line in order to once more arrest the enemy's strategic breakthrough.

Above all, the situation enforced the withdrawal of LXXXIV Inf. Corps. The German High Command had still not decided to deploy their reserves—2 and 116 Pz. Divs, which were at the disposal of Panzer Group West—to Seventh Army. This example is typical [evidence] of the fact that the Command had not yet recognized the immense danger of the situation. It also rejected the Army's request to withdraw LXXXIV Inf. Corps to the rear of the sector on both sides of Coutances. Only a limited retreat for the purpose of the straightening of the front line was approved, and this with the request to pull 2 SS-Pz. Div. out of the front line and to employ this division against the enemy penetration. On 26 July, weak elements of this division had been made available and had been committed in the strength of two Panzer and two infantry companies against the west flank of the American penetration.

Because of the lack of data—the reports of LXXXIV Inf. Corps, 2 SS-Pz. Div., 91 Luftlande Div., and 243 Inf. Div. are missing—details on the engagements and movements of the center and left wing of LXXXIV Inf. Corps are not available. In all events, it withdrew from a line La Quieze [?] – Geffosses to the Marigny – Montcuit – St-Sauveur-Lendelin Hills. Rearguards were left in the main battle line. By taking up this line on a front approximately 10 km shorter than heretofore, LXXXIV Inf. Corps was to try to pull 2 SS-

Pz. Div. and elements of 243 Inf. Div. out of the front line and to displace them to the southeast for the purposes of arresting the enemy penetration.

By evening, 3 FS Jg. Div. had been able to seal off all penetrations into the front line of II FS Jg. Corps. Local withdrawals had only insignificantly changed the hitherto existing main battle line. However, due to the tactical situation in its west flank, 352 Inf. Div. had to fall back into the line Fumichon, south of Baudret [?] –southwest banks of the Vire – village of Gourfaleur – west of Pouchiniere [?]. In the late evening, the enemy's armored spearheads, bypassing the flank of the division, advanced on St-Samson de Bon Fosse and on the crossroads of Le Mesnil-Herman. The division command post of the 352nd Inf. Div.—in position in the woods northwest of the crossroads—had to be moved to Moyen hurriedly. The advance elements of II FS Jg. Reconnaissance Battalion successfully defended the important crossroads near Le Mesnil-Hermann, while the enemy managed to take St-Samson-de-Bonfossé. At this point, the enemy retreated to the woods, after several of his tanks had been put out of action. The strategic situation of II FS Jg. Corps would have been extremely threatening if, on 27 July, the enemy could have determinedly pushed forward to the southeast.

C. 27 July

On 27 July, however, the enemy continued his offensive in full strength towards the south-southwest. The attacks on the front held by II FS Jg. Corps were continued, but no point of main effort was noticeable. On the front held by 352 Inf. Div., the enemy remained calm; nevertheless this division, i.e. 12 FS Jg. Reconnaissance Battalion, remained unable to take the initiative and attack the east flank of the enemy's penetration forces. All reserves of II FS Jg. Corps were tied down, being employed in the various penetration points.

Countermeasures set in motion by LXXXIV Inf. Corps only had the effect that elements of 243 Inf. Div. reached the area southwest of Marigny and took over the protection of the right flank of Corps. As yet, only elements of 2 SS-Pz. Div. had been pulled out of the front, which meant that Corps had no compact attack reserves at its disposal. The enemy's concentrated attack overran the remnants of Pz. Lehr Div. and 275 Inf. Div., and advanced via Marigny – Canisy on La Soulle in the Cerisy-la-Salle – Pont Brocard – Soulles sector, which he reached in the late afternoon. Remnants of the division, i.e., supply troops and emergency units, had built up a thinly manned line of security in the rear of the sector. These covering points, however, could not prevent the enemy from crossing the brook at several points—at Cerisy-la-Salle and Pont Brocard in particular—and thus unhinging the newly established defense. Under the cover of darkness, remnants withdrew to the south. Remnants of Pz. Lehr Div. assembled in the neighborhood of Villebaudon and north of Percy, those of the 275th Inf. Div. around Hanbye [?]. On 27 July the losses of those units were again extremely heavy, as very strong air activity by low-flying aircraft had been in evidence on this day. The defending forces—split up into small, weak groups as they were— were forced to the ground by intense fire from enemy fighter planes, so that the enemy's armored and other assault units could gain ground easily.

Advancing from the area of Marigny to the south, the enemy also overran the weak flank protection, formed by elements of 243 Inf. Div., on the west side of the penetration wedge.

He advanced further into the rear of 353 Inf. Div., which at the same time was being attacked on its defense front on both sides of Le Lorey. This division was unable to prevent several deep penetrations into its front. However, with the help of the still intact artillery regiment and its Panzer Jaeger battalion, it succeeded in forcing the retreat of the enemy's tanks, which had penetrated into the rear of the division. Several enemy tanks were put out of action. By the evening, the division managed to seal off the penetration into its front to such an extent that the integrity of the defense was guaranteed. However, the division's right flank was now exposed. The enemy bypassed this flank in his thrust to the southwest. Actually, there existed a gap extending to as far as the Mont-Pinchon area, in which no material defense was put up.

Owing to the withdrawal, it had been possible to arrest the enemy attacks on the remaining front of LXXXIV Inf. Corps. At this point, the enemy at first did not follow through with stronger forces and—due to the slowly southward retreating combat posts— was kept at a distance away from the main line of battle.

At noon on 27 July, Generalfeldmarschall von Kluge, OB West, had been able to obtain the following decision from the High Command: Panzer Group West was to transfer XLVII Pz. Corps (Commanding General: General of Panzertroops Frhr von Funck) with its 2 Pz. Div. (Commander: Generalleutnant Frhr von Luettwitz) and 116 Pz. Div. (Commander: Generalleutnant Graf von Schwerin) to Seventh Army, in order to be employed in the flank attack from the Tessy area against the American penetration. Generalfeldmarschall von Kluge personally gave this order at the Command Post of Panzer Group West at noon of 27 July.

Due to lack of fuel, the start of 116 Pz. Div. was delayed, while Corps and 2 Pz. Div. could begin their move to the new operational area immediately. Panzer Group West was ordered to procure—exploiting all possible resources—the necessary fuel.

Generals Frhr von Funck and Frhr von Luettwitz, who had gone ahead of their units, arrived at Seventh Army's advance command post , southwest of Percy, in the afternoon of 27 July. There they received their orders of commitment. Until such time as XLVII Pz. Corps—which was to be inserted between II FS Jg. Corps and LXXXIV Inf. Corps—could assume command, 2 Pz. Div. was assigned to II FS Jg. Corps. Advance elements (the Reconnaissance Battalion) of this division had begun the march from the billeting area south of Caen at 1600 hrs, while the main body of the division started to march at 2200 hrs. Marching on two routes, via Thury-Harcourt – Le Bény-Bocage, and St-Rémy – Montchamp – St-Marie-Lauron [?], the division reached the Vire during the night of 27/28 July. During the same night, the main body of the division crossed the Vire on the still usable (although damaged) bridge at Tessy and assembled northwest of Tessy on both sides of the road to Le Mesnil-Herman for the attack against the northwest. Advance elements of the Reconnaissance Battalion blocked the road from St-Lô to Percy, 1,500 m south of the crossroads of La Denisière [?]. It was the task of this division to establish the contact with the former left wing of II FS Jg. Corps and to block the road from Percy to St-Lô. We could not count on the arrival of 116 Pz. Div. before the night of 28/29 July.

From the position of Seventh Army on 27 July, it became clear that the enemy had completed a breakthrough, as the weak security forces still in position north and northwest

GIs inspect a 4.7cm PaK(t) auf PzKpfw 35R(f), a tank destroyer consisting of a Czechoslovak 47mm gun mounted on a French Renault R-35 chassis. There were 110 of these in service in France in 1944, and they were encountered mainly in Normandy. This one was abandoned in Littry, and was photographed on 20 June 1944.

of Percy were inadequate for a firm defense. The strategic situation on the east flank of the breakthrough no longer gave cause for great anxiety, because the front of II FS Jg. Corps was still intact and, above all, because the units from XLVII Pz. Corps were approaching this point. [However,] the remnants of LXXXIV Inf. Corps were in immediate danger of being encircled as a result of the enemy's southwestward penetration in the direction of Coutances. The Army tried once more to evade the encirclement by a withdrawal. While 353 Inf. Div. was ordered to fight its way back to the south across the La Soulle river and to reassemble in the Roncey area and secure the contact to the sea at the Sienne bend, west of Coutances, 2 SS-Pz. Div. and elements of 17 SS-Pz. Div., in great strength, were ordered to assemble east of Coutances.

During the night of 27/28 July, II FS Jg. Corps withdrew to the line Bievielle [?] creek sector (La Soulle)–north of Torigni-sur-Vire, in order to straighten the entire front line and to enable Corps to prolong its defense along this line, since the planned attack by XLVII Pz. Corps made it imperative that the east corner pillars of the Army should remain. The remnants of 352 Inf. Div. and 12 FS Jg. Reconnaissance Battalion, which had been outflanked on the south, retired to the line Pouchinière [?] – [St-] Romphaire – Le Mariage [?] – La Privelette [?], maintaining contact with 3 FS Jg. Div. 353 Inf. Div., which now, however, consisted only of small battle groups, managed to make its way back to the south, moving via Monthuchon behind the rear of the enemy tanks that had penetrated to the southwest. They had crossed the Soulles and, according to orders, prepared for the defense to the east and northeast of Roncey by morning on 28 July. The division established loose contact towards the right with the remnants of 275 Inf. Div. in the Hambye area. This division had absorbed Kampfgruppe Heinz (with about 200 men), and a further 200 men of 243 Inf. Div., and, together with the remnants of Pz. Lehr Div. in position on the hills north of Percy, was trying to establish a strongpoint type of defense line on both sides of Hambye.

D. 28 and 29 July

Due to the commitment of 2 Pz. Div., a considerable relief could be observed on the right wing of Seventh Army on 28 July, while it became impossible to halt the continuation and completion of the American penetration into the center and left wing. The battle, which had lasted for four days, had weakened the German units committed there to such an extent that no uniform and strong resistance could be offered. Due to heavy losses, the number of fighting forces was reduced to a minimum.

Further enemy attacks took place against the new main battle line on the front of the line held by II FS Jg. Corps. However, the main object of these attacks seemed to be the pinning down of our forces. The bulk of the arriving 2 Pz. Div. absorbed the elements of 352 Inf. Div., who were still fighting west of the Vire. At a later date, these remnants were incorporated into 2 and (partly) into 116 Pz. Divs. 12 FS Jg. Reconnaissance Battalion was again assigned to II FS Jg. Corps. The course of the Vire from Pont-Farcy to the north was designated as the new sector boundary between II FS Jg. Corps and XLVII Pz. Corps (Tessy was intended for XLVII Pz. Corps).

On the morning of 28 July, 2 Pz. Div., in quick assaults against the weaker enemy, had reached the Le Mesnil-Raoult – Le Mesnil-Opac – Moyon line and remained there in order to await the arrival of 116 Pz. Div. for the planned thrust by XLVII Pz. Corps. Isolated strongpoints of 352 Inf. Div. or the 12 FS Jg. Reconnaissance Battalion were still in position in front of the line reached by 2 Pz. Div. These strongpoints, however, had been overtaken by the enemy on their flanks and were fighting their way back to 2 Pz. Div. This division attempted to gain control over the crossroads of La Denisière in a quick thrust to the east, but had failed. However, 1,500 m further to the south, the road was still blocked by elements of the Reconnaissance Battalion. During the course of the day, the enemy increased his pressure against the division—particularly against 2 Pz. Gren. Regt—committed on the right flank. Above all, the effect of the enemy's air force once more prevented the continuation of the division's flank attack during daytime. We had to reckon with the commitment of one to two American infantry divisions, echeloned left to the rear of the advancing American armored units and having the task of the offensive flank protection. On its own, 2 Pz. Div. was too weak to defeat the strong enemy. Due to the delay in the arrival of 116 Pz. Div., it became more obvious to us that the flanking attack towards the northwest had now been overtaken by events, and that at this juncture only an attack towards the west could effectively strike the enemy's flank.

In the meantime, the enemy's tank units had encountered 352 Inf. Div.'s defense position in the Hambye, west of the St-Martin-de-Venilly [-Cenilly?] – Roncey line. The enemy succeeded in breaking through the front line and in advancing, with his tank groups in combat formation, as far as the Cérences area, although the division had committed the already weakened Panzer Jaeger Battalion on both sides of the road leading southwest and

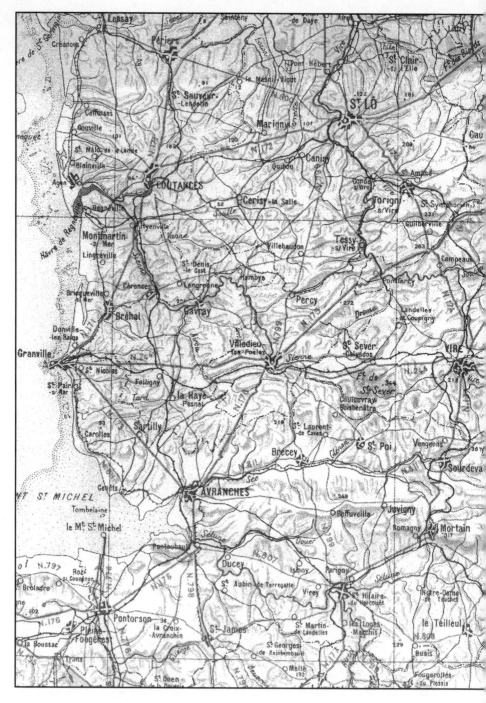

The battlefield, 25

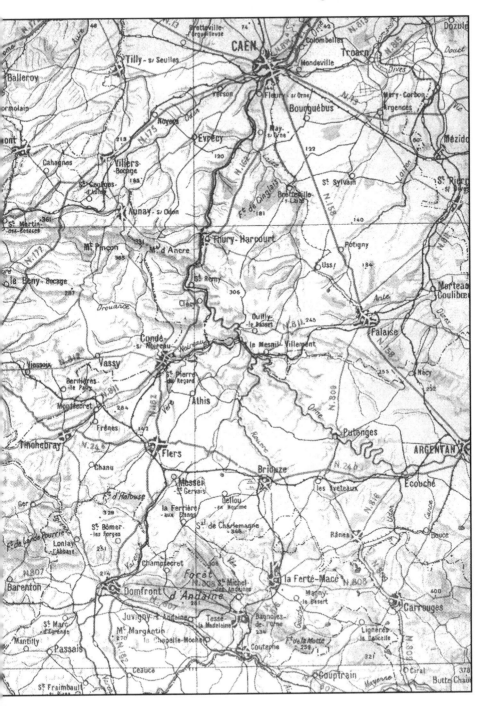

July–20 August 1944.

west from Hambye. LXXXIV Inf. Corps was practically encircled. Countermeasures by Corps, undertaken with available elements of 2 SS-Pz. Div., proved too weak to prevent the enemy's penetration on one hand and failed, as usual, on account of the enemy's air force, which prevented any movement of large extent on the battlefield. Covered by their air force, the enemy troops who had penetrated into the line affected the rear of the German units to such an extent that the unity of the defense deteriorated and the battle finally turned into separate fights for hills, localities, and individual farms. The command was almost entirely dependent on radio communication, since all wire lines had been destroyed and messengers shot in the enemy-saturated terrain. The separate units fought on their own as small combat teams, and had hardly any contact with neighboring troops.

The Commander of Seventh Army, Generaloberst Hausser, personally had the opportunity of observing this situation in its true colors, when he attempted in vain to drive from the advanced command post southwest of Percy to LXXXIV Inf. Corps' command post in the area north of Cérences. Since 116 Pz. Div., according to latest reports, could not be assembled before 30 July, a relief through a westward attack by XLVII Pz. Corps could not be expected before this date. In the evening of 28 July, the Army ordered Corps to break out to the southeast in the night of 29 July, and to try to establish contact with XLVII Pz. Corps in the Villebaudon area, in order to prevent the certain annihilation of those elements of LXXXIV Inf. Corps which were encircled in the Coutances area. The Army intended to build up a new defense in the rear of the Sienne sector and west of the bend of the Sienne river.

The Commander of Army Group B, Field Marshal von Kluge, did not agree with this decision by the Seventh Army commander, because he feared that the ordered direction of penetration—to the southeast—would tear a gap in the coastal front line, thus enabling the enemy to advance without effort to the south, and, in the course of events, to cut off Brittany. He demanded that the ordered be amended, and that contact with the coastal front line be maintained by all possible means. Under great difficulties, the Seventh Army succeeded in passing on to Corps new orders for the breakthrough to the south; however, Corps was no longer in a position to relay the necessary directions to its subordinate units, especially not to 2 SS-Pz. Div. and 17 SS-Pz. Gren. Div. After having been pulled out of the front line, it was not before 28 July that these divisions were assembled in sufficient degree for employment as compact units. During the daytime they were held down by the enemy's air force to such an extent that they could no longer effect any concentrated countermeasures. Therefore, the strongest elements of Corps, i.e., 2 SS-Pz. Div. and 17 SS-Pz. Gren. Div., were committed for the breakthrough in the general direction of Percy. The remnants of 353, 91, and 243 Inf. Divs were ordered to break through southward towards the La Baleine – Cavray [?] – Bréhal line.

During the course of the day, XLVII Pz. Corps had assumed command west of the Vire in the Le Mesnil-Raoult – Moyon – Villebaudon sector north of Percy. 2 Pz. Div., of which one Panzer battalion and one artillery battalion were still left with Panzer Group West (326 Inf. Div. sector), remnants of Pz. Lehr Div., and the arriving elements of 116 Pz. Div. were assigned to XLVII Pz. Corps.

During the night of 28/29 July, one of 2 Pz. Div.'s combat teams (15–20 tanks and two companies of 304 Pz. Gren. Regt) succeeded in advancing from Moyon to the crossroads at La Denisière and in gaining control over same. This combat team, however, had to take up a position of an all-around defense as we did not succeed in establishing a firm contact with them. However, since the main road from St-Lô to Percy was thereby solidly blocked, the first part of XLVII Panzer Corps' order could be regarded as accomplished. On 29 July, the Pz. Div. combat team succeeded, near La Denisière, in inflicting heavy losses upon the enemy, including 25 tanks.

In the meantime, Seventh Army had decided to change the direction of the Corps' intended flank attack, from the previously ordered northwest to the west. However, the start of this attack depended upon the arrival of 116 Pz. Div. The chances of success diminished by the hour on account of this delay. In the meantime, strong elements of two enemy infantry divisions were attacking 2 Pz. Div., which initially was forced into the defensive. We feared that, due to the rapid development of the tactical situation, the basis of attack had now been overtaken by events.

The main body of LXXXIV Inf. Corps succeeded in staging a breakthrough during the night of 28/29 July. 353 Inf. Div. concentrated the artillery fire of the two remaining artillery battalions on the St-Martin-de-Cenilly – Lengronne road, and, from the Cotteral [?] area in a southward direction, attacked St-Denis-le-Gast with the still combat-efficient 941 Gren. Regt. Despite heavy losses, particularly east of the Cotteral – St-Denis-le-Gast road, the breakthrough succeeded. Surprisingly, the enemy did not defend St-Denis-le-Gast, which meant that all of the division's encircled elements, including the two artillery battalions, could escape southward through the effected gap. Since the enemy had not yet blocked the Sienne crossings either, and since there was no air activity by low-flying aircraft in the morning of 29 July, we also succeeded in crossing the river, although it took until the forenoon. The enemy only applied countermeasures against St-Denis-le-Gast after the last elements of the division had passed through this place. The division prepared for the defense in the sector 2 km southeast of Hambye – Cavray (excluding the latter), which was extremely suitable for a defensive position.

Those elements of 275 Inf. Div. (Kampfgruppe Heinz) and 243 Inf. Div. (one battalion)—a total strength of 400 men—which were previously employed in the Hambye area, were put under the command of 353 Inf. Div., and were committed by this division in the right wing in the Sienne bend area, northeast of La Baleine. Because the only adjoining troops were the weak remnants of Pz. Lehr Div., the division protected its still open east flank with weak reserves. We hoped that XLVII Pz. Corps would attract the bulk of the enemy forces and thereby prevent a breakthrough to the south.

The two remaining infantry divisions of Corps, i.e., 91 and 243 Inf. Divs, which were to escape to the south, had to fight their way back by groups, thereby losing the bulk of their heavy equipment, artillery, heavy weapons, and vehicles. However, considerable numbers of the column and weak combat forces had escaped to the south, along the coastal road via Bréhal, while this road was still open.

2 SS-Pz. Div. and 17 SS-Pz. Gren. Div., facing the enemy's main point of effort, had to endure heavy fighting on, and on both sides of, the Coutances – Percy road. However, it can be assumed that these divisions' attacks came as a considerable relief to the three infantry divisions, because the thrust of these mobile units probably attracted the main body

of the enemy. There, too, the breakthrough succeeded. The main body of 2 SS-Pz. Div. combat team reached the Percy area, while 17 SS-Pz. Gren. Div. once more suffered heavy losses, and only remnants of this division managed to escape. On 29 July, the divisions were not available for combat, as they had to assemble and close up once again.

During the night, Seventh Army's advance combat post was transferred to Chavoy (6 km northeast of Avranches.)

Under these circumstances, it was unavoidable that utter confusion reigned on all roads in the rear area of the Seventh Army sector. Scattered separate columns struggled to the rear, blocking the roads. The main body of these forces turned to the southeast, or even east, when it was rumored that the enemy had penetrated in the direction of Avranches.

Seventh Army established a strict organization, the duty of which was the maintaining of order and discipline, the gathering of stragglers, and the keeping clear of the roads, necessary for supply and tactical movements. The Staff of 352 Inf. Div., 275 Inf. Div., and 5 FS Jg. Div., which had become available in the meantime, were employed in this organization. The remaining troops of these divisions had previously been assigned to 2 and 116 Pz. Divs, or 353 Inf. Div., respectively. One sector in the rear area was allotted to each of these staffs. In this sector the Staff had to assume responsibility for the gathering of the stragglers, traffic control, the blocking of the terrain and keeping localities in readiness for the defensive.

On 29 July, while the strategic situation remained unchanged, the enemy reinforced his troops in front of the right Army wing and, particularly, in front of the line held by XLVII Pz. Corps. 116 Pz. Div.'s Reconnaissance Battalion, having been the first to arrive, was ordered to seize Mont Robin, northeast of Percy, thereby gaining a base for the intended attack. This attack failed. The battalion suffered heavy losses on its first commitment. A lack of combat experience and coordination among the newly activated troops became especially conspicuous when the battalion commander was lost.

In the west, the remnants of Pz. Lehr Div. had to fall back along the Le Mesnil-Herman – Percy road to Hill 210. Reinforced by elements of the divisions that had managed to break through (i.e., 2 SS-Pz. Div. and 17 SS-Pz. Gren. Div.), they succeeded in holding this important hill directly north of Percy.

On 29 July, the enemy probed against the combat outposts which had been left behind on the north bank, but no major attacks took place. There seemed to be a lull in the fighting. The strategic situation, however, was particularly dangerous at the west wing of LXXXIV Inf. Corps, where only a few hundred men—the remnants of 91 and 243 Inf. Divs—were in position between Cavray and the coast. These troops lacked, above all, artillery and antitank weapons.

On the evening of 29 July, the Commander of LXXXIV Inf. Corps, General von Choltitz, was relieved by Generalleutnant Elfeldt, and the Seventh Army Chief of Staff, General Pemsel, was relieved by Oberst i.G. Frhr von Gersdorff [the current author]. The latter transmitted to Seventh Army the Army Group order to do everything possible to strengthen the west wing, in order to maintain contact with the sea under all circumstances. The only available unit behind the thinly manned front line of the Seventh Army wing in the area of the crossroads of Le Repas [?] was the as yet incomplete 5 FS Jg. Division's Engineer Battalion. This battalion had only just rejoined the division.

Since Army Group insisted on the commitment of XLVII Pz. Corps in the counterattack towards the west via the Tessy – Percy road, the only way out for Seventh Army was to form a combat team consisting of those elements of 2 and 116 Pz. Divs which had managed to break through, and to bring this combat team forward for the purpose of reinforcing the left wing. The execution of these measures, although ordered to be carried out immediately, was delayed to such an extent that the movements could not be accomplished during the darkness, but had to be completed during daylight on 30 July. Seventh Army's strategic situation had reached the peak of the crisis.

E. 30 and 31 July

On 30 July, activity by enemy low-flying aircraft increased to the highest point of intensity reached in the entire war. The Allies carried out continuous and uninterrupted air attacks in the American sector, and were complete masters of the situation. The Allied air forces controlled events. This situation arose on only two other occasions during the war—on 7 August, in the defense against the German counterattack on Avranches, and on 18 August, when Seventh Army was encircled in the Falaise/Argentan pocket.

The strategic situation at the front line occupied by II FS Jg. Corps remained unchanged. On 30 July, too, 3 FS Jg. Div. managed to successfully defend their main battle line against the unchanging pressure of the enemy. However, at this point, indications of the employment of the British against the left wing of Panzer Group West became noticeable. In view of the fact that the committed 362 Inf. Div. was inexperienced in battle, Corps had to consider the possibility of the east flank being endangered. Corps secured its position by employing a FS Jg. Regt and available elements of XII FS Jg. Reconnaissance Battalion in the rear of the right wing.

Field Marshal von Kluge, Commander of Army Group, arrived in person at the XLVII Pz. Corps combat post, north of St-Sever-Calvados, in order to spur the now fully assembled Corps on the attack. However, in the meantime, the enemy had reinforced his troops before the battle front to such an extent that he, too, was ready to launch an attack. Therefore, only mobile combat developed in the area west of the Vire, without any decisive gain of terrain towards the west being achieved. Therefore, any action by Corps against the main point of effort of the American penetration became impossible, leaving the main task of Corps unfulfilled. The intended thrust of the two Panzer divisions to and across the Percy – St-Lô road was unsuccessful, because the division received no relief from the adjoining 116 Pz. Div., tied down in heavy battle. Contact with the combat team, having taken up a position of all-around defense in the La Denisière area, was finally lost. Owing to the superiority of the enemy forces, this combat team was almost completely annihilated. Practically all its personnel were taken prisoner. Approximately seven tanks managed to fight their way back to Moyon.

116 Pz. Div., fully assembled in the area southeast of Tessy, and drawing up to the front from the St-Sever-Calvados area, unsuccessfully attempted to gain the basis for a further thrust against the enemy flank. Although, on the whole, the strength of the division only sufficed for a defense against the American attacks, it nevertheless succeeded in establishing contact with the left wing of 2 Pz. Div. and the remnants of Pz. Lehr Div. in the Percy area. This time, again, the division failed to capture Mont Robin northeast of Percy.

On the evening of 30 July it became evident that XLVII Pz. Corps had been forced onto the defensive, and that a continuation of the attacks against the west stood no chance of success.

The adjacent LXXXIV Inf. Corps could not prevent the continuation of the American breakthrough with its limited countermeasures. At the front line held by 353 Inf. Div., the enemy managed to force the retreat of the combat outposts still in position north of the Sienne. The enemy then attacked with his main point of effort directed against the Sienne bend, southwest of Hambye, and against the seam with 91 Inf. Div., on both sides of Cavray. The first attacks were repulsed, but later on the enemy succeeded in effecting penetrations across the Sienne, south of Hambye, at Balaine [?], and at Cavray, whereby he managed to break through as far as the regimental combat posts. At first, it was possible to seal off these attacks.

The measures ordered by Seventh Army for the reinforcement of the Army left wing had not yet taken effect. Owing to the lack of fuel and the poor transmission of orders (the cables having been destroyed by enemy fire, and the majority of the radio stations lost), the formation of the combat team, consisting of elements of 2 SS-Pz. Div. and 17 SS-Pz. Gren. Div., was delayed to such an extent that it was finally put on the march only during daylight. The newly formed Combat Team Fick (a regimental commander from 17 SS-Pz. Gren. Div.) had received orders to, first of all, reach the Beauchamps area via Villedieu [-les-Poêles?] in order to strike the enemy (whose penetration was expected mainly along the Crenes [?] – Avranches road) in the flank. Due to the air situation, however, it took the combat team all day to reach the Beauchamps area, where it arrived in a very weak condition and spread out over a wide area.

In the meantime, the enemy had broken through the thinly manned German line of security at Crenes, and had, in a quick thrust to the south, overrun 5 FS Jg. Division's Engineer Battalion, before this battalion was ready for the defense. Protected by low-flying aircraft, armored spearheads of the US 4th Armored Div. continued to advance in the direction of Avranches, without encountering any resistance worth mentioning. Seventh Army, having been able to observe the assaults of the enemy tanks from the advanced command post in the Chavoy area in the late afternoon of 30 July, had mobilized all available forces for the blocking of the Avranches gap.

The most advanced battery of the assault gun battalion (341?), in the process of being brought up, was about the only available unit for this operation. This battery was committed on both sides of the road leading northward from Avranches; furthermore, a battle commander was appointed in Avranches who was to organize a defense, using alarm units, stragglers, and construction forces. It was his task to prevent the enemy's southward thrust via the La Sée sector at Avranches. The execution of these measures, too, was delayed on account of the difficulty in transmitting orders. Only one radio station was at the disposal of the advanced Seventh Army command post. Oberstleutnant i.G. Hoffmann, the officer of the General Staff who had been sent to Avranches to supervise the defense measures, had been missing since that time.

On the evening of 30 July, Seventh Army regarded the strategic situation to be the following:

An Sd Kfz 222 armored car knocked out by the 1/8th Infantry during the fighting near St-Lô on 15 July 1944. The armor on the rear of the vehicle has been blown off, exposing the engine.

1. The strategic situation on the right wing and at the center of the Seventh Army front line seemed secure, provided that we succeeded in holding the crossroads at Percy and the important hilly terrain north of Percy. The execution of the planned flank attack by XLVII Pz. Corps, however, had become impossible. It seemed hardly possible to carry out any large-scale reorganization, or to withdraw a great number of forces from this front sector.

2. The defense of the left Seventh Army wing had collapsed. It was no longer possible to intercept or to seal off the accomplished breakthrough of the enemy. The enemy's thrust into the depth of the defense could no longer be stopped, not even if the weak covering parties at Avranches could succeed in holding this town.

In order to save as many elements as possible from certain annihilation, Seventh Army had to withdraw to the east and southeast, and had to try to establish a defense flank in the general direction of the Percy – Villedieu-les-Poêles – Avranches line. Seventh Army transmitted the necessary orders by radio, and ordered XLVII Pz. Corps to put all available forces of 116 Pz. Div. on the march in the area southwest of Villedieu-les-Poêles, in order to have combat-efficient reserves at their disposal. This reserve unit was to be used for the thrust against the east flank of the enemy's tank wedge. Seventh Army realized that the enemy forces that had advanced so far were necessarily weak, and that it was important to take advantage of this situation before the enemy could bring up stronger forces.

Considerable numbers of columns of every type poured from the Cavray area to the southeast, and, although they seemed to be lost, managed to block the roads and delay the advancing enemy.

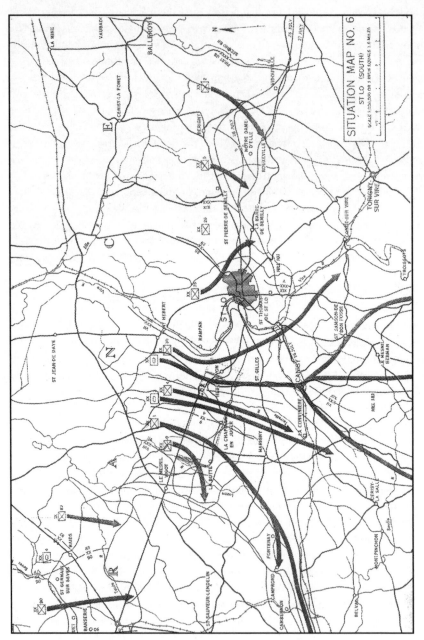

The breakout: St-Lô (south).

Field Marshal von Kluge arrived at Le Mans, Seventh Army's main combat post, in the evening. He had ordered the advanced combat post not to effect any change of position without his specific command. For that reason, the Commander-in-Chief Seventh Army remained at Combat Post 6, northeast of Avranches, even when the enemy was fighting for this town. The enemy's tanks passed only a few hundred meters from the combat post in a continuous stream. The assault gun battery, which had put several tanks out of action, had run out of ammunition. The battalion's two remaining batteries were still in the Rennes area. The combat post was evacuated at 2400 hrs when a message was received that the enemy was advancing southward on the Villedieu – Avranches road. The radio station had been blasted. Under difficulties, Seventh Army Staff had to work its way via [St-Gabriel- ?] Brécy along obstructed roads, and only arrived at Mortain at 0600 hrs. There they established the new command post. Owing to the fact that no signal communication existed as yet, and the Army therefore was not in a position of directing the strategic operations, Field Marshal von Kluge, stationed in Le Mans, assumed command. From his reports to the Armed Forces Operations Staff, and from his judgment of the situation, it is apparent that von Kluge clearly recognized the significance of the strategic situation in terms of the war as a whole.

LXXXIV Inf. Corps had ordered its units to withdraw to the southeast during the night 30/31 July, and to establish a defense front along the Percy – Villedieu – Avranches road. According to plan, 353 Inf. Div. succeeded in withdrawing to Villedieu and occupying a new line of resistance on both sides of the town. At this point, 363 Inf. Division's 957 Gren. Regt (Commander: Oberst Frhr von Call), having been the first to arrive, was assigned to the 353rd Inf. Div. The 363rd Inf. Div. (Commander: General Dettling) was in the process of being brought up. XLVII Pz. Corps moved this regiment in trucks to the front, and the regiment was de-trucked north of Villedieu-les-Poêles in the morning of 31 July. Only remnants—mostly rear services of LXXXIV Inf. Corps' other units—managed to escape during the general confusion.

116 Pz. Division's combat team (strength: one Panzer battalion, one Panzer Grenadier battalion, one artillery battalion, and elements of the Reconnaissance Battalion) managed to reach the L'Epine area, 6 km southeast of Villedieu, in the morning of 31 July.

The situation at Avranches remained obscure. On the one hand, it was reported that the enemy had penetrated into the town, while, on the other hand, Seventh Army was informed that our own columns were still driving east and southeastward through Avranches or bypassing the town. In any case, it appeared that the defense provisionally established at Avranches had collapsed. While XXV Inf. Corps (Brittany) was ordered to seal off the Avranches gap to the south and southeast at Ducey – Pontaubault and to assemble for the counterattack, after the concentration of sufficient elements from Brittany (77 Inf. Div.), in order to recapture Avranches, staffs of 275 Inf. Div. and 5 FS Jg. Div., having gathered stragglers and formed them into small combat teams, were ordered to secure the sector east of Avranches (south of the La Sée sector.)

F. 31 July

The left wing of the British invasion army launched the expected attack. The effect of heavy barrage and pattern bombing on 326 Inf. Div. at the left wing of Panzer Group West was

SITUATION MAP NO. 7
COUTANCES

The breakout: Coutances.

similar to that on Pz. Lehr Div. on 25 July. The following enemy troops (British Guards Armored Div.) managed to effect a deep penetration, thereby threatening the east flank of II FS Jg. Corps.

9 FS Jg. Regt, in a position of readiness in the rear of the right wing, proceeded to occupy a flank position west of Fierville [-les Mines?] and west of La Fouquerie [?]. 12 FS Jg. Reconnaissance Bn, having managed to fall back, secured the corps' deep flank at the Vire bend, northeast of Sourdeval (Hill 204).

Corresponding in time with the British attack, US V Corps considerably increased its pressure against the front line on both sides of Torigni [-sur-Vire]. Because the right wing of XLVII Pz. Corps (2 Pz. Gren. Regt) was pushed back to the east across the Vire at the same time, and therefore the west flank of II FS Jg. Corps was also endangered, 3 FS Jg. Div. was withdrawn to the line of small woods 6 km eastward of Torigny, on hills south of Torigny – Hill 133 – Cretteville. Due to a particularly clever conduct of the battle, the FS Jg. managed to conceal their intentions from the enemy. Local counterattacks and deception delayed the enemy, at times even forcing him to withdraw to the north.

Heavy defensive battles were fought by XLVII Panzer Corps' right wing in the general line G[ran]d Val de Vire – Moyen. Especially heavy fighting developed north of Troisgots, after the enemy had succeeded in forcing 2 Pz. Gren. Regt's right wing back to the east. At times, the hilly and wooded terrain necessitated bitter close combat. The Panzer division suffered severe losses in these close combats, above all through the heavy artillery fire. On this third day of battle, the strength of 2 Pz. Div. sank to 50–60 men per company. In the evening, 2 Pz. Div. withdrew to the line on both sides of Tessy, south of Beaucoudray.

116 Pz. Div. had managed to capture Beaucoudray, and an assault detachment from this division had succeeded in reaching the main road from St-Lô to Percy, south of La Tilandière [?]. The crossroads at Villebaudon and Mont Robin, however, remained in enemy hands, which meant that this division also failed to achieve any decisive success. The corps' attack had finally failed due to the fact that 2 Pz. Div. had been completely forced into the defensive. The recognition of this situation, and the strategic situation at the left wing of the Army, were the basis for the order to Corps to finally stop the attacks and to withdraw 116 Pz. Div. to the southeast in order to be employed at Seventh Army's left wing. 2 SS-Pz. Div. and the remnants of Pz. Lehr Div. had managed to hold Percy up to now.

The strategic situation at the front line held by LXXXIV Inf. Corps had continued to deteriorate. 353 Inf. Div., in its new position on both sides of Villedieu-les-Poêlles, managed to intercept an attack against Villedieu on the eastern perimeter of the town (941 Gren. Regt sector). Further to the southwest, however, the enemy succeeded in penetrating 942 Gren. Regt. The division reserves (remnants of 943 Gren. Regt) went into action at this point, but were completely eliminated. The enemy penetrated to St-Martin-le-Bouillant and inflicted heavy losses on the columns and rear services.

Contact with 116 Pz. Div.'s combat team, in a defensive position in the L'Epine area, was interrupted. The team was encircled by the enemy, and only managed to fight their way back to the division, in position in the St-Pois area, during the following days.

A remaining combat team from 6 FS Jg. Regt joined 353 Inf. Div. Since June, this team had been 2 FS Jg. Division's only fighting unit on the invasion front. The division committed the team (strength 30–40 men) at St-Maur-des-Bois as a covering party for the right flank.

Besides 116 Pz. Div.'s combat team, remnants of 9 and 243 Inf. Divs and alarm units were fighting in the area between Villedieu and the La Sée sector. None of these units, however, was strong enough for a defensive.

275 Inf. Div. had been ordered to secure the roads leading from Avranches to the east. The only troops available to the division for this purpose were the gathered remnants under the command of Oberst Schlee, Commander of 985 Gren. Regt (about 200 men strong), one company of NCOs of the Field Replacement Training Battalion, and one company of artillerymen. One AT gun and a few heavy arms were the only weapons at the disposal of this combat team. It did not possess a single gun [sic]. The division assumed command over the remnants of 5 FS Jg. Div., and used these forces to establish a sealing-off front in the Le Mesnil-Adelée – Reffuveille line and southwest of this line. On account of the insecure strategic situation at the northern flank, one company was left behind in the northern part of Chérencé for the purpose of protecting the flank. The division combat post was established in a farm 1½ km southeast of Juvigny-le-Tertre. However, up to this point, the enemy did not probe ahead from Avranches to the east and southeast.

In the meantime, the sector near Pontaubault had been secured by elements of 77 Inf. Div. (Commander: Oberst Bacherer). A local defense of Ducey had been organized. A combat team consisting of about two battalions of 77 Inf. Div. launched an attack against

Allied air superiority led the Wehrmacht to pay serious attention to air defense. One of its most effective weapons was the 20mm Flak 38 mounted on the SdKfz 7 halftrack. This is a vehicle from 2 SS-Pz. Div. (Das Reich), abandoned in the Roncey pocket and being inspected by some GIs.

Avranches in the evening of 31 July, and managed to penetrate to the southern perimeter of the town. These forces, however, were too weak to consolidate the success, or to hold the position. Suffering heavy losses, they had to be withdrawn to their jump-off position.

None of these measures succeeded in sealing off the enemy attack; they merely served to observe the enemy's movements. The left Seventh Army wing had in fact been annihilated. The enemy had managed to effect a large gap, through which he could roll into the interior of France whenever he chose to do so. The US Third Army stood in readiness for this purpose. It was most surprising that this Army did not take full advantage of the strategic situation on 31 July and 1 August. They would not have met with any resistance worth mentioning.

The attempts to close this gap in the front line, while moving, had failed. All that mattered now was to collect available forces as quickly as possible, in order to reestablish, in an counterattack, according to plan, the contact with the coast; this was especially important, because the High Command did not wish to take the important decision to evacuate the south of France.

Chapter 3

25–26 July

by Generaloberst Paul Hausser
Translated by EWS (B-179)

NORTHERN FRANCE, 25 July–26 July 1944

Records: 7 Army War Journal 25/26 July 1944; 4–16 August 1944.
Map: 1:100,000
Opening situation, 7 Army, 24 July 1944; evening.

ORDER OF BATTLE

Army Group B, Field Marshal von Kluge.
7 Army, Army Headquarters: Le Mans.
Forward CP: La Saurier [?] – south of Percy.

LXXXIV: Corps Headquarters
Pz. Lehr Div: Combat Gp 275 Inf. Div.
5 Para. Jg. Div., less Regt 15
17 SS-Pz. Gren. Div.
2 SS-Pz. Div.
91 Inf. Div., Combat Gp 265, 343 Inf. Div.
243 Inf. Div.

II Para. Jg. Corps:
3 Para. Jg. Div. with Para.
    Regt 15
352 Inf. Div., with Combat Gp
    266, 353 Inf. Div.

Reserves:
275 Inf. Div., less 1 combat gp
353 Inf. Div., less 1 combat gp
Staff 77 Inf. Div. – on the march to St-Malo
Brittany: Corps Headquarters XXV (LXXIV had
    been transferred to Panzer Group West by end
    of July)
265, 266 and 343 Inf. Divs, less 1 combat gp each }
2 Para. Jg. Div., less 1 regt   } not dealt with here
Channel Islands: 319 Inf. Div.   }

Evaluation of the Armed Forces

Almost every one of these units had been, ever since the beginning of the invasion, in combat with the numerically [and] materially superior US fighting forces. The only units fully fit for combat were: 3 Para. [FS] Jg. Div., 22 SS-Pz. Div., and 275 Inf. Div. with four battalions. In addition, although severely weakened, there were the Pz. Lehr Div., 17 SS-Pz. Div., and 353 Inf. Div. Other remaining units had suffered severely. The degree of training of the newly constituted 5 Para. Jg. Div. had been insufficient and incomplete, and the men lacked combat experience. The artillery had been sufficient, although it was partially equipped with captured enemy guns, and had only a limited amount of ammunition on hand.

We suffered a severe shortage of supplies. This was partially due to the extensive destruction of the railroads and bridges, as well as to the enemy's aerial patrolling of all important roads. Our own air force was no longer capable of action.

The Army's mission was to hold onto the present position. No evading movements had been planned, and although rear-area positions had been reconnoitered, they had not been fortified.

Combat instructions received stated that, due to the enemy's air superiority—fighters and bombers—and also in artillery, the MLR should be occupied only by weak forces, while all available reserves were to be assembled in the rear, near the command stations, from where they could be committed swiftly, and, by means of counterattacks, could wipe out any penetrations made by the enemy.

Reserves Available for High Command

15 Para. Jg. Regt (II Para. Jg. Corps), east of the Vire.

353 Inf. Div. (Corps Headquarters LXXXIV), west of the Vire.

275 Inf. Div. (Seventh Army), west of the Vire.

Reinforcement with additional reserves, especially of one motorized unit and one or two Werfer (rocket projector) brigades, was again urgently requested by 20 July.

The present positions had been occupied as the outcome of the previous surging battles and evading movements. They were advantageous only in the western wing, through the help of nature. Enemy forces opposing the Army were calculated to total 14–16 divisions, of which two were Panzer divisions, and numerous Panzer and artillery battalions from the Army. Nevertheless, the flow of newly arriving replacement units to reinforce others was quite possible at any time.

Preparations for the grand assault had been completed, and it was expected to take place somewhere west of the Vire. The push was expected to take place over the high terrain to the south-southwest. An expansion toward both sides had to be expected. Airborne landing operations were held possible. All these reinforcements in the front of the Army's left wing were aimed at the 3rd US Army.

On 24 July 1944, events unveiled the enemy's intention to a great extent. Although the actual infantry attack did not take place after the pattern-bombing raid—the first of its kind in the US sector—a decisive attack had still to be reckoned with, just west of the Vire.

The night remained calm. Heavy harassing artillery fire had been directed upon the major battle zones and gun positions. Reconnaissance activity was carried out to some extent. Except for widespread aerial activity—especially in the rear areas—everything remained calm in II Para. Jg. Corps' region.

After a three-hour artillery preparatory bombardment, the attack began at 1030 hrs, west of Vire. The enemy infantry had been withdrawn from its forward positions, while the enemy air force—with approximately 1,000 four-engined bombers, escorted by numerous fighters—blasted the entire MLR with pattern-bombing, including all points in the combat zone between the road Vire – Knie [?] – St-Gilles – Larigny [?] – Les Champs-de-Losque, and, in addition, attacked the Pz. Lehr Div. sector and the right wing of 5 Para. Jg. Div.

Wherever the pattern bombing took place, nearly all life ceased to exist, guns were smashed, tanks crippled, and radio and signal communications destroyed, which partially cut off the Command headquarters. But, in spite of all this, fierce battles resulted as soon as the enemy infantry began to feel its way forward; this occurred especially on the east wing. Later on, the attack expanded to the south of Remilly.

The enemy air force supported the attackers from time to time, and when their fighter-bombers intervened, a forward movement of their assault points was always evident.

Individual details can be seen from reports submitted by Maj. Gen. Bayerlein, Commander of Pz. Lehr Div. Most of the division's resistance was smashed. Thus, there occurred an approximately 3 km wide enemy penetration as far as south of Hébécrevon – Montreuil.

Besides local reserves, one regimental combat group from 353 Inf. Div., from the vicinity of Hauteville, was committed. During this counterattack, it got as far as the area southeast of Lozon, where it was stopped. To hold, or at least to delay, any further enemy advances along the Hébécrevon – La Chapelle line, a weak combat group from 275 Inf. Div. (Army Reserve) had been made available to Pz. Lehr Div. Nevertheless, this availability was never realized. because on 26 July the group became involved in an engagement between La Chapelle and Marigny, during which it was annihilated.

By evening it proved possible to intercept and to stop the enemy advance along the line south of Hébécrevon – southern edge of Lozon – south of Le Mesnil-Vigot. Everything else remained calm throughout the remainder of the front. There was extensive aerial reconnaissance activity in the Avranches – St-Malo sector. The Army calculated on a renewal of this attack, and a likely expansion to both sides.

On 26 July 1944, LXXXIV Corps Headquarters had planned to launch a counterattack with all of its available elements from 275 and 353rd Inf. Divs; those elements in the Canisy area were intended to be moved out, to be rallied during the night, and then to be moved forward toward La Chapelle. However, this attack could not be carried out.

Army Group had issued orders for the relief of 2 Pz. Div. from Panzer Group West's left wing, and replacement of same by 326 Inf. Div.

26 July 1944

After a very heavy enemy artillery barrage on the very important transit roads, and preparatory artillery fire throughout the different sectors, by 26 July 1944 the enemy attack had begun to expand over the entire II Para. Jg. Corps area. Penetrations were reported during the following afternoon near Biéville and Vidouville – Montrabot, and where 15 Para. Jg. Regt had been committed in a counterattack—St-Germain-d'Elle, Bois de la Rillerie [?], and St-Pierre-de-Semilly. To support the front, there had been committed, west of Vire, 983 Regt from 275 Inf. Div., from Canisy toward the north; and remnants of 353 Inf. Div., between Duquerie and Lozon.

This day was not like the preceding day, distinguished by pattern-bombing and artillery fire, but rather by attacks by fighter-bombers, which assaulted our moving troops and our artillery emplacements, as well as our reserves, and formed an umbrella over the enemy's spearheads. Thus the elements from 275 Inf. Div.—the only Army Reserve left—could not be sent in under unified control, and in the course of the day were almost completely annihilated. The major attack against remnants of Pz. Lehr Div. began south of Hébécrevon, to Le Mesnil-Amey, Marigny, and south of Lozon, and was supported by a large number of tanks. By committing all of the remaining reserves, it proved possible to keep, by evening, the heights near Canisy and those south of Marigny. Contact with both sides could be maintained to some extent.

Enemy attacks launched further to the west gained success against 2 SS-Pz. Div., on the Raids–Périers road, and against 91 Inf. Div. between the Seves sector and the St-Germain – Périers road. Here it was, in general, possible to seal off smaller enemy penetrations, as well as to repulse the attack.

LXXXIV Corps' situation in the center and left wing had become untenable north and northwest of Périers. It had to lead to a break, through the ranks of Pz. Lehr Div., and the consequent closing of the ring. The center and left wings had to be withdrawn. The only remaining difficulty was that of obtaining Army Group's permission.

I do not recall all details, because there is a gap in the continuity of the War Diary, but it is known that on 26 July 1944 the bulk was ordered to withdraw over the roads from Feugères, Périers, and Lessay to Coutances, to a line west of Montcuit – St-Sauveur-Lendelin–the La Quizze [?] heights – Geffosses, while leaving detachments behind to cope with the enemy. The shortening of the front permitted the withdrawal of 2 SS-Pz. Div. further toward the east. Some of its elements were already in combat on 26 July. In addition, LXXXIV Corps Headquarters made the remaining weak units from 275 Inf. Div. available.

During the evening, the Commanding General of XLVII Pz. Corps and the commander of 2 Pz. Div. reported to the Army. Coming from the Caen area, they had received orders from Army Group to proceed to and reach the area of Tessy-sur-Vire. Their arrival depended upon the weather conditions, and was not expected to take place before 28 July 1944. 116 Pz. Div. was to follow up later.

For the time immediately following, some of the statements may not be accurate, especially with regard to the Army's wings. The War Diary is sparse with regard to details up to 4 August.

PART THREE

On 26 July, the US VII Corps began to widen the Allied penetration as the 3rd Armored Division and 1st Infantry Division captured Marigny and the 2nd Armored Division advanced seven miles. VIII Corps took Périers. The "right hook" planned to envelop the German LXXXIV Corps at Coutances while its forces remained engaged trying to contain the offensive from the north.

By the 28th, much of LXXIV Corps and, critically, 2nd SS-Panzer and 17th SS-Panzer Grenadier was in what the US forces were optimistically calling the "Roncey Pocket." Some of the German forces were able to withdraw to the southeast. On 28–29 July, German forces in the Roncey pocket were largely destroyed while trying to break out. Fighter-bombers repeatedly attacked the columns trying to pull back to the southeast. The 2nd Armored Division stopped most of the breakout attempts and other US spearheads. The Germans started shifting Panzer divisions from opposite the British sector for a counterattack, but by the 28th Coutances and its key road junction were in US hands.

By the 29th, the US VIII Corps, led by the 4th and 6th Armored Divisions, were pursuing the defeated Germans, meeting only light resistance. Avranches fell on the 27th. On 30 July, the US 4th Armored Division seized the key bridge at Pontaubault. This bridge, over the Selun, was literally the gateway into Brittany.

Chapter 4

Avranches to Argentan

by General der Artillerie Wilhelm Fahrmacher
Translated by Eva Elkiner (B-724)

In the first days after 20 July, Col. Gen. Jodl had briefed Hitler about the possibility of defensive lines in the rearward areas of France. This was done under the impact of the situation, which had continued to become more critical. Hitler basically concurred with Jodl's ideas. According to them, the River Seine was to be considered only as an intermediary line. This river appeared unsuitable as a defense line because of its numerous and large bends (the same was true of the lower part of the Arno river in Italy, which increased the difficulties of the defensive line because of its meanderings). Thus the following line came into consideration—from the Somme river to the Marne, to the west edge of the Vosges mountains. The western edge of the Vosges was demanded by Hitler because the defense installations of the West Wall on the upper part of the Rhine had, in his opinion, become outmoded. The strength of the individual pillboxes was inadequate in comparison with assault weapons, which had been improved in the meantime. Besides, they were exposed to high water in the event of floods. The continuous tank obstacle formed by the Rhine was to be replaced by utilizing the forests of the Vosges, once the position had been established. There is no doubt, however, that behind this intention—even though unspoken—was a certain disinclination to give up Alsace-Lorraine. Before, he had intended defending the fortified areas at the coast with all means, and thus increase the difficulties for the enemy's supply system. This appeared to be the best way to slow down the enemy's advances.

At the same time, work was done in Italy in the "Voralpenstellung" or the "Pre-Alpine Position," following the example of the "East Prussia Position." The question was considered whether it would not be better to withdraw voluntarily to the "Pre-Alpine Position" in Italy and thus release a number of divisions for employment in the French theater. The withdrawal of further units from the east was impossible in view of the situation there. The situation in France cannot be considered by itself, inasmuch as since 22 June the attack by the Red Army against Army Group Center had thrown the whole Eastern Front into a crisis which threatened any day to become a catastrophe. Thus one has to consider the interrelation of all theaters at all times, if one wants to understand the real difficulties of the German armed forces and their leaders.

On the basis of these considerations, orders were given on 28 July to the Commander-in-Chief West, the Chief of Army Rearmament, and the Commander-in-Chief of the Replacement Army, as well as the General of the Engineers and Fortifications, to finish the Somme–Marne–Saône–Swiss Jura line. The determining of this line, especially of its left

On 28 July 1944, the Commander of the German Seventh Army ordered a retreat towards Percy to avoid encirclement. The direction of the withdrawal was ill-advised, and 2 SS-Panzer Division became encircled around Roncey. In a series of engagements with 2nd Armored Division and US P-47 fighter bombers, the division lost most of its heavy equipment. Some idea of the carnage on the way back from the road block can be seen in this photograph taken outside St-Denis-le-Gast the next day. The abandoned hulks of a number of SdKfz 251 halftracks have already been pushed off the road. The second half-track in the column is an SdKfz 251/7 bridging vehicle from an engineer company of Das Reich. Behind it is a burned-out M4 medium tank of the 6th Armored Regiment, destroyed during the night-time battles.

wing, to the Saône expresses Hitler's optimism and his desire to give up as little as possible. He wanted to move the line now from the Vosges up to the Saône in order to deny the Allies access to Switzerland. Therefore, this defense was to lean with its left wing approximately on the southeastern part of Switzerland, near Geneva, while the Commander-in-Chief Southeast also had to extend his right wing across Savoy to there. The simple question, however, was this: from where would the forces come which were, firstly, to build this long defense line and, secondly, to occupy it? (As proven later, the time at their disposal for work on the fortifications was far too short to have accomplished much). At the same time, the West Wall was to be rearmed anew. It was to be supplemented, however, in such a manner that it included Metz. In the north, it was to be extended so that it leaned upon the Iyssel Sea [Zuider Zee]. In the south, the Vosges were to be included. The Chief of Army Rearmament and the Commander-in-Chief of the Replacement Army had to finish the necessary preliminary work by 1 September, and then finish the further work within seven weeks. The Reich defense commissioners were to be called in at the given time, but not immediately, and all use was to be made of civilian labor forces, as in the East Prussian example. These plans might have rested upon a careful study of the map, but they stood in no proper relationship to the actual facts. They underestimated the speed and the occurrence of events, and overestimated the value of field fortifications, which were occupied and supplied insufficiently against an enemy who had at his disposal all modern means of science and industry.

In the face of these facts—that in the depth of the French theater there were no rearward defense lines (the refusal of such riverine defense lines characterized Hitler's command also in the Eastern theater)—the lack of mobility of the majority of the German units could cause only the most serious fears. Under these circumstances, the American breakthrough in Avranches could only be considered as the beginning of a catastrophe. Hitler attempted at the last moment to bring about a change. In his mind a plan formed which aimed at regaining Avranches in a sudden counterattack, leading to a favorable decision. Even now, Hitler had no thoughts of withdrawal, and had decided to continue the battle and fight it through.

Thus the question arose whether it would be possible for the Americans to maintain the corridor which they had along the west of the Cotentin peninsula near Avranches, and to extend it in order to bring their troops to the rear of the German lines and to supply them there, or whether it would be possible for the Germans, on the other hand, to close up this corridor and thereby cut off the American forces which had already broken through.

The following units were believed to be in the American sector on 1 August 1944: four armored divisions and eight infantry divisions. Apparently, it was their aim to encircle the German II Para. [Fallschirm Jaeger] Corps and XLVII Pz. Corps and open the road to Paris. The center of the battle was partly on the boundary of Panzer Group West and the German Seventh Army and partly on the left German wing, where II SS-Pz. Corps tried to close the gap to the sea. Here, however, the enemy could advance further and reach the area of Vitres [Vitré?] with tanks. A blocking unit near Avranches had been pushed back into the area on both sides of the Ole [?] river.

On 1 August 1944, Commander-in-Chief West reported at 1100 hrs, by telephone, that the situation near Avranches had become more critical. The German forces had to be withdrawn behind the sector near Pontaubault. Only a few tanks were fighting on to the northeast of Avranches; the area was open to the enemy. It was expected that 116 Pz. Div. was engaged in battle in the vicinity of Brezay [Brécey?]. Further to the north, the situation at the front seemed stable, with the exception of the furthest right wing of the German Seventh Army, where the situation could not be cleared. Field Marshal von Kluge had the intention of employing 116 Pz. Div. as well as the other approaching forces on the German left wing.

But at 1150 on the same day, Commander-in-Chief West had to report that the enemy had broken through the defenses near Pontaubault and had reached several villages in Brittany. Probably this was the insertion of a command group for the organization of the French Resistance movement. Now a further block was formed near Dinan. Because of this situation, Hitler agreed to withdraw the German 2 Para. Div. from Brittany and to put it into the Normandy front. He refused, however, to permit the withdrawal of the German 319 Inf. Div. from the Channel Islands.

Commander-in Chief-West transmitted on the same day an exact evaluation of the situation. In it, he considered a second landing as improbable. Because of the arrival of new troops (especially Canadian units), the enemy had been reinforced to 45 divisions and numerous Army troops. With these, he would want to break through to the south and cut off Brittany. One had to reckon with the possibility of the simultaneously renewed employment of glider and parachute troops. Furthermore, Commander-in-Chief West reported that he intended to prevent the breakthrough at all costs, and considered the complete evacuation of the remaining sectors of the front. However, this required special attention, as the lack of armored and other mobile units would bring unfavorable results. The fight against the Resistance movement in the rear areas took a favorable course, as before.

In accordance with this idea of Field Marshal von Kluge's, 9 SS-Pz. Div. launched an attack in the direction of Avranches on 2 August 1944. With the intention of freeing other forces, Commander-in-Chief West ordered the release of XLVII Panzer and LXXXVI Corps. II Para. Corps withstood all enemy attacks. The enemy, however, reached the north edge of the town of Vitres [Vitré?] as well as St-Barthélemy and advanced to the south of St-Hilaire. Rennes and Dinan, however, could not be held.

There could, however, be no doubt that the forces of one single Panzer division were insufficient to retake Avranches. If Commander-in-Chief West, nevertheless, permitted this attack there, it was done apparently with the idea that the Americans had not yet found time to built up a defensive flank east of Avranches. In this case, the possibility of success was more probable with a fast, surprise attack by the single Panzer division, whereas, later on, their success could not be insured even with much stronger forces.

Hitler, however, was of the opinion that it was already too late for such an undertaking. He did not approve of the attack. In his opinion, there was a risk that the enemy's attention would be called to the great danger which threatened him from this direction. Commander-in-Chief West received orders to parry the enemy breakthrough by means of a counterattack by strong German forces. For this undertaking, the motorized divisions which were still on the front were to be relieved by infantry divisions. In order to make this possible, the infantry divisions which were approaching from the north were to be put into the line between the Vire and the Orne rivers. This front was to be held by infantry forces. If necessary, the line was to be taken back as far as Thury-Harcourt – Vire – Fontenermont. A withdrawal to this line need not exert any influence on the success of the plan proper. In this manner, at least four Panzer divisions were to be gathered for the breakthrough to the west coast of the peninsula. No consideration whatsoever was to be given to the American forces which had penetrated into Brittany and to the south of Avranches. If the breakthrough succeeded, they would be cut off and would then have to face annihilation.

On 3 August, after the receipt of this order, Commander-in-Chief West ordered that the Panzer divisions were to be concentrated for an attack on the left wing under the command of the German Seventh Army. Commander-in-Chief West advised the Fuehrer's Headquarters by telephone that he evaluated the situation as being extremely critical on the right as well as on the left wing. He would, however, accept all risks and employ the last means available in order to make a breakthrough by the Americans impossible.

Hitler agreed to the reinforcement for Panzer Group West which was to be used for the breakthrough. All tanks available were given to it, partly without crews, as crews were available at Panzer Group West. Hitler, however, refused any weakening of the German Nineteenth Army in southeastern France by withdrawing 11 Pz. Div.: it was the only armored unit which this Army had at its disposal. With the extended front line, this unit seemed essential as a mobile reserve. A landing in southern France was still expected. (Subsequently the presence of 11 Pz. Div. proved to be the lifesaver for Nineteenth Army. During the withdrawal, this armored unit kept the Rhône valley free to the north and thus kept open all communications for Nineteenth Army.)

On 3 August, at 1100 hrs, Commander-in-Chief West agreed by telephone to the basic idea of the order that he had been given, and reported on the continuation of the measures to concentrate the armor. He did not deem possible the moving up of 9 and 10 SS-Pz. Divs as well as the 21st Pz. Div. He maintained that he saw the necessity to employ every means available and to accept every risk.

Subsequently, he sent the order which he had planned for the attack. According to it, the front was to be closed and a strong armored attack group was to be created. Furthermore, Panzer Group West and the German Seventh Army were to withdraw during the night of 3/4 August into a line east of the Orne river (as up to now) – St-André-sur-Orne – the Orne near Thury-Harcourt – north of St-Martin-de-Balley [?] – Hill 279, south

The clear superiority of the Panther over the Sherman, demonstrated in the Normandy fighting, led US Army officers to try to develop antidotes. A few captured Panthers were subjected to the fire from various types of weapons at a test field near Isigny, in an effort to determine the Panther's weak spots.

of Le Plessis [-Grimoult?] – Lassy – the south bank of the Allière river – the heights north of the Vire – Champ-du-Boult – St-Michel-de-Newatjoie [-Montjoie?].

At the same time, Panzer Group West and the German Ninth Army were to release two Panzer divisions each. On the west wing, the armored spearheads of the enemy were to be thrown back by attacks from the forces available there. On both sides of Sourdeval, the attack by the Panzer group was to be prepared in such a manner that the front could be closed again with a thrust to the west. For this, the following units would probably be available: Headquarters XLVII Pz. Corps; and LXXXVI Corps, with 2, 9, and 116 Pz. Divs, as well as combat teams of 2 SS-Pz. Div. The threat against Normandy was to be ignored in the meantime.

About the front, it could be said that it had achieved a certain success on 3 August. The gap between Panzer Group West and the German Seventh Army had been closed. The northwest and western fronts had been stabilized. To the south, a new front had been built up against possible encircling attacks by the enemy. A further advance by the enemy to the south and southeast, however, could not be stopped. The enemy could penetrate Rennes and reach Vitré, as well as Châteaubriant and Redon. The enemy forces in Brittany were estimated to be two armored and three infantry divisions. During the night from 3 to 4 August, the front was withdrawn to the Orne river, and a line extending from there in a westerly direction.

No important actions took place on 4 or 5 August. However, it proved necessary to secure the Loire river against the continuous advances of the enemy. The bridges were prepared for demolition. The position of the security details, however, was so thin and far-extended that it did not offer reliable protection. There could be no further doubt that the enemy had already brought strong forces through the bottleneck of Avranches to the south. With these he attacked Mayenne and Laval on 5 August.

On 6 August, Vire was lost at the front. The pressure of the enemy at the front west of the town was reinforced anew. That made it clear that the enemy now now sufficient forces in the area east of Avranches, where heavy battles could now be expected. It was critical, because the German Seventh Army was cut off from its supply base. The ammunition and fuel situation became threatening.

Simultaneously, the enemy appeared at the gates of the fortresses of the Brittany peninsula. East of Brest, he managed to break through the defense line of 2 Para. Div. Around St-Malo, which had no strong garrison, there developed heavy battles. In the area south of the point of penetration, which had been completely evacuated by the defenders, the advances by the motorized American forces developed an ever-increasing tempo. The hastily assembled rear-echelon troops could hardly offer any serious resistance. On 7 August, enemy armor appeared in the area south of Le Mans, and, on 8 August, at the Loire river.

In the face of these developments, Field Marshal von Kluge made the request that the German First Army should be relieved by LXIV Corps in the command along the Biscay front. The German First Army was to be in charge of the formation and in command of a task force which was to put up a barrier against the enemy advances south of the Normandy front. There still existed the hope of preventing a disaster once again. It was obvious, however, that the German forces in Normandy would be encircled and brought into an extremely difficult position if the breakthrough to the coast did not succeed soon. Everything now depended upon the success of this thrust.

The situation came to a head in a very dramatic way, because, obviously, each of the two opponents had the aim of encircling the other. Without any thought of retreat, and therefore without sufficient preparation in the event of failure, Hitler wagered everything on this one card. In the meantime, he developed his attack theory even further. If the breakthrough to Avranches succeeded, the enemy forces which had broken through to the hinterland in the meantime would themselves be in the greatest danger. But perhaps the enemy had already weakened his front on the Contentin peninsula in favor of his encircling wing, which had broken through! Then there was, perhaps, an opportunity, if the breakthrough to Avranches succeeded quickly, to annihilate the enemy forces which were in position along the north front. The destruction of those forces further to the south was then only a question of time. For this purpose, the attack group had to exploit the initial disorder of the enemy once it had reached the coast at Avranches, in order to turn off to the north immediately and to roll up the enemy front. Then, perhaps, it would even be possible to retake the enemy's harbors and landing beaches. According to Hitler's theory, the utmost daring was necessary for the carrying out of this undertaking, but to him the idea seemed within the realms of possibility.

Of course, one had to ignore the streaming in of American forces into the rear areas with extreme cold-bloodedness. This could even be of advantage for the success of the final plan, if one could only prevent a premature attack by the enemy against one's own back. In the meantime, one had to accept, equally calmly, the risk of removing the best armored units from the front and putting them aside for the thrust which then had to bring about a decision.

There is no need to criticize these thoughts here: they were typical of Hitler. One has to be aware of them in order to understand the ensuing events.

Hitler ordered, by telephone on 6 August, that Gen. Eberbach was to lead the attack with XLVII Pz. Corps and four divisions. Thus, he wanted to employ the experienced armored commander in the decisive spot. Field Marshal von Kluge, however, protested that Gen. Eberbach was indispensable as Seventh Army commander and that he wanted to put SS-Obergruppenfuehrer Mausser in charge of the attack. This, by the way, was to commence the following night, and therefore a change of commanders was no longer advisable. Field Marshal von Kluge explained the early attack time by saying that he had no choice; he could not wait any longer. The surprise of the enemy had to remain the biggest issue. But, most of all, one would have to prevent attacking troops from being destroyed through enemy air attacks when they were in their assembly areas. For these reasons, he did not want to postpone the time of the attack, even though the assembly of the troops had not yet been completed. At 1700 hrs, he telephoned this opinion to the acting chief of the WFStab, and discussed it with him.

Hitler, however, was of the opinion that the attack only had a chance of success if all available forces could be used for it. To him, this did not yet seem to be the case. He had the impression that Field Marshal von Kluge had not yet fully understood his real intentions.

On 7 August, therefore, he sent his Chief of Staff of the Army, Gen. Buhle, to the front by plane. He wanted, once again, to bring his ideas to the attention of the commanders at the front by personal contact with a representative of his own headquarters.

Simultaneously, at 1515 hrs on 7 August, he had the following order sent to CinC West: The attack offered a unique opportunity to step into an area from which our forces had almost been completely withdrawn, and thereby the situation could be completely turned around. He would have to break through to the sea, daringly and unswervingly. By accepting every risk, CinC West was to bring up 2 SS-Pz. Corps and 12 SS-Pz. Div. or 21 Pz. Div. as the third wave. The rearward attack waves were to turn off to the north. Their purpose was to annihilate the enemy by thrusting deep into his flank and his rear, and to collapse his Normandy front. As soon as success could be noticed here, the other infantry divisions further east along the front were to join the general attack. Interrelated to this was the order that St-Malo was to be defended to the end. This was to prevent those American forces which had broken through from gaining a harbor.

In the meantime, the attack had begun on the morning of 7 August, and had got bogged down without any success. The reason for this failure was the enemy air force, whose carpet-bombing had suffocated it. The question why Hitler had not prevented it on the afternoon of 6 August cannot be explained solely by technical difficulties: the main cause was based in Hitler's own character and in his other peculiarities. He still trusted the Field Marshal, even though voices were already raised against him. Foremost among them was the Chief of Staff of the Army, Col. Gen. Guderian. As such, he only handled the problems of the Eastern Front, whereas Col. Gen. Jodl, as Chief of WFStab, was the responsible adviser to Hitler in questions concerning the command in France. Col. Gen. Guderian, however, in his capacity as Inspector General of Armored Forces, demanded the right to criticize the command of armored units and the use of armor on the part of the CinC West. His unusually sharp attacks were, in the final analysis, of course, a criticism of the abilities of Field Marshal von Kluge, with whom Guderian personally was not on the best of terms. It is improbable that at this time there were reports about the supposed membership of von Kluge in the treasonable circle [Bomb Plot] of 20 July.

In the face of the fact that the attack had bogged down, CinC West now decided to bring up 9, 10, and 12 SS-Pz. Divs, as well as the bulk of 9 Pz. Div. and two mortar brigades. With these, the attack was to be continued on 10 August. This bringing up of further forces agreed with the new orders issued by Hitler, which Gen. Buhle also transmitted. The postponement of the attack date to 10 August, however, enraged Hitler. It surprised him that the Field Marshal had refused even the smallest delay, but now wanted to wait three more days. This was a later time limit than Hitler had imagined. In these three days, the encircling move of the enemy at the south of the attack group could reach an extent which could not be foreseen with certainty.

In his estimate of the situation of 7 August, CinC West was of the opinion that a second landing from England was now not to be expected. Possibly, on the other hand, there could be a new landing by air in order to open the roads to Paris. For more than two months, the enemy, who was superior in all three departments—land, sea and air—had been confronted. Now, however, he had come closer to this aim. CinC West believed a landing in southern

France now to be less probable. This would be substantiated by the transfer of French forces from North Africa to the Channel. Peculiar, however, were the heavy air attacks against southern France which had started the 3 August; at the Fuehrer's headquarters, now, as before, the possibility of a landing in southern France was considered to be real.

Gen. Buhle, who in the meantime had arrived in the west, reported the following to Hitler on 8 August: The Commander-in-Chief had, from the beginning, advised all officers of Hitler's ideas. He had permitted the attack in the night 6/7 August in order to guarantee the element of surprise and to prevent the troops from being dispersed by enemy air attacks. CinC West had therefore made the decision on 8 August for a new (and planned) attack, which was to begin on 10 Aug. This intention, however, was not realized because of deep penetrations east of the Orne and Vire rivers. CinC West had gained the impression on the front that a quick success was impossible, as the German units had already been weakened. The enemy, however, could reinforce himself at any time he pleased. Furthermore, the good weather favored his superior air force. Gen. Buhle reported, further, that an increase in the depth of the enemy's penetrations could make the planned attack possible.

In reality, therefore, one of the weakest points of the whole plan had been touched upon. Up to now, we had not succeeded in holding the front *with* the Panzer divisions. We were unable to prevent the breakthrough. Consequently, it was improbable that we could now hold the front *without* the Panzer divisions in order to plug up the breakthrough with a heavy attack—especially so as it was obvious that the enemy continued to be reinforced while the German forces were becoming increasingly depleted. The plan could only succeed if the enemy remained inattentive and inactive. The former could not be expected and the latter could be dismissed with certainty. The enemy was attacking and had no reason to rest just at the right time.

On the basis of the reports about the advances of the enemy, CinC West—as Gen. Buhle reported on 9 August at 0030 hrs—saw himself forced to use some of the units planned for the attack in the threatened parts of the front. Independently, he moved 9 SS-Pz. Div.'s tank battalion and employed it in I SS-Panzer Corps' sector, as well as the spearheads of the approaching 85 Inf. Div. Other parts of the Panzer divisions had to protect the southern flank, because the enemy had taken Le Mans in the meantime and threatened the area around Alençon, which was especially important because it contained the only supply point close to the front.

Thus there remained only 10 SS-Pz. Div., as well as one mortar brigade, to be fed into the attack. As the tanks which were approaching from the replacement Mailly-le-Camp, as well as the tanks of 11 SS-Pz. Div., could arrive only in a few days, Gen. Buhle gained the impression that the main force had now been taken from the attack wedge. CinC West held fast to his intention to attack, and was conscious, fully, of the effect of his decisions. In the face of the situation east of the Orne, however, he saw no other possibility. He had to consider this situation as critical. One has to remember here the earlier remarks about the significance of the area around Caen. Now, a breakthrough on the German right wing had to have still more serious consequences as the left wing had already been pierced and encircled.

Hitler informed CinC West at 2035 hrs on 9 August that the attack of 7 August had been started too early and therefore had been too weak, and, furthermore, had been started during a period of weather which was favorable to the enemy air force. CinC West was to start the attack anew with strong forces, but in a different position. The basepoint of the attack was to be the area around Domfront and northwest of it. From here, the attack was to be led at first in a southwesterly, and later on in a northwesterly, direction. With this, Hitler hoped to avoid the place where the enemy had to expect the attack after previous events. In order to gain forces, the German Seventh Army could be withdrawn.

A further attack group was to be formed to the south of Domfront under LXXXI Corps from the already available forces and from the infantry divisions approaching from the German Fifteenth Army. These had to follow the armored attack, echeloned to the left, and thereby protecting it in the flank. If necessary, this attack group should itself thrust to the south, into the northern flank of the Americans. Hitler reserved for himself the decision concerning the timing of the attack.

It was recognized as a requirement for this attack that the breakthrough by the enemy through the north front had to be prevented under all circumstances. The area around Falaise was considered to be the most dangerous spot. Therefore, I SS-Pz. Corps would also have to be supported rapidly. All counterattacks along the defensive front were forbidden, in order to avoid the losses connected with them, in case the situation could be cleared by withdrawing the front. In conclusion, CinC West received guiding directives for the composition of the forces along the Loire and for the infantry attack groups.

The Commander-in-Chief first reported at 2030 hrs on 10 August that the enemy was advancing via Le Mans towards Alençon. To the west, the enemy was in position in the area around Mayenne. Forces which were advancing in the direction of Nogent-le-Rotrou via La Ferté-Bernard were at first believed to be reconnaissance. CinC West had refused the proposal to withdraw his own forces into a line from Domfront to Nogent-le-Rotrou. The large area around La Ferté-Bernard was not secured at all. Here there existed a gap. With this, Chartres seemed threatened, and forces had to be put together for its security. It has to be remarked here that all these hurriedly deployed rear-echelon security forces had considerable shortcomings—age and health, as well as training and equipment. Full performance was not to be expected from such units if opposed by a modern army.

On the evening of 10 August, at 2115 hrs, CinC West reported further that the American encircling wing had turned off to the north after an initial thrust in an easterly direction. It had reached and crossed a line Mayenne – Beaumont – Bonnétable – La Ferté-Bernard. That proved clearly that there was a connection between these moves and the British attack on Falaise. The enemy intended a double envelopment. Exposed to it were the troops of the Seventh Army, as well as the Panzer Army which had relieved Panzer Group West. The use of strong pursuit and bombing squadrons with the enemy spearheads—the latter, especially, had prepared and supported the attacks near Beaumont and Bonnétable with carpet-bombing—was the characteristic sign of how much value the enemy attached to this move. LXXXI Corps forces had not been able to protect the extended southern flank, nor to keep open the Alençon–Flers road, which was vital for the movement of supplies.

Therefore, CinC West asked for permission for a short and audacious armored thrust. This was to hit the enemy armored spearheads which were advancing to the north and thus secure a basis for the further battle—especially for the planned attack which was to come from the area of Domfront toward the coast. This latter attack could not start before 20 August in any case, because of the weather and because of the time which was needed for the concentration of troops and matériel. Therefore, the proposed short thrust to the south would not involve any delay in the main attack.

The same evening, CinC West ordered the bringing up of 15 Lw. Field Div. from the Fifteenth Army Sector. This division was to relieve 220 Inf. Div. in Le Havre, which was to be attached, like 344 Inf. Div., to the German Seventh Army. It should be mentioned, however, that all the necessary marches and movements could proceed only very slowly because of the air situation. The crossing of the Seine below Paris was possible only with ferries. Furthermore, the gradual withdrawal of forces from Fifteenth Army is significant. It corresponded to the opinion that a second landing along the Channel coast had become unlikely. With this, the last large group of forces which still existed as a compact unit was dissolved and used up.

On 11 August, at 1215 hrs, CinC West made a far-reaching report after a conference with his commanders. SS-Obergruppenfuehrer Hausser, who was charged with the command of the attack in the direction of Avranches, did not deem it possible any more. The breakthrough to the sea could succeed now only after tenacious and lengthy battles. For this, however, the armored units were lacking forces. Field Marshal von Kluge agreed with this opinion, and added on his own part that, through the sharp turn to the north by the enemy, who was in position in the south, as well as through the heavy employment of his air force, the situation had become worse. At the moment, 9 Pz. Div. was fighting near Alençon. The first units of the approaching 6th Para. Div. amounted to only a comparatively small reinforcement. For this reason, Gen. Eberbach was to start a counterattack immediately with his armored units on the threatened wing. For this purpose, the following units could be released: in the night 11/12 August, 116 Pz. Div.; and in the following night 1 SS-Pz. Div and 2 Pz. Div. These measures required, of course, a shortening of the Seventh Army front, out of which the thrust to the sea was to come. In practical terms, this meant a sacrifice of this attack plan. CinC West, however, was of the opinion that a final decision had to be made now, as the situation was becoming more critical hour by hour. Such a decision would have the following objectives:

1. To defeat the enemy with the available forces near Alençon.
2. To bring further divisions to this wing in order to secure the flank of Army Group by means of attacks to the west.

This report excited Hitler a great deal. He criticized the command of Field Marshal von Kluge. It was obvious that he now distrusted him. He emphasized that it was inexplicable that von Kluge had started the attack against Avranches with insufficient forces because the right moment had passed; then, however, he had again and again postponed the attack, despite the fact that the troops continued to be exposed to the disastrous effects of the enemy air force. This latter had moved him to rush the attack, whereas now he had ignored it completely. The shortening of the Seventh Army front meant not only that a later attack would be more difficult, but also it would offer the enemy air force an increased opportunity to attack the more concentrated assembly area. These would have an even mere destructive effect as long as Seventh Army was concentrated in an ever-narrowing area. Therefore, it would have to be CinC West's first priority to avoid this. Hitler also criticized the counterattack which von Kluge had proposed against the armored spearheads which were attacking from the south. He claimed the attack was planned too frontally, and therefore against the strength of the enemy. It would be better to start it from the area south of Domfront in a southeasterly direction. Thus the thrust would lead to the left flank of the attacking enemy. That would not only make it more effective, but it also increased the assembly area for the attack against Avranches. If this were not possible, the attack would have to aim into the right flank of the enemy and start from the area to the west of Alençon.

Hitler was almost bitter about the Field Marshal's statement that a "total decision" had to be made. He maintained that, in the course of his life, he had proved often enough that *he* was the man to make "total decisions." But the "total decision" asked for here meant only retreat. In fact, one should note that here was the deciding difference between Hitler's way of thinking and Field Marshal von Kluge's: Hitler refused, now as before, any retreat; Kluge, however, was attempting to avoid a catastrophe for both armies.

Thereupon, the Chief of the WFStb, Col. Gen. Jodl, exchanged messages with Kluge at 1515 hrs, on Hitler's orders. CinC West replied that no decision had yet been made about the basepoint of the planned attack against the Americans in position to the south. In order to release forces, he intended to clear the salient east of Avranches. This withdrawal was to be made only to a line from Sourdeval to a point east of Mortain. A further withdrawal had not been planned. The attack planned up to now could no longer be carried out. If success was to be achieved at Alençon, then perhaps it could still be executed. The Chief of WFStb expressed Hitler's wish that the new attack against the American pincerpoints was to be led north of Le Mans, halfway between Alençon and Le Mans, in a northwest-to-southeast direction.

Thereupon, Hitler cancelled the order that he had given on 9 August. He set the as first aim of the new operation the elimination of the threat against Army Group's southern flank. For this purpose, the First Army was to concentrate its forces around Chartres (it was not able to do that later on). Hitler, however, stuck obstinately to the idea of an attack in the direction of Avranches. Main efforts were to be formed on both wings of the northern front. For this purpose, he permitted a shortening of the front near Tourneval [?], and this was executed in the night of 11/12 Aug.

Hitler had an order transmitted to CinC West on the afternoon of 12 August through Jodl. The enemy in the south was not to be attacked frontally, but as deep as possible in the flank and rear. At the same time, it was necessary to secure the German rear against the enemy near Mayenne. The same evening, the CinC West reported at 2100 his intentions for the attack. He added, however, that they could not be executed in that manner as enemy armor had already penetrated the German assembly areas.

In the meantime, the situation on the northern front had also continued to worsen. The enemy had begun a large-scale attack on 7 August to the east of the Orne river. This was accompanied by a second attack to the west of the river. A serious crisis developed on 8 August south of Caen. It was still possible, though, to build up a new MLR along the Dives and to the west of it. Furthermore, at the same time the Americans continued their attacks around Vire, which again necessitated a withdrawal of the front on 8 August. Further

A third of the US Army's tank strength at the start of Operation "Cobra" was its 694 M5A1 light tanks, in addition to 1,269 M4 Shermans. The M5A1—one is seen here advancing through a French town— was useful for reconnaissance, but its 37 mm gun and thin armor (here reinforced with sandbags) was inadequate for the battlefield in 1944. (US National Archives)

territorial losses, which occurred on 9 August, would be retaken by means of counterattacks. These attacks could have as their only aim the tying down of German forces within a pincer, whose outlines could already be noted. It was clear that the enemy intended a breakthrough south of Caen with his British forces, so as to meet the Americans approaching from the south and to close the circle. It was significant that they did not attack the Loire front. Here, they had only little protection, and brought all their forces to the north for the thrust into the rear of the German armies. On 10 August, the enemy reached the outskirts of Chartres.

The front lines gradually took on the form of a snail. The south front ran initially in an easterly direction and then turned considerably to the north. In the new salient thus created stood Group Eberbach, in order to thrust into the flank of the enemy who was attacking from Alençon to the north. His forces were estimated to be two armored and three infantry divisions. Communications and supplies had already become critically difficult. Fifth Panzer Army had to take charge of supplying Seventh Army, as the latter had already lost its rearward installations. Furthermore, the armored forces could not remain in this area for reasons of the situation in the air.

The enemy recognized the danger which threatened the flank of his attack here. On 13 August, therefore, he turned west and thus [denied us] the opportunity of attacking his flanks. Simultaneously, however, he thrust to the north via Alençon. Thus the supply train for both armies had finally been forced to canalize on one single road. Even now Hitler did not abandon his plan, and allowed no decisions which anticipated an abandonment of the battle or which aimed at retreat; nor did Nineteenth Army, which had been in southern France, receive any orders for retreat. It was desired, however, to create a contact between the forces along the Loire blocking our crossing and the German First Army. In reality, however, First Army had few forces at its disposal. It was not capable of protecting its own territory. The forces along the Loire could help only as long as they could attack rather than block. It was obvious that here was a strategic castle built on sand. Its stability was highly questionable.

CinC West reported at 1800 on 13 August that the British had assembled for an attack to the east of the Orne river in the direction of Falaise and to the northeast of it. They were estimated to have seven infantry divisions, two armored divisions, and two armored brigades. The north and west front were tied down by British-American forces with a strength of fifteen infantry divisions and four armored brigades.

Opposite the southern front there were at first three motorized divisions and one armored division. Here, on 12 August, the Americans had turned sharply to the west, while blocking to the north with two further infantry divisions and two more armored divisions. With this force, they were to thrust into Seventh Army's rear. Their aim probably was to anticipate the German counterattack which they had recognized in the meantime. Therefore, the enemy attempted with all means to encircle Seventh Army and Fifth Panzer Army. 116 Pz. Div., on the other hand, was to hold up the enemy, but could not prevent his turning off. It had been pushed back to the north and was now ready for battle near Argentan.

1 SS-Pz. Div. and 2 Pz. Div. could proceed only slowly on their way to the assembly area. Probably they would have to enter the battle and give up their move toward the east in order to keep their rear free. The bringing up of further armored units (9 and 10 SS-Pz. Divs, and 21 Pz. Div.) would be necessary as the combat strength had decreased considerably and the assembly area became ever smaller. The situation made it necessary, therefore, to fight in order to keep the rear free. This was especially necessary with regard to the supplies and communications.

For these reasons, CinC West proposed to withdraw to a line on either side of Flers during the night of 14/15 August, in order to gain armored units. All armored units were to be attached to Group Eberbach, with the exception of 2 Pz. Div., which was to protect the southern flank. If the front were to remain extended, it would be penetrated and encircled. The units which were required to fight free of the circle would then be lacking. Therefore, CinC West asked for new orders.

The situation grew rapidly worse after the evening of 13 August. The Canadians pushed the front 2–4 km back toward Falaise and continued their attack on 14 August, making new and deep penetrations. The northwest front was also crushed. Subsequently, the west front was withdrawn and 9 SS-Pz. Div. and 21 Pz. Div. were released to Group Eberbach. On the southern front, the enemy advanced near Dompierre and in the area around Tourneval.

There could be no doubt that the final encirclement of both armies had come threateningly close. It was high time to give up the phantom hope of a breakthrough to Avranches. The success of such a breakthrough was most improbable under the present ratio of strength. The rigid adherence to this plan meant that more and more German forces would come into the pocket and be tied down. In this limited area, they were exposed to constant losses inflicted by the enemy air force, which could not help but find valuable targets in every stretch of woods and every valley. The troops, therefore, were exposed to a continual drain comparable to Falkenhayn in the Maasmuehle [Verdun] of 1916. It was high time to employ all forces in an escape from this predicament.

Hitler answered the report and request of CinC West for new orders on 14 August. He blamed the Field Marshal for the situation in the rear of Army Group and told him that it was a consequence of his first abortive attack against Avranches. The turning of the enemy spearheads to the west would bring the danger that Panzer Group Eberbach, which was too far to the north, would again be forced to a frontal commitment of its forces.

Therefore, Hitler ordered once more that the battle was to be fought in the Alençon – Carrouges area, and in such a manner that a large part of the American XV Corps would be annihilated. For this purpose, 9 and 10 SS-Pz. Divs and 21 Pz. Div. were to be brought up. The Panzer Group thus reinforced would then have to be committed far enough to the south that the enemy would be gripped deep in its flank. He was not to be permitted to thrust into the right flank. In order to release the two SS-Panzer divisions, it was permissible to

An artist's impression of a German headquarters in action. Notice the relatively small size, and the lack of communications equipment. (US National Archives)

withdraw the front west of Flers. It was to be possible, however, that the enemy could then lead stronger forces much more quickly against the southern front. Therefore, this move was to be executed only in so far as it was absolutely necessary, in order to release the divisions. The security forces northwest of Chartres and the troops returning from leave to there were to be driven energetically to the west against the line Mortain – Nogent-le-Rotrou. With this, enemy forces were to be tied down. The complete mission for the next day, therefore, was the annihilation of the enemy near Alençon and the defense of the south coast against the coming landing. All further orders would be dependent on the result of the battle near Alençon.

In the face of the landing which was pending in southern France, this attitude was more than risky. Particularly, the fact that it had been impossible to create a task force capable of operation under the First Army should have made it evident that the battle should be discontinued.

CinC West gave an estimate of the situation at 0200 hrs on 15 August. In it, he called attention to the fact that the anticipated British attempt at a breakthrough was approaching and that he was counting on the use of glider troops. The advances of the enemy from Le Mans to the east and north east were to be considered a diversionary movement. The enemy had been satisfied with encircling the fortresses in Brittany, except for St-Malo. The release of the armored units for the battle of the south front had been ordered on 14 August. At the same time, First Army had been given the mission of blocking the line from Chartres to Orléans, with the main effort near Chartres. There were no indications of an enemy advance across the Loire.

In the interior of France, the revolution announced for 13 August had not occurred, not even in Paris. The newest directives by the enemy to the Resistance movement were to avoid open battle. In south and northwest France, German forces had been concentrated on the main communication lines. Control over the adjacent territories had become a secondary matter, on the other hand.

A further report by CinC West arrived at 0500 hrs. According to this report, the enemy had now begun the expected large-scale attack but had been stopped, despite deep penetrations. 21 Pz. Div., however, would have to be attached to 1 SS-Pz. Corps, as otherwise the situation north of Falaise could no longer be held. In Gen. Eberbach's opinion, the attack by his group could no longer be executed with the forces available. The necessary ammunition and fuel were also unavailable. The roads were completely blocked. Therefore, the General had been forced to give the order to defend.

CinC West himself would go to Gen. Eberbach's CP on 15 August, and there also meet SS-Obergruppenfuehrer Hausser. If the idea of an attack had to be given up, there would remain only the possibility of a breakout from the pocket in a northeasterly direction.

This was the last report by CinC West in the early hours of 15 August, the same day on which the landing in southern France occurred. Right afterward, CinC West left his CP in order to go to Group Eberbach. As he did not arrive there, he was inaccessible for the whole day. Thus, the crisis in the command reached a climax.

One had to consider the possibility that CinC West had suffered an "accident" similar to Field Marshal Rommel's, or had become a victim of enemy air activity. Even at 0220 on

16 August, there was uncertainty of his whereabouts. In anticipation, Hitler had ordered on 15 August that Field Marshals Kesselring and Model report to the Fuehrer's headquarters in order to appoint one of them as CinC West. In the meantime, SS-Obergruppenfuehrer Hausser was given acting command of Army Group B, which had been taken over by von Kluge after Rommel's "accident."

In the morning of 16 August, a report reached the Fuehrer's headquarters that Field Marshal von Kluge had reached Gen. Eberbach. In the meantime, the situation had become more critical as the Americans succeeded with their breakthrough toward Sées, while, on the other hand, it had not been possible to thrust into the flank of the southern pincer. Hitler, however, held fast to his decision to change the CinC. The criticism by Col. Gen. Guderian contributed considerably to that. The Chief of the Wehrmachtfuehrungsstab, Col. Gen. Jodl, had not stood by Field Marshal von Kluge during the last weeks. Hitler had reported that the Field Marshal had been connected with the traitors of the 20 July. The SS-leaders in Normandy had not always been in agreement with the Field Marshal and had ways to bring their opinions directly to Hitler. In this manner, Hitler received news later on that von Kluge had intended to desert to the enemy on 15 August. Enemy patrols had already been on their way to meet him. The meeting had been foiled only by accident. Hitler still wavered for some time during the noon conference of 16 August, and then withdrew for a short period for a private conference with Col. Gen. Guderian. Then he gave the order that Model was to be recalled, as he had already returned to his Army Group in the east.

Field Marshal Model arrived at the Fuehrer Headquarters during the night of the same day. Here, Hitler briefed him about the developments up to now, about the present situation, and about his intentions. He thanked him for his achievements, gave him the new mission, and decorated him with the Diamonds for the Oakleaves and Swords. A few hours later, in the morning of 17 August, Model departed by plane from Fuehrer Headquarters and arrived in the course of the same day at the Headquarters of Army Group B. He handed von Kluge a letter written by Hitler in which he told him that he was relieved of his command.

In the meantime, at 1600 hrs on 16 August, Hitler had given the order to fight out the battle near Falaise. SS-Obergruppenfuehrer Hausser was to annihilate the enemy spearheads near Sées by attacking with Group Eberbach from the west and with LXXXI Corps from the northeast. Furthermore, Fifth Panzer Army was to hold the area north of Falaise at all costs. The forces approaching from Rouen were to be attached to LXXXI Corps. It was the mission of the German Seventh Army to protect the attack at its rear, to the west. Its breakout to the east was to depend upon the situation on the southern flank and along the attack front.

If SS-Obergruppenfuehrer Hausser were unable to reach and command the divisions approaching from the northeast, they were to receive their orders from the Rear CP of Army Group B. For this purpose, Field Marshal von Kluge was to go there. On the way there he committed suicide. As Group Eberbach was already short of fuel, 100 transport planes were alerted to fly it there. Furthermore, Gen. Eberbach had also been relieved of his command.

Hitler's suspicion was directed against the whole Staff of Army Group B, whom he believed [to be] in agreement with the traitors of 20 July. He suddenly maintained that von

Kluge had taken over the command of Army Group B in place of Rommel in order to have access to its Staff. The Staff of CinC West had not been agreeable to him because it had remained loyal. The whole Staff of Army Group B, however, had been infected. In connection with this, the Chief of Staff of Army Group B, Brig. Gen. Speidel, was arrested. Nothing could be proved, however, and he was later released and sent to Kuestrin under house arrest. The son of Field Marshal von Kluge was removed from the Staff of Group Eberbach. Furthermore, Bedenburg admitted that the suspicions directed against Rommel were closely connected with Hitler's opinion of the whole situation.

On 15 August, Hitler finally admitted that the situation in Normandy was beyond repair, and he gave directives for new measures to be taken. The order of 17 August, which required the evacuation from France, was based on these directives. On 16 August, he had permitted the evacuation of all operational staffs from Paris. Now the evacuation of all officers and units of the armed forces had been ordered, with the exception of those who were fighting units and were west of the line Orléans – Clermont-Ferrand – Canal de Bourgogne. The evacuation of southwestern and southern France, which had thus been introduced, had become unavoidably necessary. Simultaneously, the withdrawal of Army Group G was ordered. It was under the command of Col. Gen. Blaskowitz. He was to leave behind fortress garrisons in Toulon and Marseille. With the mass of his forces, Army Group was to disengage from the enemy, and was to link up with the left wing of Army Group B. Some of its divisions, deployed in the mountains, were to turn to the east into the mountains, be detached from Army Group G, and join CinC Southwest in Italy. It was now their mission to occupy the mountain passes facing west. Their task was to protect the rear of the Italian front against a thrust from southern France.

On the front, in the meantime, the difficulties increased. The developments were irrevocably conditioned by the ratio of strength and by the position of the front lines. The arrival of Field Marshal Model, who had proved himself in the east, could not change anything any more. On 15 August, the German forces had to withdraw to the Dives river. That interrupted communications with 1 SS-Pz. Corps. In the night of 15/16 August, the German Seventh Army withdrew its western salient. The enemy pincers were separated only by 8 km south of Cannes and north of Argentan. In the east, the enemy advanced to Dreux. Chartres was held only by weak German forces. Now there was a danger that the enemy, anticipating a withdrawal across the Seine river, might block it with a large-scale enveloping move. The German First Army took charge at Fontainebleau in order to counteract that. It had, however, only limited forces which could be considered as fully combat efficient. As a whole, the German First Army could not be expected to accomplish very much.

On Hitler's order as CinC for all German Armed Forces, von Choltitz was appointed in Paris. It was his mission to mobilize and use all available forces in the city for battle against the enemy.

On 16 August, the enemy managed to push German forces across the Dives river at some locations. The center of the battle was again in the I SS-Pz. Corps sector. This Corps had to withdraw, however, so as to be able to bear the attack in a new MLR. The loss of Falaise could not be prevented. In the west, [the Germans] commenced a withdrawal consisting of several phases. Group Eberbach was reorganized. Even the fact that we had been successful in pushing apart the enemy pincer points just a little further could not conceal the fact that the enemy had been successful in encircling most of the troops. In the south, enemy armor reached Châteaudun and Orléans.

Inasmuch as the enemy attacked on 17 August, the German forces had to be withdrawn here across the Vire river. There was only a very narrow link to I SS-Pz. Corps, which was holding the enemy south of Morteau[x?]. The enemy achieved a new penetration west of Falaise. However, air transport and land transport succeeded in bringing up enough fuel to Group Eberbach to create the conditions required for an attack.

In the south, the enemy pushed as far as Houdon [?] through the gap which had been created near Dreux. Furthermore, he advanced with armor as far as Fontainebleau. Orléans had also to be ceded. The dangers which were caused by the advances of the mobile American units were obvious.

The enemy could concentrate his forces and strike with them at the Seine river below Paris. Thus he could have caused a catastrophe for all German armies and troops in positions west of Rouen. On the other hand, he could also cause a national revolution by a drive through the east and thus threaten the withdrawal of the German forces from southwestern and southern France.

The first possibility, that of a thrust from Dreux toward Rouen, seemed to be the more dangerous. CinC West therefore received orders on 18 August to halt the withdrawals in the German First Army sector west of the Seine. The reinforcement of the German First Army was to be accelerated if possible. Group Eberbach was to be used for this purpose, if it succeeded in breaking out of the enemy pocket.

On 18 August, however, the British managed to tear open the MLR in the north across a width of 4 km, and to advance to Trun. Some elements thereby reached the American objective. Now the German Seventh Army, with four to six units, Fifth Panzer Army, with two units, and Panzer Group Eberbach were completely encircled. As the enemy had reached the Seine east of Paris, a further crisis could be expected here.

The main forces of the Germans had become engulfed in a serious defeat west of the lower Seine, and for the most part had been encircled in their rear with a wide river without bridges which the enemy had already reached upstream. The German forces from southern France were engaged in a difficult withdrawal along the Rhône valley. In between, there was a huge gap not even covered scantily by the extremely weak forces. It offered the enemy all sorts of possibilities for practically any kind of operation.

May it be permitted here to make some critical remarks, as we now face a turning point in the battles? This turning point finds expression in the aims of the respective enemies. Up till now, the German forces had fought in order to gain the initiative from the enemy, and to force a decision by means of a German attack. Now this decision had been made [for them], and it could only be a question of saving as many units as possible from collapse, so as to gain at least the chance to regroup troops for future combat. Only a withdrawal created the prerequisite for a later defense. Whether there existed any chance of regaining the initiative and staring a German attack appeared more than questionable. It is true that by far the largest part of France had now to be considered lost. The serious consequences which would result from the loss of France as regards strategy and armaments have already been mentioned.

Throughout these pages up till now, one can see the contrast between the Hitler's ideas and those of Field Marshal von Kluge. The Field Marshal does not always seem to pursue a consistent line in his reports. On the one hand, he emphasizes again and again that he and his subordinates were fully aware of Hitler's ideas; then he outlines the necessity for a breakthrough to Avranches. On the other hand, he fails to find the correct starting point. Again and again, there are last-minute obstacles which make it impossible for him to carry out Hitler's orders. This causes Hitler to become gradually suspicious, and once the situation repeats itself he becomes convinced that the Field Marshal is a traitor. Finally, he believes that the Field Marshal is deliberately sabotaging his orders. He also believes that he has been in secret accord with the enemy. His final desertion has only been foiled by an accident.

As a matter of fact, von Kluge acknowledged shortly before his suicide that, when he received the order for the breakthrough to Avranches, he immediately had the feeling that an undertaking was ordered here which was grandiose but could not be carried out. Of course, he was fully aware of the daring and audacity of he plan, but did not believe it was in accord with the true situation and the ratio of strengths. From the beginning, he had the feeling that, with this order, the historical responsibility for the defeat was to be put on his shoulders.

Secretly, he was of the opinion that, even after a successful advance to Avranches, he could not hold the front between the east and west coasts of the Cotentin peninsula. Just at the point when the flow of American forces into the rear areas had been stopped, the pressure against the front had to increase. Even without that, the front could hardly stand this pressure, and in the opinion of the Field Marshal would have to break just as at the end of July, when the pressure increased anew. Besides the general relation of forces, he saw the main weaknesses of his own position as the failure of the GSF and the insufficient number of tanks. He believed that the personal enmity between him and Col. Gen. Guderian, the Chief of Staff of the Army and simultaneously Inspector General of Armored Forces, had made it impossible for him to correct this latter shortcoming.

There had already been friction between von Kluge and Guderian in the first month of the campaign against Russia in 1941. Then von Kluge commanded Fourth Army in he Army Group Center sector, under Field Marshal von Bock. Fourth Army was in control of the Panzer group which was commanded by Guderian. Even the temperament and characters of the two commanders might then have made difficult any smooth cooperation. With Guderian, it was also a question of personal ambition, and the pride of the armored force. He did not want to be dependent upon an infantry army, but rather to have the means available to such an army for his own operations. In this, he and the other Panzer groups succeeded soon after the beginning of the campaign. When, however, a crisis began soon after winter had started, von Kluge had to take over command of Army Group as von Bock had become sick. Thus, again, he became a superior of Guderian. When Guderian proved himself obstinate in the ensuing operations and withdrew in a direction with his Second Panzer Army—which created a wide gap between himself and the Fourth Army—von

Kluge asked that Guderian be relieved of command of the Second Panzer Army. Hitler answered this request. He had just then taken over as Army CinC and used his power to dismiss quite a number of generals. Here was the big cut in Guderian's career. In these events lies the root of his enmity with Field Marshal von Kluge, which was to play an important part.

It cannot be said with certainty that it was completely impossible to carry out Hitler's plan, as luck and unforseen circumstances have often played an important part on the battlefield. But it can be said that the chances of success were very small from the beginning. Furthermore, of course, it was very unfortunate that the man charged with implementing this difficult and risky plan on the battlefield was torn by personal doubts; and it was obvious that the criticism by the Field Marshal of Hitler's plan was perfectly justified.

It is characteristic of Hitler's way of thinking that in this plan the final success was dependent upon a number of conditions which were modified by each other and whose partial non-realization would make the whole scheme questionable. It was a requirement that, even after the withdrawal of the armored units, the partly exhausted and poorly armed infantry divisions should be in a position to hold the front. Then the element of surprise had to be guaranteed for the attack, despite the fact that the enemy would have noticed the absence of the armored units, and despite the fact that he would have noted the build-up of larger forces for an attack in the face of the aerial situation. Besides, the plan was based upon the hope that the enemy had not yet built up a defensive line. His main strength, however, was based upon the mobility of his efficient combat troops. The foremost of these were his bombers and his tanks. If the forces were hardly sufficient for a breakthrough to the sea, it could hardly be expected that they could carry out a powerful thrust to the north and into the enemy's flank in order to roll up his front. Here also, the enemy's greater mobility would prove to be his decisive advantage. In addition, he was in a position to bring numerous units from England in a very short time and employ them in battle.

Von Kluge knew Hitler too well not to realize that he had fallen in disgrace. He also knew that he was on the list of war criminals. Therefore he chose suicide. In his last letter addressed to Hitler, he justified himself and begged Hitler to make peace.

Hitler and Col. Gen. Jodl saw in this letter only an admission of guilt. Perhaps one misses sequence and firmness in Kluge's reports. That, however, is a consequence of the fact that he lost confidence in Hitler—as can be seen from his letter. Only thus it can be explained that he frequently puts the judgment of his subordinates into the foreground.

On the other hand, Hitler and Jodl themselves had become completely estranged from the front. Earlier, at least, Hitler frequently telephoned the commanders at the front. This was not done any more. He limited himself exclusively to briefings by Jodl. But he, too, had become too much engulfed in his own office. He was always at Fuehrer Headquarters, never at the front. Even the connection with his own Staff, the Wehrmachtfuehrungsstab, could not by any means be considered as close. Thus one cannot avoid the occasional conclusion that the thinking and planning of Jodl and Hitler toward the end belonged more to the realms of grey theory and had lost any firm relationship with reality.

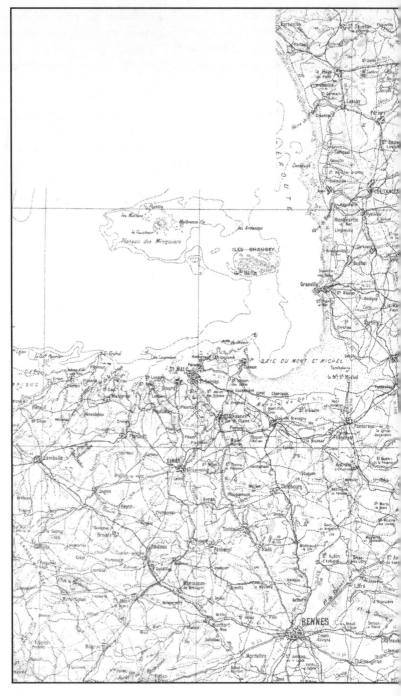

Normandy and th

Maßstab 1:500 000

ittany approaches.

Chapter 5

27–31 July

by Generaloberst Paul Hausser
Translated by Thomas Woltjer (B-179)

27 July

The ultimate breakthrough occurred on 27 July 1944. The attacks were launched with unceasing viciousness, with the center of gravity from St-Gilles to Marigny, in a southwesterly direction, against remnants of Pz. Lehr Div., and weaker enemy units attacked 353 Inf. Div. The Americans succeeded in advancing up to Soulles, after heavy combat engagements, as far as the village of that name. Pont Brocard and Cerisy-la-Salle were captured during initial engagements, and a bridgehead was established on the opposite bank of the Soulle river, southeast of Pont Brocard, on Hill 125. The road from Pont Brocard to Notre Dame-de-Cenilly, as well as Montpinchon, remained in our hands. The 353rd Inf. Div. was in a very critical situation: its front had remained intact, also the flank attacks had withstood; the situation on their right flank, however, was still not cleared up. It appeared that the area up to Montpinchon was open. Strong elements seemed to have broken through in the direction of Coutances.

Enemy attacks continued in the II FS Jg. Corps sector; local withdrawals enabled a coherent front to be maintained. The left wing was drawn back behind the river, north of Funichin [Fumichon?] and west of the Vire river, into the elevated terrain of Pouchinière [?]. Local security groups were located at Le Mesnil-Herman. A further withdrawal of 3 Para. Jg. Div. was desirable in view of the proposed shortening of the front, and could be carried out without the danger of breaking the link with Panzer Group West. The Biéville Heights naturally offered a favorable solution for this purpose, south of the Forest of Rouxeville – St-Jean-des-Baisants – 176 Ste-Suzanne-sur-Vire. This line had to be held in view of XLVII Panzer Corps' attack from Tessy. The date upon which the occupation began cannot be given.

Also, in regard to the period in which troop movements on the left wing of LXXXIV Corps took place, some facts remain unclarified. Here are the divisions, named in sequence: 17 SS-Pz. Div., 91 Inf. Div., remnants of 243 Inf. Div., which retreated to the line Monthuchon – 147 – 125 – the Sienne loop on the evening of 27 July.

This offered us the opportunity to organize the main body of 2 SS-Pz. Gren. Div. and parts of 17 SS-Pz. Gren. Div., in the district east of Coutances.

28 July

During the day of 28 July, the US First Army could pluck the fruit of its success of the three-day battle from 25 to 27 July. The breakthrough appeared to be a success. Over the same period, however, things became easier west of Vire.

II Para. Jg. Corps successfully contested all enemy attacks, the purpose of these apparently being to keep the troops situated west of the Vire river drawn into the defeat of the right wing of LXXXIV Corps. No further recognizable role was played by them in succeeding events.

The withdrawal of the front to east of the Vire river—to the heights south of Rouxeville forest, during the night of the 26th—was presumably ordered to shorten the defensive front and to assure the link with 2 Pz. Div. This division, under command of XLVII Pz. Corps, commenced an attack in the early-morning hours from western Tessy-sur-Vire, in a northwesterly direction. It encountered an enemy of approximately one to two infantry divisions, which were following up, in deep formation, the tank attack of 27 July against our east flank. Moyon was taken from 2 Pz. Div. as well as terrain along the Tessy – Le Mesnil-Herman – Hill 133 road, and northeast thereof, in heavy battles. We succeeded in holding the Le Mesnil-Raoult – 133 – Moyon – Hohenruecken area, and the forest northeast of Villebaudon, until the evening. Battles occurred in addition to this on the Le Mesnil-Herman and Villebaudon road, where local parts of 2 Pz. Div. and collected groups of Pz. Training Div. encountered enemy pressure which could be checked. Other parts of 2 Pz. Div. succeeded in capturing the La Denisière [?] road network during the night of 29 July 1944, and were able to hold it.

The enemy armored elements, which had advanced from Cuislain [?] – Notre-Dame-de-Cenilly, and which were now bending more to the west and southwest, encountered the 353rd Div. in combat in line west of St-Martin-de-Cenilly – Roncey. They encountered only weak resistance farther south, which enabled them to advance far in the direction of the coast and to reach the Cérences district, which consequently resulted in the encirclement of LXXXIV Corps.

This armored thrust prevented the Commander of Seventh Army from making a trip to the Commanding General of LXXXIV Corps in the Cérences area, to give personal instructions. After the return of the Commander-in-Chief to the advanced CP southwest of Percy, the Army High Command (AOK) succeeded in making a very brief telephone call to the General Command, to whom the Commanding General was able to report: "An American breakthrough to the west, enemy tanks in the vicinity of the CP." Consequently, only a short period of time remained to issue the following short command: "A breakthrough during the night, with spearheads of 2 SS-Pz. Div., in southeasterly direction towards the rear of the Sienne district and in a westerly direction. The rear security cover to the north. Contact right of Villebaudon." Following the completion of this command, our communications were severed.

Field Marshal von Kluge of Army Group B did not agree with this command. He feared that the connection with the coast would be lost and, consequently, that a clear road to Avranches would be offered to the enemy. He requested that everything possible be done to prevent this from happening, and to switch to the south with the main strength. Corresponding orders reached Corps Headquarters only after great hazards had been surmounted.

The question remained, however, whether a breakthrough by the enemy to the south could still be prevented with our weak defenses. Our immediate mission was to prevent the threatening encirclement and the splitting of our Army in two. We succeeded in both cases, but this did not prevent the breakthrough near Avranches on 30 July. Here was the operative complicated point: the advanced army CP was transferred to a point 8 km northeast of Avranches, on the road from Villedieu to Avranches, which enabled it to intervene directly in the battle.

The instructions issued to LXXXIV Army Corps are not known in their full particulars; it can be stated with certainty, however, that confusion and changes were the direct result of interference from Army Group.

It appeared that the following orders had been given:

2 SS-Pz. Div., with parts of 17 SS-Pz. Gren. Div.: General direction of attack—Percy.

353 Div.: La Baleine,

91 Div.: Gavray-Cérences,

24 Div.: Bréhal

The two last-named divisions were to advance under cover of their rearguards, to the north. Remnants of 275 Div. were assembled at Hambye.

This blockading line tended up to the Sienne bend, and its location was favorable. The territory situated between the Sienne river and the coast consisted of open country; two divisions would have been the most required to defend it against strong enemy elements.

For the imparting of orders within the chain of command between II Para. Jg. Corps (right) and LXXXIV Corps (left), XLVII Pz. Corps was inserted in the area east of Percy, and the two Panzer divisions (116, and the remains of Pz. Lehr) subordinated to it at that time in the St-Sever-Calvados region. They were assigned either side of Percy.

29 July

No engagements of any operational significance occurred on 29 July east of the Vire river, to which II Para. Jg. Corps had been assigned. Preparations were made for a retreat to the rear of the river sector, north of Torigni.

2 Pz. Div. fought within the region assigned to XLVII Pz. Corps, west of the Vire , in the period around 29 July. Combat engagements were mainly of a defensive nature, against an enemy whose strength was rapidly increasing. The enemy was mainly interested in diverting the retreat to his flanks in the southwest. The road network around La Denisière remained in the hands of 2 Pz. Div.

The Reconnaissance Battalion of 116 Pz. Div. was committed to take Mont Rubin—a hill 3 km north of Percy—to establish it as a point of departure for future attacks. This did not succeed. The hill fell into enemy hands. It would not be possible to send in 116 Pz. Div. until the next day at the earliest, and probably not before 31 August. The point in question would depend on how matters progressed for 2 Pz. Div. at Percy, in the interior.

To the west were the remains of Pz. Lehr Div., which was compelled to yield gradually on the Mesnil-Herman–Percy road, up to Hill 210. It was replaced in the morning by parts of 2 SS-Pz. and 17 SS-Pz. Gren. Divs. The latter held the hills north of Percy.

The instructions now issued by the Army, in particular those imparted to XLVII Pz. Corps, are not known. Their object must certainly have been—by means of an attack, with

This 150 mm Hummel self-propelled gun (named "Clausewitz") and SdKfz 251 halftrack, were at the head of a retreating column from 2 SS-Panzer Division, followed by about 90 other vehicles and 2,500 Waffen-SS-troops, which was stopped at the crossroads near Notre-Dame-de-Cenilly at around midnight on 28 July at a 2nd Armored Division roadblock. The ensuing traffic jam along the hedgerow-lined road left the remainder of the column exposed to American fire, and a savage night time battle began in which the column was largely destroyed.

a limited objective against the flank of the wedge of the US First Army—to relieve the pressure on the middle and the left wing of LXXXIV Corps and to restore the coherence of the formations within the Army.

During the night, LXXXIV Corps was relieved of its strain thanks to the breakout, which had succeeded during the night. This relief, however, was not long-lived. Our own breakthrough had been successful, despite some material losses. 2 SS-Pz. Div. encountered the heaviest fighting on the way from east Coutances to Percy; this was in the exact direction of the main strength of the enemy, but was of great relief to the movements and combats of the other divisions. Further particulars are not available.

Also, 353 Inf. Div. experienced night combat in its advance to Cotteral [?] via St-Denis-le-Gast to La Baleine. It succeeded, however, in reaching its destination behind the Sienne, without losses worth mentioning. The rest of 275 Div. was placed under its command.

The western adjoining divisions, 91 and the 243, and the released parts of the coastal batteries, which had a long journey rearward before them, naturally lost more equipment. The situation here remained critical. The aim was achieved, however.

The Sienne area and the region south of Hambye up to the bend were thus satisfactorily occupied and blockaded; advanced combat posts were still located north of this region. A temporary blockade and guard patrol was established west of the Sienne river, which assured general security.

The enemy felt his way toward our foremost combat positions on the 29th. The enemy situation on the east wing of the LXXXIV Corps was still unclarified. No acute danger existed here. Things appeared different on the west wing, however: no reinforcements were available. It was certainly no help that, just at this moment, the Commanding General of Corps, Maj. Gen. von Choltitz, was replaced by Maj. Gen. Frhr von Gersdorff. This change of command had nothing to do with the order to break through on the 28 July; it had been planned earlier.

The conditions behind the front in regard to the troop columns and rear sections were, naturally, not very encouraging. All unengaged staffs, especially those of 275 Div. and 5 Para. Jg. Div., were assigned the organization and collection of bands of stragglers.

30 July

The US First Army now reaped the fruit of its previous struggles—the breakthrough to Avranches on 30 July.

To the east of the Vire, II Para. Corps withdrew to a position south of the river sector and north of Torigny [Torigni] in the evening. This was done to maintain the link with the left wing of Panzer Group West and the portions assigned to positions west of the Vire. Attacks on XLVII Pz. Corps had become tougher here. They were successful on the right wing of 2 Pz. Div., and compelled it to withdraw from the Vire bend to Hill 133.

The actual commitment of 116 Pz. Div. was delayed. Changes regarding the planned area of commitment, and the confusion which was wrought by enemy air raids across this difficult terrain, were the reasons for the delay. The division completed its preparations during the night, southwest of Tessy. Despite increased pressure, the heights north of Percy were held, even if, as it happened, Mont Robin could not be recovered from the Americans. The Sienne defense line up to Gavray was held against enemy advances; a penetration of our lines by the enemy occurred further to the east.

Conditions remained critical on the left wing. All sources of assistance were taken advantage of in order to blockade the area between the Sienne river and the coast. The weakness of the available units, (parts of 91 Div. and 243 Div., and the former coastal batteries) allowed only a more concentrated occupation of strongholds of Cérences, Bréhal and the area north of Chanteloup. V Para. Engineer Bn was situated behind this region, around Le Répas [?]. A combat group consisting of portions of 2 SS-Pz. Div. and other elements advanced towards Beauchamps.

The Staff of 77 Inf. Div., which was marching to St-Malo, was stopped near Avranches and assigned to the defense of the region here. Only alarm units were available for this purpose, reinforced at the last minute by a newly arrived assault gun battery. The LXXIV Staff, with its headquarters in Brittany, was to see to the blocking of the narrow strip of Pontaubault, just in case this was attacked.

That afternoon, very strong Panzer [i.e., US armored] units advanced under heavy air cover (fighter-bombers) through Cerenées and westward through Le Répas and St-Jean des-Champs toward the south. From the vantage point of Seventh Army's field headquarters at La Marche, northeast of Avranches, the attacking spearheads, with the planes circling and diving round them, could be clearly seen every now and then. Strict traffic control delayed all troop movements on the roads; even single dispatch riders were often held up interminably. It was so very difficult to gain any clear picture of the state of affairs at Avranches. Units of the Army Staff and couriers sent out failed to return. We had to consider the possibility that the enemy had reached Avranches, and that inconsiderable portions, especially those with heavy weapons, or artillery, or columns from the west wing, had been cut off, which meant that their only path of retreat was to the southeast.

The Commander-in-Chief evacuated his advanced CP at midnight and transferred it to the region southeast of Mortain, where he succeeded in again establishing contact with Army Group and Corps.

31 July

31 July brought with it the completion of the breakthrough; the Cotentin peninsula was thereby lost to the enemy. The most important decision had now been given.

East of the Vire river, the front occupied by 2 Para. Div. was transferred farther to the rear, into the line of Waeldchen [?] 166 – 6 km east of Torigni (and the heights thereof) – Hill 133 – Cretteville. The planned retreat, especially that by 3 Para. Jg. Div., ran very smoothly, guided by cautious and clever minds, the destinations envisaged were reached on scheduled time without noticeable losses, and no enemy penetrations occurred.

2 Pz. Div. had heavy defensive battles to go through, west of the river, which resulted in an enemy penetration of our lines near Troisgots and forced a withdrawal of the right wing. The opposition of the combat unit on the road crossing of La Denisière was broken. Nearby, on the left, the attack by 116 Pz. Div. developed, in very uneven terrain, difficult to see over, along the great road leading west from Tessy. This terrain unfortunately did not lend itself to the commitment of compact Panzer formations; the capture of Beaucoudray succeeded, and later the main road north of La Tilandière [?] was reached. This could be credited to an infantry attack by the Grenadiers. The enemy resistance in Villebaudon, however, could not be broken. Likewise, an attempt to recover Mont Robin also failed. Near Percy, where parts of 2 SS-Pz. Div. and 17 SS-Pz. Gren. Div. were fighting under the control of Pz. Training Div., we succeeded in holding the heights hard north of Percy and also achieved some success in our endeavor to recover Mont Robin.

The course of events for LXXXIV Corps soon resulted in a command to XLVII Corps, in the afternoon, to cease the attacks, and to prepare the retreat of 2 Pz. Div. to the area southwest of Villedieu (with some detachments sent on ahead), so that it would be able to support the south wing of Corps. In the meantime, 116 Pz. Div. was subordinated to LXXXIV Corps Headquarters for this purpose.

The vanguard of the newly sent 363 Inf. Div. (brought up by Army Group) was to reach the Villedieu area so as to blockade the roads north of this village. They were subordinated in the first instance to 353 Inf. Div. Attacks on LXXXIV Corps in the Sienne sector had resulted in enemy penetrations on the road from Hambye to Sourdeval, near La Baleine and near Gavray on the day previous, of which the first threatened our connection with Villedieu.

It was to be presumed that 2 SS-Pz. Div. was on the road from Villedieu to Beauchamps. On our south wing, the weak combat group from 77 Inf. Div. had not succeeded in holding Avranches; it had been lost to the enemy. The blockade defense had been moved back to the Salune [?] line between Ducey and Pontaubault, lightly reinforced by detachments from St-Malo.

The attacks against Villedieu, where 353 Inf. Div. was blocking, were successful. A breakthrough could be checked on the road from Hambye on the northern outskirts of Villedieu, but, on the other hand, a strong enemy Panzer [i.e., tank] attack succeeded west of the city, brought with it heavy losses, severed the connections with our neighbors on the left, and advanced far in the direction of Brevey [Brécey?].

Details are not available regarding the events which occurred on the Villedieu road and in the Le Pave forest. Parts of 91 Inf. Div. were fighting here, along with a Panzer group of 116 Pz. Div. The latter was encircled in this forest, and only sections of it could break through to the east. Assembled elements of 275 Inf. Div. (not including parts of 353 Div.) were to blockade the main road from Avranches to Mortain in the vicinity of Juvigny, and were accordingly set in march.

The first great chapter of the battles of Seventh Army ended on 31 July 1944. The US First Army had achieved its operational goal, namely, a breakthrough from the Cotentin peninsula. An opening had been created. enabling the US Third Army to go into action. The invasion was undoubtedly a great feat, and is to be credited as such regarding planning, preparation, and execution.

It is no discredit, however, to the US First Army when the accomplishments of the German Seventh Army—the enemy—are praised. The invasion was directed at, and struck against, the weakest of our armies —an army with inadequate reserves—and against the section of the coast where the defenses against a seaborne enemy were least developed. Nevertheless, the struggle, unsupported by our own air force, and carried on against an enemy superior both in men and material, was kept up for 56 days.

Four western divisions, reinforced piecemeal, and four additional divisions from Brittany (including single combat groups), as well as four fully equipped divisions (two Panzer divisions, one Panzer Grenadier and one Para. Jaeger) and at the very end by still two others, were putting up a fight against the US First Army—now swollen to no fewer than eighteen or nineteen divisions, among them four armored divisions. At least four divisions were newly organized formations, in some instances with inadequate training, whose first action was to face the enormous pressure of the enemy superiority in matériel. The first American pattern-bombing attack struck full against Seventh Army.

At the end of the fighting on 31 July, seven divisions could be counted as destroyed (Pz. Lehr, 352, 275, 243, 77, 91, 5, and 5 Para. Jg.); only insignificant remnants gathered together. 17 SS-Pz. Gren. Div. had only about the same value.

These sober figures show that the troops had done their duty. The troop command proved, likewise, to be up to the job. They judged the situation and development of events quite correctly. Seventh Army stood alone in combat not far from Panzer Group West and the extreme western wing of Fifteenth Army, through almost two months of fighting, with inadequate support, against all the American forces initially committed, while the main body of the German Army in France looked on, waiting until it was too late.

A subsequent study of the Report of Operations up to 1 August 1944 shows that the west wing of this Army, during the second and third days of the great breakthrough battle west of the Vire river, covered surprisingly little territory. It appears as though the German west wing was still waging battle on 27 July, near Périers and Lessay. Nevertheless, I believe that in the night of 26 July, this wing had retreated far back to St-Sauveur-Lendelin, and part of it as far as Coutances. Considerable portions of 91 and 243 Inf. Divs had no doubt been annihilated north of Coutances; the remainder broke out during the night of 28 July. The principle battles ensued with the US 1 Inf. Div. and 2 and 3 Armored Divs, which, in particular, 2 SS-Pz. Div. (including remains of 17 SS-Pz. Div.) and 353 Inf. Div. ran up against. Any uncertainty in this regard can be dispelled only by a member of the LXXXIV Corps Headquarters, or better still, by the commander of 91 Inf. Div., Brig. Gen. Koenig.

PART FOUR

On 1 August, the US reorganized its command structure. The First Army Headquarters became Twelfth Army Group, and Patton's Third Army Headquarters were activated. As Third Army became operational, Gen. Bradley relinquished command of First Army to Lieut. Gen. Courtney B. Hodges, and assumed command of the 12th Army Group. The German Seventh and Fifth Panzer Armies were opposed to the two US Armies under Bradley, and the Second British and First Canadian Armies, both under Gen. Sir Bernard L. Montgomery's 21st Army Group.

However, at this point the US advance into Brittany, intended to clear the ports, began to appear to some US commanders to be a diversion from the main effort of defeating the German Army. On 3 August, the Brittany campaign was identified as a "minimum force" mission. Now, the US would swing their right flank toward the Seine, in order to push the Germans back against the lower part of the river,. The Germans would be pressed, unable to escape: Allied airpower had dropped all the bridges. Germans west of the Seine would be encircled.

Despite this, the US operations in the opening days of August were still focused on the Brittany campaign. On 1 August, the US 4th Armored Division was halted around Rennes. On 2 August, the Luftwaffe failed in an attempt to use Hs 293 guided missiles, launched by Do 217Ms of KG 100, to destroy the bridge at Pontaubault. Rennes was abandoned by the Germans on 3 August. US spearheads moved throughout Brittany, except for the fortresses, as most deployable German forces had been moved into Normandy. The FFI was also strong in Brittany. CCA of the 4th Armored Division reached Vannes on Quiberon Bay on 5 August, while on 5 August the US 83rd Division made its initial attack on the defenses of St-Malo, with heavier attacks starting two days later. St-Malo would not be taken until 14 August: the citadel would hold out until the 17th, requiring point-blank fire from heavy guns to force its surrender. Offshore fortresses would hold out even longer. CCB of the 4th Armored Division reached the defenses of Lorient by 7 August. The 6th Armored Division and Task Force A advanced to the defenses of Brest. The Third Army liberated Le Mans on 8 August.

The long-delayed German counterattack, insisted on by Hitler, brought the focus back to Normandy. In the first week of August, the Seventh Army front had been pushed over the Vire river, as the US First Army took Mortain and Vire. Panzer divisions had been concentrated for the counterattack by replacing them in the line with infantry divisions brought up from Fifteenth Army. On the night of 6/7 August, the Germans launched

Operation "Luettich" (Liege), the counterattack on Mortain. Hitler aimed to strike across the base of the US penetration to Avranches on the coast. Von Kluge thought, if it was lucky, it might buy time to pull back the forces in France.

The couterattack hit troops of the US 30th Infantry Division and pushed them back, re-entered Mortain, and penetrated the VII Corps front. The defenders of Hill 317, including the 2/120th Infantry, held their ground and directed artillery fire on the advancing Germans. Over the next few days, stubborn US resistance, counterattacks, and air attacks—especially from RAF rocket-firing Typhoon fighter-bombers—decimated the Panzer spearheads. Offensives by the British Second and Canadian First Armies, starting 30 July and 8 August, respectively, forced the Germans to shift armored forces. The German offensive ground to a halt on 8 August. Hitler went into a rage and ordered more Panzer divisions sent into the attack, moving them from the front opposite the British and Canadian forces. It was only on 10 August that Hitler was persuaded that other threats were emerging in the form of a potential envelopment.

The concentration of German forces for the counterattack gave Gen. Bradley the idea of countering the attack by trapping the Germans. In the presence of Gen. Eisenhower, he telephoned Montgomery and secured approval for a change in plan. XV Corps had already taken Laval and was on its way to Le Mans—an enveloping Allied arm around the German left flank, eighty-five miles southeast of Avranches. A northward thrust by XV Corps from Le Mans toward Alençon would threaten the German counterattacking forces from the south. Plans were made to use paratroops, if required, to block German escape routes.

Chapter 6

The German Counterattack
Against Avranches

by Generalmajor Rudolf-Christoph Freiherr von Gersdorff
Translated by C. L'Lorsa (B-725)

A. Decision, Mission and Intention of Seventh Army

On 21 July, the CinC of Army Group B, Genlfdm. von Kluge, arrived at Seventh Army's new command post in Mortain, to discuss the further conduct of battle. Considering the overall situation—into which he had been forced by the inflexibility of the High Command, which obviously did not appreciate the impossibility of restoring the tactical situation, he persisted in the decision to close anew the Normandy front line and, for this purpose, regain connection with the coast through attacking. He ordered us to pull all available mobile forces out of the front defensive line and to assemble them for a counterattack against Avranches. For this, he wanted to bring forward to Seventh Army all available armored forces of Fifth Panzer Army (from 1 August, Panzer Army West was renamed Fifth Panzer Army), as well as further forces which were in the process of being brought up, from the Fifteenth Army, from the south of France and from elsewhere. For the execution of this order, however, speed was the most important factor, since, following the successful enemy breakthrough, the situation in France became more and more untenable every day.

Thereupon, Seventh Army reported its intention of sealing off the breakthrough area as long as possible with the weak forces available, and to organize a defense in the deep southern flank, by calling up all forces fit for action, so as to at least delay an enemy thrust into the interior of France. Furthermore, Seventh Army intended to pull out 2 and 116 Pz. Divs and the 2 SS-Pz. Div. from the defensive front line north of the La Sée sector and to assemble same in the area of Bourdavalle [?] – Mortain for the purpose of counterattacking Avranches. The execution of this move, however, necessitated the bringing forward of infantry units, in order to relieve the Panzer divisions, as well as a withdrawal to the approximate line Vire – St-Pois. In addition, the Army requested the immediate bringing forward of the strongest possible Panzer forces, artillery, mortars (Werfer), reserve tanks, ammunition and fuel for the counterattack, and additional forces to secure the open southern flank. The Seventh Army reported that the execution of the counterattack depended, tactically, upon the development of the situation at the southern flank and upon the Seventh Army right wing holding out, and, with regard to time, upon the arrival of reinforcements. After calculating the time element, it was established that the reorganization within the Army could be completed by 5 August, so that the attack could be launched on 6 August at the earliest. Finally, Seventh Army again requested the evacuation of the Channel Islands, and that 319 Inf. Div., as well as additional forces from the fortresses of the Brittany, be brought up for the protection of the area south and southeast of Avranches.

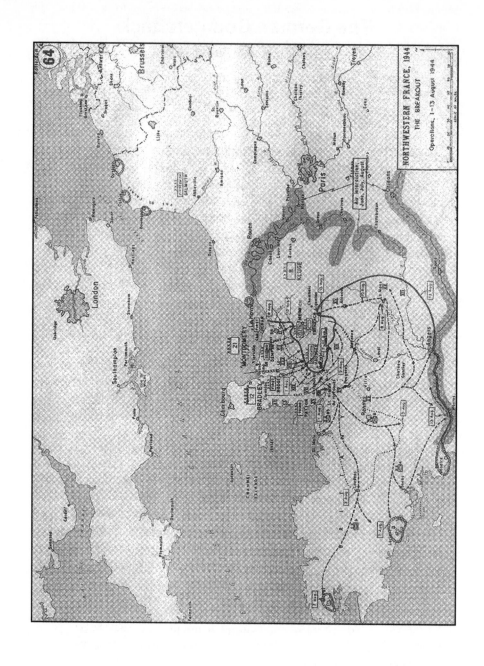

NORTHWESTERN FRANCE, 1944
THE BREAKOUT
Operations, 1–13 August 1944

The Army suggested the assignment of XXV Inf. Corps to the First Army in Brittany, because Seventh Army was no longer able to command this Corps due to the development of the tactical situation.

Genlfdm. von Kluge agreed with the intentions of the Seventh Army. He promised to bring forward, by the most direct route, one or two Panzer divisions from Fifth Panzer Army, 9 Pz. Div. from the south of France, three or four infantry divisions (including 708 Inf. Div. from the south of France as well as 84, 331, and 363 Inf. Divs and, later, additional divisions from Fifteenth Army), and also two mortar brigades (Werferbrigaden) and Army-level (Heeres) artillery. He emphasized, once more, that the counterattack had to be launched at the earliest possible moment.

On 1 August, the Army transferred its advanced command post to a farm one km southeast of Flers, in order to calmly prepare the counterattack from there. The Ia (G-3) of the Army, Colonel of the General Staff Helmdach, was sent to the main command post at Le Mans with the following mission:

a. To organize any and all possible means of defense in the area between Mayenne – Loire and Brittany, so as to delay by every means an enemy advance in this area.

b. To conduct the movements of the units approaching from the south of France and to accelerate them as far as possible.

On 1 August, Corps Staff of LXXXI Inf. Corps (Commanding General: Gen. Kav Kuntzen) was first brought forward to Seventh Army, which then appointed it as Operations Staff for all forces to be committed south of Domfront. The Operations Staff had to protect the southern flank of the Army, and at the same time Army Group. The nerve center of Seventh Army was located in the Alençon area, where the bulk of all supplies was stocked. The protection of this area was, therefore, of decisive importance for the entire conduct of battle.

The proposal of Seventh Army, transmitted by Army Group, to bring forward 319 Inf. Div. from the Channel Islands as well as additional forces from Brittany, was refused by Supreme Command. Beginning about 3 August, XXV Inf. Corps was directly subordinated to Army Group B.

Since 1 August, elements of 84 Inf. Div. had been arriving in the Sourdeval area. This division, which had only recently completed its activation in the Rouen area, was brought forward and assigned to LXXXIV Inf. Corps.

708 Inf. Div. (Commander: Gen. Wilk) and 9 Pz. Div. (Commander: Gen. Jolasse) were in the process of being moved up from the south of France. The first of these divisions was a static unit, insufficiently armed and equipped. The artillery had only one horse team section; the crew had an age average of 30–35 years. The division was only partly qualified for defense. 9 Pz. Div. had not quite completed its reorganization in the south of France. The division could not be assembled in the Alençon area before 6 or 7 August. A motorized security regiment was to be brought forward from the Paris area towards Laval by way of Le Mans.

B. Estimate of the Enemy Tactical Situation

It was obvious that the already identified US Third Army would push forward to the south by way of Avranches, in order to make an assault towards the east into the deep flank of Army Group B, and also, with some elements, push into Brittany. This divided France into two parts, and contact between Army Group B and Blaskowitz was interrupted. The planned encirclement and annihilation of Army Group B was thus already indicated in connection with the expected attacks of the British invasion army and US First Army.

Using considerable forces (US First Army) in offensive operations, the enemy protected the penetration he had succeeded in making towards the east. In this connection, however, the main body of his forces had swerved north of the La Sée sector to the southeast and east, while, south of the river, only elements of the US 3 Armored Div. had as yet made their appearance. However, this same division was also reported north of La Sée. On the whole, we had to reckon with eight or nine infantry divisions and one or two armored divisions of the enemy in front of the so-called defense line of Seventh Army, composed of II FS Jg. Corps and LXXXIV Inf. Corps. In addition, the extreme right wing of the Army was also being attacked by considerable British forces. However, only local importance was attributed to these attacks at the seams between the British and Americans against the seams between the 5th Panzer Army and Seventh Army, which, it was assumed, were launched in order to support the decisive American offensive and to tie down German forces. The point of main effort of the British forces was still supposed to be in the area of Caen, and was therefore a continuous serious threat against the deep north flank and the rear of Seventh Army. This threatening situation increased each time armored forces were withdrawn from Fifth Panzer Army.

In the American breakthrough area of Avranches, the enemy appeared at first to move slowly, first of all drawing up forces from the rear. In view of our own intention, this was favorable, because the assembling of forces for the counterattack required time; therefore, each hour in which the enemy hesitated was to our advantage. It was also to be hoped that Brittany would tie up considerable enemy forces, and in this way weaken the expected thrust against the southern flank and the rear of Army Group B. Nevertheless, it would definitely have been better to have evacuated Brittany and the Channel Islands, and to have employed all available forces for the protection of the deep flank, or for blocking the American strategic breakthrough. The German Supreme Command, however, expected better results from the defense of the fortresses (ports in Brittany) and therefore deliberately sacrificed all forces employed in the fortresses and on the islands.

In view of the tactical situation of the enemy, it was important that Fifth Panzer Army and the defensive front line of Seventh Army hold out, even while facing an enemy superiority of four to five times its size, that the enemy advance in his breakthrough area be delayed, and that all available attacking forces be assembled as rapidly as possible, so as to advance toward the coast, making use of the momentarily favorable situation east of Avranches, and, in this manner, cut off the rear contact of the enemy forces which had broken through towards the south. Each day tended to change this situation to the detriment of the Germans. Therefore, the earliest possible time had to be made full use of.

C. Estimate of the Terrain

The La Sée sector formed an antitank obstacle which offered natural protection for the north flank of the counterattack. The attack terrain itself was the usual hedge terrain of Normandy, with its restricted possibilities for deployment. South of La Sée, however, it was higher, and offered a better opportunity for observation by artillery and heavy weapons, both in the direction of attack and to the north. In addition, the Juvigny-le-Tertre – Avranches, and Mortain – Montgothier – Avranches main roads were favorable for conducting an attack and for supply. Then again, on the southern flank, the Selume sector provided natural flank protection and a foothold. Therefore, the Army had already decided on 31 July to conduct the counterattack on the isthmus between La Sée and La Selume [?], and, for that reason, assemble the attack forces in the area of Sourdeval – Mortain. This assembly area was favorable for moving into position for the attack, because it offered cover and also possibilities for a covered approach in the area to the east. However, it was important that Mortain itself and the dominant heights east of it remained in our hands, particularly since great difficulties were to be expected for an attack in this deeply intersected terrain near Mortain.

D. 1–2 August

In the early morning of 1 August 1944, Seventh Army was organized as follows:

1. II FS Jg. Corps (Corps command post: farm west of St-Martin-Don). With 3 FS Jg. Div., reinforced by 15 FS Jg. Regt of 5 FS Jg. Div. and XII FS Jg. Reconnaissance Bn. Right Corps boundary, which formed, at the same time, the seam between Seventh and Fifth Panzer Armies: Vire (Seventh) – Vire river towards the north – La Lande-sur-Drôme. Boundary between II FS Jg. Corps and XLVII Pz. Corps: Mesnil-Clinchamps – Pont-Farcy (XLVII) – Tessy-sur-Vire (XLVII) – Vire river.

2. XLVII Pz. Corps. With 2 Pz. Div. and 2 SS-Pz. Div., with subordinated elements of 17 SS-Pz. Gren. Div. and remnants of Pz. Lehr Div. Boundary line between XLVII Pz. Corps and LXXXIV Inf. Corps: La Jouardière [?] – St Aubin-des-Bois– La Bloutière – Sourdeval-les-Bois (localities for LXXXIV Inf. Corps).

3. LXXXIV Inf. Corps (Corps command post: west of Gathemo). With 353 Inf. Div., with a subordinated regiment of 353 Inf. Div. and the Kampfgruppen of 243 and 275 Inf. Divs; 116 Pz. Div.; remnants of 91 and 243 Inf. Divs; remnants of 275 Inf. Div., with subordinated remnants of 5 FS Jg. Div.; and 84 Inf. Div., whose elements were arriving in the area east of St-Pois.

4. In the process of arriving: LXXXI Inf. Corps, for commitment at the Army left wing.

5. XXV Inf. Corps (Corps command post at Lt. [?] Lorient). With 77 Inf., 266 Inf., 343 Inf., 255 Inf., 2 FS Jg. and 319 Divs (without the Kampfgruppen which had been transferred to the Normandy front line).

On 1 August, the Army occupied the general line La Fouquérie [?] south of Cretteville – Tessy-sur-Vire – Beaucoudray east of Villedieu-les-Poêles. From there, the big gap started, which the following Kampfgruppen tried to seal off:

1. 116 Pz. Div., which, during the night, had been pulled out, arrived in time in the area south of the Forest [Forêt] de St-Sever to stop the enemy, who was advancing towards the southeast, near Coulouvray-Boisbenâtre and in the line St-Laurent-de-Cuves – [St-Gabriel-] Brécy.

2. South of the La Sée sector, 276 Inf. Div. held securing positions in the line Le Mesnil-Adelée – Reffuveille and southwest of it.

3. Kampfgruppen of 77 Inf. Div. held blocking positions in the line Ducey – Pontaubault. Although an assault on Avranches, executed with two battalions and supported by some assault guns, had reached the southern edge of the town, it remained unsuccessful in the end. On 1 August, the enemy continued his attacks along the entire front line.

The situation in front of II FS Jg. Corps became more and more untenable due to the fact that both flanks were threatened. The main body of 326 Inf. Div. at the left wing of Fifth Panzer Army (LXXXIV Inf. Corps) had obviously been annihilated. The full effect of the counterattack by II SS-Pz. Corps did not yet show. When, in the afternoon of 1 August, Tessy, on the right wing of XLVII Pz. Corps, was captured, a withdrawal to the rear of Vire was ordered.

The center of 3 FS Jg. Div. slowly fell back towards the south during the day, while the two wings attacked the pursuing enemy on both his flanks. These tactics succeeded in not only stopping the surprised enemy, but even in forcing him to withdraw towards Torigni. This made it possible to move the division without difficulty to the south bank of the Vire river during the following night, and to leave strong combat outposts on the north bank in the line Mont-Bertrand – Beuvrigny. XII FS Jg. Bn continued to protect the exposed right Corps and Army flank on the Vire river east of St-Marie-Lanmont [Ste-Marie-du-Mont?].

In the XLVII Pz. Corps sector, it had been possible to pull the bulk 116 Pz. Div., as the first unit, out of the front line and to bring it forward to LXXXIV Inf. Corps in the area southwest of the Forest de St-Sever. But the elements remaining in the front line were engaged in heavy, intensive fighting.

The enemy continued to attack strongly, especially the right wing of 2 Pz. Div., and was able to capture Tessy-sur-Vire on the afternoon of 1 August. The division's left wing was still fighting south of Beaucoudray. After the breakthrough was accomplished and Villedieu captured, Percy lost its importance. Thus, XLVII Pz. Corps received orders to fall back to the line north of Pont-Farcy – Binet [?] – Montabot – Montbray – northwest corner of the Forest de St-Sever, in the course of the intended withdrawal movement, during the night of 2 August. Additional forces could not yet be made available through this evading movement, with the exception of the remnants of Pz. Lehr Div., which no longer played an important role and was not considered for the planned counterattack on Avranches.

In the XXXIV Inf. Corps sector, 353 Inf. Div.—which, in spite of the heavy fighting, the severe losses and the continuous breakthroughs, still remained a highly compact Kampfgruppe—had fought its way back to the western edge of the Forest de St-Sever, offering tenacious resistance, and had moved into defensive positions in the line St-[Georges-d'?]Aunay – Le Gast. The small Kampfgruppe of 6 FS Jg. Regt, subordinated to 353 Inf. Div., was kept in readiness as division reserve.

116 Pz. Div., with one Kampfgruppe, which was to liberate the south flank of 353 Inf. Div., had encountered enemy tanks near Coulouray-Boisbenâtre. They did not succeed in capturing the locality, but the enemy assault was halted, and several enemy tanks were put out of action. Other elements of the division succeeded in establishing an obstacle line in the direction of St-Laurent-de-Cuves – Brécey, and also prevented further advances there by the enemy. In the rear of the division, the first elements of 84 Inf. Div. had arrived, and

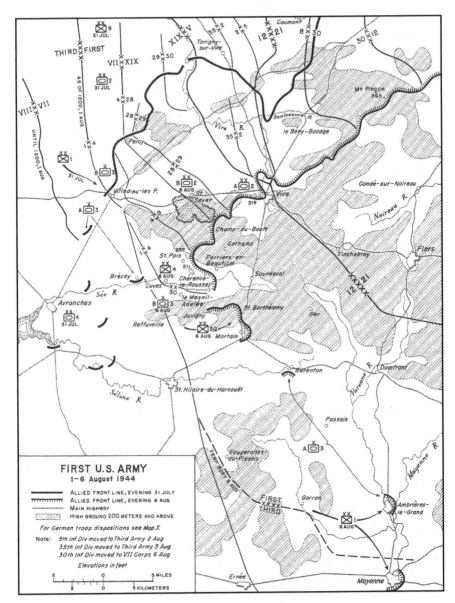

FIRST U.S. ARMY
1–6 August 1944

ALLIED FRONT LINE, EVENING 31 JULY
ALLIED FRONT LINE, EVENING 6 AUG
MAIN HIGHWAY
HIGH GROUND 200 METERS AND ABOVE

For German troop dispositions see Map X

Note: *5th Inf Div moved to Third Army 2 Aug*
       35th Inf Div moved to Third Army 5 Aug
       30th Inf Div moved to VII Corps 6 Aug

Elevations in feet

5   0   5 MILES
5   0   5 KILOMETERS

were, at first, assigned to 116 Pz. Div. Corps intended to relieve 116 Pz. Div. after the arrival of the entire 84 Inf. Div., and to bring 116 Pz. Div. forward to the south bank of La Sée for the planned counterattack on Avranches.

In the course of 1 August, the Kampfgruppe of 275 Inf. Div. had completed its assembly in the thinly manned security line, where, except for heavy enemy air activity, no enemy was as yet encountered. Further to the south, local defense was located in St-Hilaire [?] and Fougères [Feugères?].

It was already possible to foresee that the protection furnished by 77 Inf. Div. would not suffice even to delay the enemy's exploitation of his breakthrough, because enemy reconnaissance had succeeded several times in breaking through the thinly manned security line and to thrust forward up to the area north of Rennes. The tactical situation near Pontaubault – Ducey was obscure.

On 2 August, the tactical situation on the Seventh Army's right wing was decisively influenced by the breakthrough of British armored forces in the area north of Vire. While, at first, this penetration was not considered of strategic importance in the estimate of the overall situation, it still affected the general situation inasmuch as II SS-Pz. Corps was pinned down and could not be made available for the counterattack on Avranches. Furthermore, the situation at Seventh Army's right boundary made it necessary to withdraw the front line, and to tie up forces which could here no longer be employed for the defense against the US First Army. It was important that the road center of Vire, with its crossings, should, for a while, fall into enemy hands.

On 2 August, the counterattack by II SS-Pz. Corps reached only the Courte [?] area, 4½ km east of Vire. There was a wide open gap from there to the locality of Vire. II FS Jg. Corps had moved some 88 mm flak batteries into position, along the line Vaudry (2 km east of Vire) – La Papillonière [?] (three km north of Vire), which succeeded in forcing the retreat of the British tanks thrusting forward on Vire. Corps withdrew in the line La Graverie – La Beltière [Bellière?]. The boundary line to the unit adjacent to the right was transferred approximately to the line Flers (Seventh)–Tinchebray (Seventh)–Courte (3 Pz.)–Le Bény-Bocage (5 Pz.), so that the left boundary line to XLVII Pz. Corps could also be shifted to the line of Truttemer-le-Grand–west of Vire – Pont-Farcy.

XLVI Pz. Corps had received orders to successively pull out from the front line elements of 2 Pz. Div. and 2 SS-Pz. Div., in the course of the withdrawal in the line of Vire – Forest de St-Sever, and to send them into the assembly area of Sourdeval – Mortain. The last elements of these divisions were then to be relieved by the gradually arriving forces of 363 Inf. Div. During the night of 2/3 August, Corps withdrew for this purpose in the line of La Fosse – La Saulnerie [?] – Les Long Champs [Longchamps?] – northwest corner of St-Sever, under continuous rearguard actions. At the same time, 2 Pz. Div. withdrew its reconnaissance battalion and additional elements from the front line and sent them ahead into the area south of Sourdeval. Elements of Pz. Jg. Bn of 2 Pz. Div. had to be committed temporarily for the defense against the British tank attacks northeast of Vire, because the division command post at the western edge of the city appeared to be endangered. 2 SS-Pz. Div. also had its first elements assembled in the rear of the front line.

Considerably stronger fighting took place in front of LXXXIV Inf. Corps, which had to continue defending the former line. 353 Inf. Div. was able to hold its position at the western edge of the Forest de St-Sever against heavy enemy attacks. The division was also able to rehabilitate itself to some extent by bringing forward replacements and the remnants of the Kampfgruppe, which, as a first part of the division, had been originally committed at the invasion front line within the framework of 352 Inf. Div. Thus it was possible to reactivate at least the cadres of 3 Regt (943 Gren. Regt) and the Fus. Bn. From all elements they assigned to the division, two regiments of about medium strength were activated, to which the meanwhile still subordinated 957 Gren. Regt of 363 Inf. Div. was added as a third regiment.

The battle fought by 116 Pz. Div. in the area southwest of the Forest de St-Sever led to the abandonment of the strongpoint of Brécey, which was echeloned to the front, but, on the whole, the tenacious battles, which were conducted flexibly by defense and counterattack, succeeded in preventing an enemy breakthrough at St-Pois. In this connection, it was unfortunate that 116 Pz. Div., which was to participate under all circumstances in the counterattack, clung, with ever-increasing tenacity in costly battles, to their positions, and that the relieving portion of 84 Inf. Div. had a very low combat efficiency. Therefore, 116 Pz. Div., at first, could only release the reconnaissance battalion, which received orders to reconnoitre south of La Sée, in the direction of Avranches, and to delay enemy advances to the east. On 2 August, too, however, only weak enemy armored reconnaissance [units] felt their way forward toward the 275 Inf. Div. security detachments west of Juvigny-le-Tertre.

On the other hand, the enemy then energetically attacked the blocking front line of 77 Inf. Div. at Pontaubault, He not only succeeded in rapidly piercing it, but also in capturing the important crossing near Pontaubault still intact. It had been prepared for demolition, but the local command and the security detachment at the bridge had failed. With that, the threat in the deep southern flank had reached its decisive stage. Except for local security detachments in the form of local strongpoints, nothing was left which could have halted the enemy advance. Therefore, it was of great importance to hasten by every means possible the reorganization, moving up to position and the beginning of the intended counterattack.

F. 3 August

It was deemed essential at II FS Jg. Corps to close the gap toward the neighboring unit on the right by attacking. For this reason, Corps had to pull out forces from the front line which, in turn, was only possible provided 3 FS Jg. Div. withdrew further to the south. Since the newly projected separation lines of Corps narrowed down in the rear towards both adjacent units, it was possible to make available 8 FS Jg. Regt, committed on the left wing. Simultaneously, 5 FS Jg. Regt was also pulled out from the front line and assembled in the Viessoix area (5 km east of Vire) in order to have a reserve available at the threatened Army seam. 9 and 15 FS Jg. Regiments and XII FS Jg. Reconnaissance Bn defended Vire and the Vire river to the north of the town, with the front facing east and northeast. 8 FS Jg. Regt succeeded in making contact with the left wing of II SS-Pz. Corps near Courte, and, with that, the crisis was alleviated for the time being. However, enemy elements were still located in the rear of the front line, which was closed again. In the face of a pursuing enemy, the reorganization, for the purpose of releasing mobile units, was continued at Army center.

On 3 August, the bulk of 363 Inf. Div. had arrived in the Tinchebray area and had advanced into the area of Gathemo – [St-Germain-de-Tallevende-] la-Lande-Vaumont. The occupation of the final position of LXXXIV Inf. Corps in the line Vire – Champ du Boult was prepared.

During the night of 3/4 August, XLVII Pz. Corps withdrew to the line Coulonces – Mesnil-Clinchamps – St-Sever-Calvados, and thus was able to relieve the main body of 2

Pz. Div. and additional elements of 2 SS-Pz. Div. from the front line. The strong enemy pressure was unchanged in front of LXXXIV Inf. Corps. At the right wing of 353 Inf. Div., the enemy succeeded in breaking through into the northern part of the Forest de St-Sever; this breach, however, was eliminated through a counterattack by the division reserve and the small Kampfgruppe from 6 FS Jg. Regt. 353 Inf. Div., fighting bravely, was, moreover, able to hold its MLR at the western edge of the wooded area against all enemy assaults during that day.

Although additional elements of 84 Inf. Div. had meanwhile arrived, it was not yet possible to relieve 116 Pz. Div. There, too, local heavy battles again occurred, during which the division had to abandon terrain west of St-Pois, but was able to hinder the breakthrough attempted by the enemy by way of St-Pois toward the east. On 3 August, the main body of the Inf. Div. reached the area of Sourdeval – Clément [?] and had to remain there for security duties, until sufficient forces from XLVII Pz. Corps had arrived, as the area was of the utmost importance for the assembly for the attack. As a result, a further delay in relieving 116 Pz. Div. had become unavoidable. Likewise, the newly brought up 394 Assault Gun Bde had been subordinated for the time being to XLIV Inf. Corps, although, according to plans, it was also to take part in the attack.

On 3 August, for the first time, severe enemy pressure was also noticeable south of La Sée, toward the east. It had been possible to have 275 Inf. Div. reinforced by two assigned march companies (400 men) and two assault guns. The forces of the division, however, were

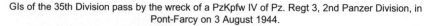

Gls of the 35th Division pass by the wreck of a PzKpfw IV of Pz. Regt 3, 2nd Panzer Division, in Pont-Farcy on 3 August 1944.

still too weak to be able to repel the heavier enemy attacks, which began on 3 August. The defense could only be established on a system of strongpoints. The enemy, by frontal fire and air force action, forced the crews of the strongpoints to take over and, simultaneously, passed them on both sides. Thus the enemy succeeded in capturing Reffuveille and then also Juvigny-le-Tertre by enveloping attacks, inflicting severe losses upon the elements of 275 Inf. Div., which were considerably inferior in equipment and in strength. The assault guns were put out of action through direct hits by the enemy air force.

The enemy, by a rapid assault towards the east, succeeded in capturing St-Barthélemy, north of Mortain, and in pushing forward to the heights west of Mortain. Here, the enemy encountered the Reconnaissance Bn of 2 Pz. Div., which took over the protection of the divisional strategic concentration area south of 84 Inf. Div. A counterattack on St-Barthélemy was unsuccessful, because the enemy committed considerable air power and attacked, especially, Mortain—the point of departure for the counterattack—very heavily from the air. Reconnaissance forces from Pz. Lehr Div., which were also employed in the depth of the Army flank for reconnaissance, provided cover for Mortain, Barenton and Passais, and at the same time reconnoitered the southwest.

On 3 August, as expected, the enemy assaulted with strong forces also from the breakthrough area of Avranches towards the south. Directly north of Rennes, he encountered a flak barrier, which was established there, and the elements of 341 Assault Gun Bn, so the first attacks could be repelled. However, there, too, the highly mobile enemy armored force succeeded in circumventing the static and nonmobile flak batteries; they encircled Rennes and penetrated into the city from the east. From Rennes, as well as from the area of Fougères, which was also captured by the enemy, he continued advancing to the south and southeast.

Obviously, the US 6 Armored Div. had been turned towards the west against Brittany. Their spearheads were halted on both sides of Dol-de-Bretagne by security detachments from 77 Inf. Div., which, after the collapse of the defense near Pontaubault, had withdrawn in the direction of St-Malo.

In the meantime, LXXXI Inf. Corps had taken over command of all security forces in the area south of the line Barenton – St-Hilaire, and had established its command post southeast of Alençon. Of those forces which were in the process of being brought forward, advanced elements of 9 Pz. Div. were just arriving in the area west of Alençon, while 708 Inf. Div., advancing on foot, and widely dispersed, had reached the area south of Laval – Nantes – Angers. On 3 August, 1 Security Regt had left Paris.

The remnants of 352 Inf. Div. were assembled in the area southeast of Alençon, and the division, by order of the newly assigned divisional commander, Gen. von Schuckmann, was brought up to strength by reserves, in order to again make available, as quickly as possible, a battle-efficient unit.

F. 4–6 August

In spite of the enormous danger for the entire western front line, the tactical situation had developed more favorably than could have been expected at first. The crisis at the boundary between Fifth Panzer Army and Seventh Army was eliminated by the employment of II SS-Pz. Corps and by the excellent fighting qualities of 3 FS Jg. Div. However, the divisions of

II SS-Pz. Corps, which originally had also been intended for the counterattack on Avranches, had become tied down for the time being. It could hardly be expected that they could still be pulled out, considering the pressure of time.

However, such strong elements of the Army had still been able to escape the battle of extermination at St-Lô – Percy – Avranches that it had been possible once again to establish a connected front line between Vire and the La Sée sector, i.e., before the main body of the US First Army, from which front line it was possible, by 5 August, to pull out two Panzer divisions (2 Pz. Div. and 2 SS-Pz. Div.). The heavy pressure against this front line, the holding of which was a prerequisite for the intended counterattack, however, compelled a further shortening of the line into the general line Vire – Champ du Boult–Chérencé. It was to be hoped that this line could be held with the help of the newly arrived divisions (84 and 363 Inf. Divs). However, mobile antitank forces (remnants of Pz. Lehr Div., and 394 Assault Gun Bde) had to be left in this front line. Furthermore, it hardly seemed possible to pull out 116 Pz. Div. from the front line before 6 August. Either this division, therefore, had to launch an attack on the same evening across its former front line north of La Sée, or the time of attack had to be postponed in order to move the division into an assembly area south of La Sée.

Even though the enemy, with, for the time being, still weak forces, was attacking directly west of the concentration area at Sourdeval – Mortain, we nevertheless succeeded in holding this area and carrying out the initial assembly as planned. With the exception of 2 Pz. Div. and 2 SS-Pz. Div., we could—after the commitment of II SS-Pz. Corps had become necessary at the seam of the Army—only reckon with the support of 1 SS-Pz. Div., which was to be brought forward from Fifth Panzer Army to Seventh Army by 6 August.

In the area of the breakthrough, precious time had been gained by the enemy's hesitation on 31 July and during the first days of August, and also by our commitment of the various security detachments. According to enemy orders captured at the beginning of the invasion, it was expected that the US Third Army would at first turn its main effort towards Brittany. In any case, we gained the impression that no strong enemy forces were advancing towards the immediate flank of Seventh Army at the Mortain – Domfront line, but rather that the enemy only went under cover there. An assault north of the Loire towards the east would require more time, and all means had to be used to delay it. Since, however, we had to reckon with the execution of such an enemy intention, it was important to start the counterattack as soon as possible—by 6–7 August at the latest. We hoped that the enemy would react to the counterattack in such a manner that the tactical situation in Brittany, and first of all in the deep flank of Army Group, would be eased, and finally again become stabilized.

Seventh Army then faced the difficult decision to either—with regard to the tactical situation at the deep flank—launch the counterattack with the forces available on 6 August, that is, with four or five Panzer divisions (1 SS, 2 SS, 2, 116, and elements of 9 Pz. Div.), or to disregard the developments of the tactical situation in the wider area of Le Mans and await the concentration of stronger forces. In the latter case, the time for commencing the attack could not be foreseen. In any case, it did not then seem possible before 10 August. As a result, however, the entire plan for the offensive might have become questionable, because, in seven to eight days, the defensive front line north of La Sée could have been broken through, and also, first of all, the deep southern flank of Army Group might have become encircled to such an extent that the contact to the rear and the supply base in the Alençon area would have been directly threatened.

Therefore, Seventh Army decided to launch the counterattack on the evening of 6 August, with the forces available at that time. All forces which were later brought forward were urgently required for the further task of holding the Avranches area. The Army considered this task the more difficult one. On 4 August, Seventh Army gave an estimate of the tactical situation, which will be quoted in excerpts:

"Exploiting the breakthrough at Avranches, the main body of the American forces pushes towards the south and tries to cut off and capture Brittany. Up to now, the development of the tactical situation shows that the enemy elements, advancing towards east and southeast, have the mission to protect the enemy east flank. After the British breakthrough at the left wing of Fifth Panzer Army has been successfully sealed off, it can no longer be assumed that the enemy will commit considerable forces for a combined operation with the British Army towards the east. The confirmation of these enemy intentions is of decisive importance for the preparation and execution of the planned operation. The Army intends to attack towards Avranches in a straight line south of the La Sée sector, with concentrated forces, echeloned to the left.

"For a successful command of the attack, it is of decisive importance that enemy air supremacy be reduced by committing all available German fighter airplanes. The previous engagements have shown that the enemy successes were achieved only because of their absolute air supremacy.

"It has to be assumed that the enemy will commit strong forces for the defense against the German tank attack, because it is vital for him to protect his lines of communication to the rear. Therefore, the attacking units will have to concentrate all forces toward the north and partially toward the south during the course of the operation and following its successful termination. For this reason, reinforcements are absolutely necessary for the retention of the gained area . . .

"It is of decisive importance that this operation start as early as possible, in order to regain the initiative. Every delay makes it increasingly difficult to disengage from the enemy and thereby endangers the execution of the entire operation.

"Therefore, the Army has decided to launch the attack as soon as XLVII Pz. Corps and 9 Pz. Div., with their combat elements, have been assembled. Thus, we give only the shortest time to the enemy to take countermeasures, as our assembling cannot be concealed from his air reconnaissance.

"To summarize, the Army points out again the decisive importance of sufficient fighter escort and the bringing forward of reinforcements."*

---

* From *War Diary* of the Seventh Army, Document VI: Phone Calls and Conversations (re-translated from English).

The combined operation with the British Army mentioned in the estimate was understood to mean only a possible American attack by the way of the Domfront–Mortain line in the general direction towards Flers, and not the big encirclement over Laval – Le Mans – Alençon, with which one had to reckon later in any case. On 4 August, this intention was not yet evident.

Genlfdm. von Kluge agreed with the estimate, the decision, and intention of Seventh Army. He promised to use all his influence for the fulfillment of the Army's requirements.

The Army issued the orders necessary for the attack. In the evening of 6 August, XLVII Pz. Corps was to launch the attack with three divisions, in an advanced front line as follows:

On the right: 116 Pz. Div., directly north of the La Sée sector;

At the center: the reinforced 2 Pz. Div., in the La Sée – St-Barthélemy sector;

On the left: 2 SS-Pz. Div., on both sides of Mortain.

LXXVI Inf. Corps, with the available elements of 9 Pz. Div. and 708 Inf. Div., was to follow the attack by XLVII Pz. Corps, being echeloned at the left to the rear.

The point of main effort was to take effect in the center of XLVII Pz. Corps, by reinforcing 2 Pz. Div. with elements of 116 Pz. Div. and 1 SS-Pz. Div., and also the organization of the artillery and Werfern (mortars), and especially by bringing forward 1 SS-Pz. Div. (Leibstandarte).

The objective of the attack was Avranches. After having reached this area, the Army intended to establish a connected front line towards the north, at the south bank of the La Sée river, with a bridgehead at Avranches, and to cover same with some elements at the La Selume sector to the south. The name "Luettich" [Liége] was ordered as the codeword for this operation.

On 4 August, the tactical situation at the Army's right wing, at II FS Jg. Corps, remained critical. The objective of attack, i.e., the reestablishment of the front line at Lassy – Etonvy [Etouvy?], had not been accomplished. The front line had not yet been firmly closed again, in spite of attacks by II SS-Pz. Corps and 3 FS Jg. Div. Strong enemy forces had been cut off behind our own front line, and were annihilated in the course of 4 August in an attack by 10 SS-Pz. Div. and elements of 3 FS Jg. Div. Such an enemy group, was, in particular, annihilated in the Viessoix area. Individual enemy tanks, however, still remained behind the front line. Burcy and Fergues [?] were captured by 5 FS Jg. Regt, while Presles was taken by 9 SS-Pz. Div.

The enemy, who obviously had recognized the withdrawal of the armored forces, attacked XLVII Pz. Corps more intensively than before, in order to tie down forces. He succeeded in making several penetrations into the front line, which was weakened by the pulling out of the Panzer division, south of Coulonces and southeast of St-Sever, where the enemy was able to advance up to Le Mesnil and the crossroads 1 km west of it. Corps could no longer commit for counterattacks those elements of 2 Pz. Div. and 2 SS-Pz. Div. which had already been pulled out, in order not to endanger the timely assembly of the attack group. Thus, the penetrations were only sealed off, and, during the night of 4/5 August, the troops fell back, according to plan, to the line Vire – St-Martin-de-Tallevende – St-Manvieu-Bocage – Champ du Boult, which was already occupied by 363 Inf. Div. Thus, the last elements of 2 Pz. Div. and 2 SS-Pz. Div. then also became available, and were brought forward to the assembly area south of Sourdeval. The small Kampfgruppe remnant of Pz. Lehr Div. was brought forward to II FS Jg. Corps, with orders to assemble same as reserves at the boundary to the neighbor on the left, southeast of Vire.

The enemy also renewed his severe attacks towards the east against LXXXIV Inf. Corps. At 253 Inf. Div., he succeeded in breaking through on both sides of Le Gast and penetrating the southern part of the Forest de St-Sever. This penetration, however, could be sealed off. The right division wing, in which 957 Gren. Regt of 363 Inf. Div., which was still battle trim, was committed, successfully repelled all attacks.

116 Pz. Div. received orders to pull out its elements by platoons from the front line, in the course of the arrival of 84 Inf. Div., in order to assemble them for the counterattack. This, however, was only partly possible, because of the slow arrival of the infantry and the continuous severe enemy attacks. Above all, the inevitable penetrations into the front line again had again rendered necessary the commitment of elements of the Panzer division, which had been relieved. On 4 August, the most dangerous enemy penetration occurred at the left division wing, north of Le Mesnil-Gilbert up to Hill 211 (1½ km southeast of St-Pois). Elements of the Panzer regiment launched a counterattack against it.

South of La Sée, elements of 2 Pz. Div. had succeeded in establishing a security line in the direction of Chérencé – La Graverie, and in preventing further enemy advances there. On the other hand, the enemy had been able to capture Mortain, and the important Hill 273 northwest thereof, during the night. Our own security detachments (275 Inf. Div. and elements of 2 SS-Pz. Div.) were now located in a line from St-Clément to the hills directly east of Mortain. In addition, 275 Inf. Div. had established security lines at the south edge of the Forest de Mortain for the protection of the left flank, and had organized local defense lines in Barenton and St-Georges-de-Rouelle[y]. XLVII Panzer Corps' assembly area had thereby been pushed back considerably, and was directly in front of the enemy. This was a great disadvantage for the various reasons of enemy action, difficulties of camouflage, and systematic preparation.

During the night of 4–5 August, according to orders, LXXXIV Inf. Corps, following XLVII Pz. Corps, withdrew to a line Champ-du-Boult – hills west of Gathemo – hills west of Sourdeval so as to make possible the pulling out of 116 Pz. Div. Along the wide area of LXXXIV Inf. Corps, the only thing of importance that occurred was a weak enemy assault, conducted from the Fougères area in the direction of Ernée. But, as the enemy tried to push forward with stronger forces from Fougères towards Vitré and from the Rennes area in a southerly direction on Nantes, it was not yet evident, on 4 August, that considerable enemy forces intended to swerve toward the east. It seemed, at first, that the enemy was advancing only to the south towards the Loire, in order to cut off Brittany. Ernée and Vitré remained in our hands. The enemy advancing on Nantes had turned back again.

On 5 August, the reorganization of Seventh Army was completed. The right Army boundary towards Fifth Panzer Army was removed to a line Presles – Flers, towards the east. Therefore, II FS Jg. Corps had to be relieved on its left wing. The new left Corps boundary was shifted to a line east of Vire and west of Tinchebray. The entire adjacent sector up to La Sée was subordinated to LXXXIV Inf. Corps, which was thus in command of 363, 353 and 84 Inf. Divs in the line of Vire – Champ-du-Boult – Le Mesnil-Gilbert. 957

Gren. Regt of 363 Inf. Div., which, since 30 July, had been assigned to 353 Inf. Div., was reassigned to its former division. During the previous commitment it had suffered severe losses.

XLVII Pz. Corps also took over command in the attack sector west of Sourdeval and east of Mortain. The left Corps boundary towards LXXXI Inf. Corps was fixed along a line Barenton–St-Hilaire-du-Hargouët. XXV Inf. Corps, in Brittany, was subordinated directly to Army Group B, because it could no longer be directed by the advanced Army command post at Flers.

5 August was characterized by strong activity on the part of the enemy, namely the US First and Third Army. II FS Jg. Corps had intended to establish a continuous front line along the south bank of the stream which flows south of Presles and Burcy to the Vire river. This front line was to make contact in the direction of Lassy with the front line of Fifth Panzer Army. The stream crossing south of Presles had been fixed as the point of contact between the two armies. However, a critical tactical situation continued to exist in this sector, because of constant strong British pressure, which again and again made such contact impossible. Thus, at first, it was impossible to make available even a single division from II SS-Pz. Corps. During the fluctuating battles around Burcy, Presles, and Sourdeval, 3 FS Jg. Div. fought with outstanding bravery. This division was able to repeatedly eliminate enemy penetrations by successful counterattacks, and to put out of action numerous enemy tanks.

In the LXXXIV Inf. Corps sector, a deep enemy penetration with US tanks—obviously one combat command—at the right wing of the newly committed 363 Inf. Div. was particularly disturbing, because it directly threatened Vire, which was important as a road center. Corps, therefore, ordered a counterattack by the division reserve (one battalion), and, for this purpose, subordinated elements of 394 Assault Gun Bde (Commander: Maj. von Jena) to the division, together with one heavy antitank company with twelve 105 mm guns. The execution of the counterattack, however, was delayed by the strong activity of enemy low-flying airplanes, which made simply impossible the assembly and launching of an attack during daytime. Thus, the launching of the attack was only possible after darkness had fallen. The operation was successful, and the enemy tanks were put out of action.

The same occurred at a local enemy penetration in the neighborhood of Champ-du-Boult, where 80 prisoners were captured during a counterattack by elements of 353 Inf. Div. The heaviest battle developed at the south wing of Corps, where Hill 211, southeast of St-Pois, was again lost, and where the enemy was able to push forward up to the eastern edge of Perriers-en-BeaufPcel in a thrust from Chérencé towards the north and northeast.

84 Inf. Div. was particularly affected by the lack of combat experience and the absence of a well-coordinated lower command. Therefore, elements of 116 Pz. Div. repeatedly had to be moved in for sealing-off and counterattack purposes. Preparation, systematic assembly, and the moving up to position for the attack of this division was therefore hardly possible. The division received orders to bring up one Panzer battalion of 2 Pz. Div. into the area southwest of Sourdeval by 6 August, so as to form the local point for the intended attack.

The tactical situation of XLVII Pz. Corps was not substantially changed on 5 August. However, conditions for the conduct of the attack had been further aggravated by the critical tactical situation in the Chérencé area, and by the pinning down of strong elements of 116 Pz. Div. at the left wing of LXXXIV Inf. Corps. 2 Pz. Div. and 2 SS-Pz. Div. had both reached their assembly areas, as had 460 Artillery Bn, which was the only reinforcement artillery available for supporting the attack. No elements of 1 SS-Pz. Div. had as yet reached the Army area. The relief of the division at Fifth Panzer Army by the newly brought up 85 Inf. Div. was delayed. The Panzer Army, however, reported that the main body of the division, with the exception of one regiment and one Panzer battalion, would be available in the assembly area by the evening of 6 August. 394 Assault Gun Bde could not be taken away from LXXXIV Inf. Corps, because this front line would then have lacked any mobile antitank defense. This, too, resulted in an undesirable weakening of the attack group.

The tactical situation was subjected to a decisive change in the deep flank of LXXXI Inf. Corps' sector. After the US Third Army, with its VIII Inf. Corps, had on 4 August pushed forward into Brittany and obviously had become aware of its own superiority over the weak forces of XXV Inf. Corps, it turned off towards the east with strong forces from the breakthrough area of Avranches – Rennes. During the assault on Mayenne by way of Ernée, about 120 tanks alone were observed. Additional enemy forces attacked Laval, where, aside from the local garrison, the security regiment had just arrived in good time from Paris. It was thus proved that the enemy intended to launch a large-scale envelopment operation north of the Loire, which threatened the entire Army Group B, and it was to be feared that a partition of German-occupied France into two would occur. Seventh Army was aware of the great danger of this tactical situation.*

It was imperative that LXXXI Inf. Corps should employ all possible measures, in order to arrest and delay the enemy advance until our own armored attack on Avranches could make itself felt. It could not be assumed that Corps would be able to stop the enemy for a longer period of time, but Seventh Army hoped that it would be possible to do so for three or four days. For this, however, 9 Pz. Div. had to be put entirely at the disposal of Corps. It seemed impossible to still use this division at full capacity in an attack, which was echeloned to the left and driving in the direction of St-Hilaire.

LXXXI Inf. Corps had established a defensive front, based on a strongpoint system, in a general line Domfront – Ambrières [-les-Vallées] – Mayenne – Laval, with elements of 708 Inf. Div., which had by then arrived, together with the Reconnaissance Bn of 9 Pz. Div., the reassembled Pi Bn of 5 FS Jg. Div., alarm units, and 1 Security Regt. In the main, this only involved defending the main crossings at [La?] Varenne and Mayenne. It was possible to bring up Pz. Jg. Bn of 17 SS-Pz. Gren. Div., which was newly activated south of the Loire, as reinforcement into the Laval area. Corps also cooperated with 13 Flak Div., whose elements, committed in front, had to form the backbone of the antitank defense at the various Kampfgruppen.

The assembling of 9 Pz. Div. was not yet complete. The air situation had greatly delayed and prolonged transportation of the division. In order to make available additional forces

---

* See *War Diary* of the Seventh Army, Document VI: Phone Calls and Conversations, Daily Report of 5 August, Paragraph 1: "All reconnaissance reports confirm that, today, the enemy is pushing forward with strong forces against the general line of Mayenne–Laval into the deep Army flank. The *former estimate*, that the enemy is merely feigning an attack in this direction, *has to be revised*."

A battery of US M7 self-propelled 105 mm howitzers ready to go into action, with additional ammunition dumped by their position. (US National Archives)

for the protection of the flank, the Commander of Pz. Lehr Div., Gen. Bayerlein, received
orders to activate a Kampfgruppe from the rear elements of the division, which were
located east and southeast of Alençon, and to put same at the disposal of LXXXIV Inf.
Corps. The division Kampfgruppe, which was still located south of Vire, remained there
for the time being, so as to support the defense combat of II FS Jg. Corps and LXXXIV
Inf. Corps. On the other hand, a small Kampfgruppe of Pz. Lehr Div., located near 275 Inf.
Div. and committed in the Barenton area, was put on march to reach the division in the
Alençon area.

Meanwhile, OB West had ordered Army Group Blaskowitz to establish defensive
strongpoints at the main crossings along the south bank of the Loire with elements of First
Army, and to prevent the enemy from crossing the Loire towards the south. There,
however, the enemy only felt his way forward with strong reconnaissance troops, which
were repelled at all points.

Due to the newly established situation, Seventh Army had to face difficult decisions.
The only proper decision, as seen retrospectively, would have been to abandon the
counterattack and to fight the south flank free with the available Panzer forces, at the same
time withdrawing the Army to the east. However, this was impossible, since approval by
Supreme Command could never have been obtained. It was not to be discussed. Any
proposal to move back the front line would have resulted in the immediate recall of the CinC
and strongest counter-orders. Therefore, the Army decided to execute the counterattack,
even with the weakened forces (i.e. without II SS-Pz. Corps, 9 Pz. Div., 394 Assault Gun
Bde, the Werfer Bde, and other supporting weapons). But it was evident that this decision

could only be executed up to 7 August, since any further delay would cause the tactical situation at the south flank, and probably also at the right of the Seventh Army wing, to become untenable. The success of this attack seemed to be the last chance to relieve the endangered front-line sectors, and to frustrate the strategic intentions of the enemy. Therefore, Seventh Army reported the following intentions for 6 August:

Relief of 116 Pz. Div. by 84 Inf. Div.;

As far as the tactical situation at the Army right wing allows, the effort to eliminate the penetration is to be continued in cooperation with elements of Fifth Panzer Army;

Sealing off the penetration west of Vire;

The intended operation "Luettich" is to be launched in the evening after elements of 1 SS-Pz. Div. are completely assembled;

Attack by advanced elements of 9 Pz. Div., in order to recapture Mayenne;

Motorized transportation of the missing elements of 708 Inf. Div. in the direction of Mayenne, with the intention to relieve elements of 9 Pz. Div., which had been committed there.*

Army Group and OB West agreed with these intentions of Seventh Army. However, they requested, repeatedly, that the main body of 9 Pz. Div. participate in the attack on Avranches. This created a divergence of opinion, which was expressed again and again over the following days.

From 6 August, the boundary between LXXXIV Inf. Corps and XLVII Pz. Corps was changed to the line St-Pois (XLVII) – Vengeons (LXXXIV), since 116 Pz. Div. had now to lead the attack north of the La Sée sector. The elements of 84 Inf. Div. which had been committed in the attack sector were assigned temporarily to 116 Pz. Div. for the beginning of the attack.

Heavy battles took place again during 6 August along the defense line of Seventh Army. During the whole day, a counterattack by 10 SS-Pz. Div. at the Army seam did not come off, due to the unfavorable air situation. On the other hand, the right wing of 3 FS Jg. Div. was able to successfully repel an enemy attack in the Burcy area. Further attacks directed against the center of II FS Jg. Corps were also repelled.

LXXXIV Inf. Corps was engaged along its entire front line in heavy defensive operations. By means of strong artillery fire on Vire, and with heavy support by air, the enemy tried repeatedly to break through west of the city. It was possible to mop up a penetration to Hill 219 southwest of Vire by counterattack. On the other hand, the enemy had broken through in the area of St-Manvieu-Bocage. 363 Inf. Div., with its focal point at its right wing, was not able to eliminate this penetration, especially as the enemy had also captured Forêt de la Haye and had deeply penetrated the line of the neighbor adjacent to the left. A blocking front line was established in the line Le Veux [?] (southwest of Vire) – La Clartière [?] – La Jullière [?]. 353 Inf. Div. had lost Champ-du-Boult, and had not been able to prevent a deep enemy penetration toward the southeast. The tireless division, however, had been able to gain a footing again in the line east of Forêt de la Haye – L'Endrie [?] (2½ km west of Gathemo) and to establish a compact front line. A considerable number

---

* See *War Diary* of the Seventh Army, Document VI: Phone Calls and Conversations.

of enemy elements, with one armored group, were still located in the rear of our own front line in the Gathemo area. The severity of the battles was manifested by the fact, that, on 6 August, 363 and 353 Inf. Divs alone put a total of 28 enemy tanks out of action.

At the right wing of XLVII Pz. Corps, too, the enemy had again launched an attack against Perriers-en-Beauficel and east of it, and had succeeded in making penetrations. In order to prevent a breakthrough, elements of 116 Pz. Div. again had to be committed, and, at the same time, had to protect its northern flank at Gathemo against an enemy who had broken through.

Originally, the evening was fixed for the beginning of the attack. But, since the Panzer Battalion of 1 SS-Pz. Div., which was to be brought forward to the attack group of 2 Pz. Div., had not yet arrived, the beginning of attack was postponed until midnight.

While the enemy, on 6 August, remained relatively quiet in front of the attack sector, he attacked the southern flank of Corps near Barenton. However, 275 Inf. Div., which was protecting this area, was able to repel this enemy attack.

In the LXXXI Inf. Corps sector, the troops had not succeeded in recapturing Mayenne. However, elements of 9 Pz. Div. and 708 Inf. Div. committed there had been able to recapture Aron (4 km east of Mayenne) and thus prevent an extension of the enemy bridgehead at Mayenne. It was more unfortunate that, at the deep flank, Laval had suddenly fallen into enemy hands, and, because of that, the Mayenne front line was broken through at a second point. It seemed doubtful whether the thinly manned blocking front line northeast and east of Laval would hold out.

These events justified Seventh Army's decision to launch the attack without waiting for additional reinforcements. A subsequent reproach, made by the High Command, that the Army had not awaited unfavorable flying weather, was absurd, because then it might have been necessary to wait for weeks. In addition, in the afternoon of 6 August, Gen. der Flieger Buelowius, Fighter Commander West, arrived at the Army Command post and reported that, in the morning of 7 August, 300 German fighter planes would be committed in waves over the attack area. Based upon this promise, the Army hoped for a temporary neutralization of the enemy air force, which would make it possible to continue the night attacks also by day against an inferior and surprised enemy. The enemy tactical situation in the attack sector seemed still favorable, because, until then, only elements of the US 3 Armored Div. and 30 Inf. Div. had been observed.

Genlfdm. von Kluge, who was constantly being informed about the tactical situation and intentions, and who had, several times, appeared at the Army Command post, agreed with the decision. He personally made an effort to bring forward additional reinforcements for the attack. His request that 10 SS-Pz. Div. be ready and available on 5 August in the Vassy area could not, however, be complied with by Fifth Panzer Army, because of the tactical situation at II SS-Pz. Corps. Likewise, 638 Heavy Pz. Jg. Bn, which had been brought forward by Fifteenth Army, could not be made available. 331 Inf. Div., the advanced elements of which could reach the Army on 9 August at the earliest, was directed into the area of Tinchebray, in order to be employed either in the defense line or in the attack front line, according to the tactical situation. At that time, the Army intended to employ the division, after the successful attack, as a link between LXXXIV Inf. Corps and XLVII Pz. Corps in the Brécy area, but reserved the decision concerning the final employment.

An advanced command post was established for Genlfdm. von Kluge west of Alençon, from which he wished to personally supervise the conduct of the counterattack.

G. From the Evening of 6 August–11 August

The following units took part in the first counterattack:

116 Pz. Div.;

2 Pz. Div.;

2 SS-Pz. Div., with the subordinated Kampfgruppe from 17 SS-Pz. Gren. Div.;

1 SS-Pz. Div., minus one Panzer Grenadier regiment and one Panzer battalion (both remaining with Fifth Panzer Army);

Elements of the Reconnaissance Bn of Pz. Lehr Div.

While studying the operational plan, it must be borne in mind that the numerous frictions which occurred during the strategic concentration, and the impossibility of preparing an accurate schedule for the relief and concentration movements, continuously caused unrest. The staffs, units, and Army troops which arrived subsequently also caused constant changes during the course of operations.

The operational plan called for pushing through with the strongest possible Panzer Group on the isthmus between La Sée and La Selume, the direct way to Avranches, taking advantage of the favorable enemy situation, reaching the west coast of the Cotentin peninsula, and thereby cutting off the rear contact of the American forces which had broken through via Avranches. By reinforcing the operation with all the reserves that could be made available, a new front line, facing north, was at first to be established at the La Sée sector; furthermore, enemy attempts to break out at La Selume, conducted by those enemy forces that had penetrated to the south, were to be repelled. Considerations as to whether to first conduct the attack in a southwesterly direction on St-Hilaire and then turn in towards Avranches were rejected, because this was bound to create a danger that the attack would be stopped at St-Hilaire and because, furthermore, time would be lost conducting the battle in this way.

The point of main effort was in the center, and was to be pushed forward like a wedge via Juvigny against Avranches. For the first attack, during the night of 6/7 August, one Panzer battalion each from 116 Pz. Div. and 1 SS-Pz. Div. were assigned to 2 Pz. Div., which was attacking in the center, in order to concentrate the local point of attack. 2 Pz. Div. was first to assault towards the west between the La Sée sector and the St-Barthélemy–Juvigny road, and then, with the support of the Panzer Bn of 1 SS-Pz. Div. (Leibstandarte), was to open up the Juvigny–Avranches road by means of a thrust via St-Barthélemy. There, the entire 1 SS-Pz. Div. was to be committed as the most combat-efficient unit, and was to break through against Avranches in a brisk advance.

116 Pz. Div. was to support the attack north of the La Sée sector, echeloned right to the rear. The main task of this division was to protect the northern flank of the operation, to bind the enemy forces north of La Sée, and to keep up contact with the defense front line of the Army (LXXXIV Inf. Corps).

2 SS-Pz. Div. was to capture, by means of a surprise raid, Mortain and the hills west of it, by an attack encircling both sides, and then support the attack at the local point, echeloned left

to the rear. Elements of the Reconnaissance Bn of Pz. Lehr Div. were assigned to the division for reconnaissance purposes at the southern flank.

LXXXI Inf. Corps, together with the assigned 9 Pz. Div., 798 Inf. Div., and fragmented units, was to protect the deep flank of Seventh Army at the Mayenne front line and, most importantly, prevent a thrust by American armored forces into the Alençon area.

For the first attack, the armored strength was about as follows:

116 Pz. Div. (without detached forces)   20–25 tanks
2 Pz. Div. (including reinforcements)   80–100 tanks
2 SS-Pz. Div.   20–25 tanks
1 SS-Pz. Div. (without detached forces)   30 tanks

A sufficient number of Panzer replacements seemed to be secured by the remnants of the Pz. Regt of the Leibstandarte, which were still expected, and the announced 9 and 10 SS-Pz. Divs and a Panther (tank) battalion of 9 Pz. Div., which had to be newly brought forward.

The assembly for the attack had to take place during constant contact with the enemy. 116 Pz. Div. was already fighting at Perriers. The northern flank was much endangered by the critical tactical situation at Gathemo. 2 Pz. and 2 SS-Pz. Divs, in their assembly areas, were also in contact with the enemy near Chérencé, near St-Barthélemy, and east of Mortain. Therefore, no distinct boundary could be drawn between the moving into position and the beginning of the attack, which was especially detrimental for 116 Pz. Div.

At first, supplies for the operation did not cause any special difficulties, because Seventh Army was able to rely upon its well-equipped supply bases, which were favorably situated in the Alençon area. Shortages occurred only with certain types of ammunition, which, however, were caused more by production difficulties than those of supply. The supply train, naturally, suffered because of the strong air activity of the enemy, and was limited exclusively to periods of darkness.

H. 7 August

On 6 August, the Army defensive front line had had nine days of heavy fighting, which had resulted in particularly high losses. On the other hand, heavy losses of personnel and material had also been inflicted upon the enemy. Although terrain was lost, we nevertheless succeeded in preserving the cohesion of the front line and preventing the enemy from breaking through.

On 7 August, II FS Jg. Corps finally succeeded in making safe contact with the troops adjacent to the right. On the other hand, the left wing of Corps remained threatened, because the enemy had penetrated into Vire and an obscure situation had arisen there. 3 FS Jg. Div. echeloned 9 FS Jg. Regt left to the rear, as flank protection. The Kampfgruppe of Pz. Lehr Div. was committed at Hill 303 south of Vire as seam protection, and for this purpose was assigned to LXXXIV Inf. Corps because, above all, the Kampfgruppe had to fight together with 363 Inf. Div. Enemy attacks during the afternoon were repelled by the right wing of 3 FS Jg. Div., inflicting heavy losses upon the enemy.

On 7 August, LXXXIV Inf. Corps was engaged in heavy battles along the entire width of the front line. Vire, situated in the plain, was given up, and the main battle line was

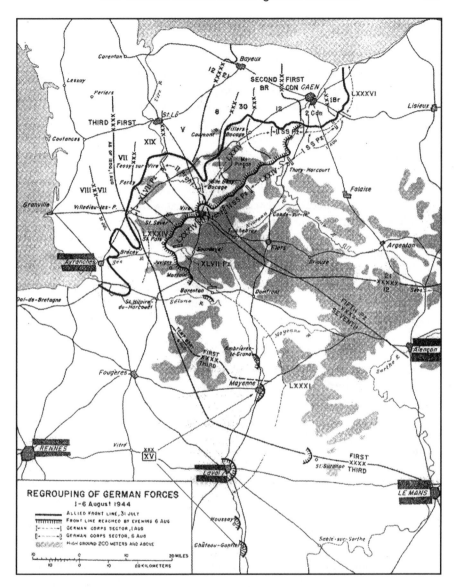

REGROUPING OF GERMAN FORCES
1-6 August 1944

ALLIED FRONT LINE, 31 JULY
FRONT LINE REACHED BY EVENING 6 AUG
GERMAN CORPS SECTOR, I AUG
GERMAN CORPS SECTOR, 6 AUG
HIGH GROUND 200 METERS AND ABOVE

20 MILES
20 KILOMETERS

withdrawn to the hills south and southwest of the town. The combat outposts remained in the locality into which the enemy penetrated at first with only weaker forces.

A special point of pressure developed on both sides of the boundary line between 363 and 353 Inf. Divs, where the enemy succeeded in making a deep penetration in the direction of St-Germain-de-Tallevende [-la-Lande-Vaumont], which, at first, could not be sealed off. Furthermore, the enemy continued to launch attacks northwest of Gathemo, strongly supported by tanks. These attacks were, however, for the most part repelled by the bravely fighting 353 Inf. Div. Again, all reserves were committed in order to seal off the penetrations or to eliminate them by counterattacks. Both Corps and Army hoped that the attack by XLVII Pz. Corps would have a relieving effect for the severely struggling defense front.

Immediately before the beginning of the attack, friction occurred at XXXVII Pz. Corps. Due to mistakes made by the lower command, the Panzer Bn of 1 SS-Pz. Div. (Leibstandarte), which was to be brought up to 2 Pz. Div., was greatly delayed, and was still not ready for action at 2400 hrs. The battalion was in close formation in a defile when an enemy fighter-bomber, which had been shot down, fell on the first tank and thus blocked the entire battalion. Backing out and turning round the vehicles took up valuable hours. Therefore, the left attack group of 2 Pz. Div. was only able to launch the attack on Barthélemy at dawn on 7 August.

However, Corps launched the attack at 2400 hrs, according to plan. 116 Pz. Div., which with its right attack group intended to attack Hill 211 and with its left attack La Mardelle [?] (1½ km north of Chérencé), was not at all able to advance. This division, however, had to face the hardest fighting conditions. The division had been weakened by having detached strong elements, but it had to face the strongest enemy. The surprise element was missing. It was, therefore, a breakthrough attack against an enemy ready for defense and superior in forces, especially in artillery. In addition, the division was threatened in the rear by the tactical situation near Gathemo, and some of its elements had to secure toward the north. However, in view of this situation, Divisional Command had not exerted itself to the full to influence the conduct of the attack, so both troops and officers lacked the necessary impetus in attack.

The right attack group of 2 Pz. Div. (reinforced 304 Pz. Gren. Regt) had been very successful. It advanced in a brisk attack on Le Mesnil-Adelée via Le Mesnil-Tôve against an enemy who, it is true, was only weak. Some elements were turned off toward the north as protection against Chérencé. At Le Mesnil, some troops from the US 9 Inf. Div. were captured. This division had been, up to then, only observed north of La Sée, in front of the center of LXXXIV Inf. Corps. The Pi Bn of the division was committed against an enemy counterattack from the direction of Juvigny-le-Tertre towards the north. The left Kampfgruppe (reinforced 2 Pz. Gren. Regt) took Bellefontaine, and encountered very tenacious enemy resistance at St-Barthélemy. Well dug-in American antitank guns at first prevented every penetration by our own tanks. Only during the second attack did we succeed in capturing the locality against the bravely defending American forces, and in advancing beyond it in the direction of Juvigny. Over 100 prisoners fell into German hands. Then, 1 SS-Pz. Div. was committed for the continuation of the attack against Juvigny-le-Tertre.

2 SS-Pz. Div. (Das Reich) also succeeded in the attack, encircling Mortain on both sides. It was able to capture the locality, and then advance on the hills west of Mortain and towards Romagny. However, several enemy groups, which had been cut off, still remained in the rear of the front line. Small single groups still defended themselves in houses of Mortain. A stronger group held out on the hill east of Mortain. During the subsequent period, this enemy group had a very disturbing effect and constantly pinned down forces of the division.

In the meantime, it had become light. 7 August was a clear and sunny day, with ideal flying weather. According to plan, our own fighter formations had taken off from their bases in the Paris area, but already they were engaged in air combat or, on their approach to the attack area, were being forced away by Allied fighter formations. In fact, not a single

German airplane reached the ordered operational area. Thus the Allied air force was completely unhindered in the heavy defense which had started here, and the flak forces of 13 Flak Div. were also too weak to bring about any noticeable relief. The absolute air supremacy of the Allies made any further movement by the attack units impossible.

Towards noon, the attack by 1 SS-Pz. Div. was stopped about 2 km east of Juvigny-le-Tertre, because the situation—due to losses of tanks caused by the tremendously strong low-level attacks—became untenable. Specially constructed British rocket-firing planes were very successful in individual attacks against tanks. Corps had no choice but to halt its attack towards 1300 hrs until dusk.

The attack was stopped from the air. This had a decisive effect, inasmuch as the alerted enemy was now able to prepare countermeasures and thus render any continuation of the attack considerably more difficult. The spearheads advancing in narrow wedges at Le Mesnil-Adelée and east of Juvigny were exposed to heavy enemy counterattacks in unfavorable positions. The right flank of 2 Pz. Div. was greatly endangered when 116 Pz. Div. halted its attack.

The enemy continued his attacks simultaneously at the left flank of XLVII Pz. Corps against Barenton – St-Georges. Owing to the withdrawal of the Kampfgruppe from Pz. Lehr Div., as well as the fact that the flak units of 13 Flak Div. had been transferred in order to support the attack, 275 Inf. Div., committed there, had been weakened to such an extent that it was unable to prevent the enemy from taking Barenton.

On the other hand, St-Georges-de-Rouelley was still able to hold out. The Army then repeatedly ordered LXXXI Inf. Corps to commit 9 Pz. Div.'s Reconnaissance Bn against the flank of the enemy, who was attacking to the north. This battalion, however, was still tied down in the Mayenne area, and could not go into action.

Enemy pressure against the deep Seventh Army flank increased considerably. Thirty enemy tanks were observed south of Domfront. Further to the south, the enemy took Ambrières and established a bridgehead across the Varenne river. Our own counterattack on Mayenne could not advance against an enemy who was growing stronger. There, through prisoner's statements, the presence of the US 90 Inf. Div. and 357 Armored Bn was newly revealed. The nonmobile elements of 708 Inf. Div. were not able to prevent the assault in the direction of Javron [-les-Chapelles?] by the highly mobile enemy force from the Mayenne area.

The enemy advanced with one to two divisions from the Laval area towards the east and northeast. There, LXXXI Inf. Corps had ordered stronger elements of 9 Pz. Div. into the Evron area and also committed the Kampfgruppe from Pz. Lehr Div. on the heights near Sillé-le-Guillaume. The completely defeated 1 Security Regt withdrew with some elements to this Kampfgruppe, and, with its main body, to Le Mans. Its combat efficiency was low. It seemed that the main body of the enemy was turning off in front of Sillé-le-Guillaume in the direction of Le Mans, which could only be insufficiently protected.

In spite of the situation, which became more and more critical, Seventh Army decided to ruthlessly continue the attack, because it seemed that relief to the deep Army Group flank could only be obtained in that way. Hence, the Army issued the following orders:

1. As soon as the air situation allows it, XLVII Pz. Corps has to continue its attack with all its forces, and to force a decisive breakthrough on Avranches. This attack has to

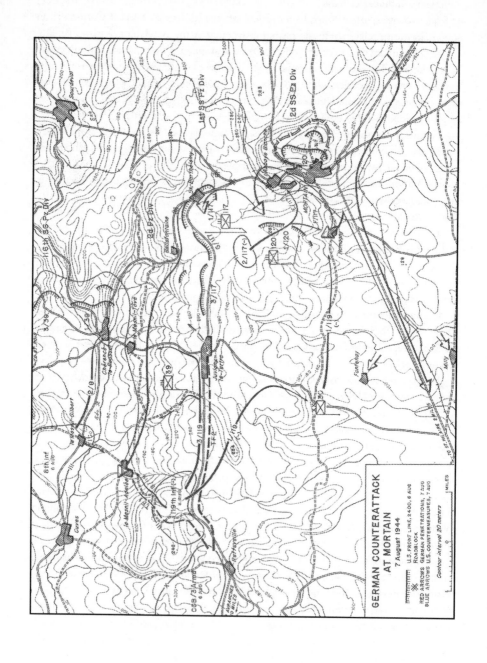

GERMAN COUNTERATTACK
AT MORTAIN
7 August 1944

U.S. FRONT LINE, 2400, 6 AUG
ROADBLOCK
RED ARROWS GERMAN PENETRATIONS, 7 AUG
BLUE ARROWS U.S. COUNTERMEASURES, 7 AUG

Contour interval 20 meters

0   1   MILES

be carried on, without consideration being given to the tactical situation in the south or on the north flank.

2. In contrast to previously issued orders, the main task of LXXXI Inf. Corps will now be the protection of the deep south flank of the Army. Available forces of 9 Pz. Div. have to be employed according to the tactical situation for an attack in the direction of St-Hilaire, as heretofore ordered.

3. A successful continuation of the defense battle by II FS Jg. Corps and LXXXIV Inf. Corps is of decisive importance.*

By telephone calls, the Army repeatedly requested from Army Group a decision concerning the further conduct of battle in general, and especially on its left wing. For the latter, Seventh Army set up the following three alternatives in a telephone call at 1930 hrs:

a. To hold out and to fight up to annihilation;

b. To withdraw towards the east, whereby an enemy breakthrough towards northeast becomes unavoidable;

c. To fall back towards the northeast, whereby the way towards the east in the direction of Paris will be opened up.†

Towards 2200 hrs, the remnants of 1 SS-Pz. Div., including 25 assault guns, were made available for the continuation of the attack. Elements of 331 Inf. Div., which were approaching, were, however, in turn, brought forward to Fifth Panzer Army, in order to relieve elements of 1 SS-Pz. Div. Thus, 331 Inf. Div. was broken up.

Immediately thereafter, Army Group informed Seventh Army that 10 and 12 SS-Pz. Divs were to be brought up to it on 8 August. LVIII Pz. Corps was to be sent up as operations staff for these units (Commanding General: Gen. der Pz. Tr. Krueger). This Pz. Corps had relieved II SS-Pz. Corps of Fifth Panzer Army in matters of command only at the beginning of August in the sector southwest of Caen. These decisions were personally approved by Adolf Hitler, at the suggestion of OB West at Hitler's headquarters in the field.

Thus a new tactical situation arose for the Army. It intended at first to let LVIII Pz. Corps follow up the attack in the second line behind the left wing of XLVII Pz. Corps. In this way, the attacking forces were to be guaranteed greater depth and force of penetration, as well as a greater protection for the southern flank of the operation.

I. 8 August

II FS Jg. Corps, which, by then, had made contact with the troops adjacent to the right in the line Chênedollé – Viessoix – Hill 247 (3 km southeast of Vire), was not attacked on 8 August. Corps had deeply echeloned its left flank by employing 9 FS Jg. Regt and XII FS Jg. Reconnaissance Bn, and was thus strongly covered. The Corps command post had been transferred into the region 2 km south of Cerisy (5 km northeast of Tinchebray).

On the other hand, US First Army continued its attack against LXXXIV Inf. Corps with undiminished impetus. Supported by the heaviest artillery fire, low-flying airplanes, and tanks, the enemy succeeded in deeply penetrating at the right Corps wing and to rip up the

---

* See *War Diary* of the Seventh Army, Document VI (re-translated from English).

† *Ibid.*, Vol. 4, Paragraph 4, pages 9a, 10a, 11, and 12.

front line of 363 Inf. Div. The situation in the area of St-Germain-de-Tallevende became extremely critical. Now enemy penetrations also took place in the Gathemo area. The Army could only help Corps by putting all available transportation space at its disposal, in order to accelerate the forward movement of the most advanced regiment of 331 Inf. Div., which was then in the process of approaching.

In committing their last reserves, the heroic troops of LXXXIV Inf. Corps, and in particular those of 363 and 353 Inf. Divs, succeeded once more in blocking the enemy penetrations, and thus preventing a breakthrough. On Hill 321, at the southeast corner of the Bois de la Haye, alone, five heavy enemy attacks, supported by tanks, were repelled. But it became ever clearer that LXXXIV Inf. Corps' front line could not be held any longer without the bringing forward of reinforcements.

Meanwhile, the enemy had grown stronger in front of XLVII Pz. Corps. The main body of the US 4 Inf. Div., which, until then, was believed to be north of La Sée, was confirmed to be actually concentrated in front of the center of the Corps front line. Furthermore, it had to be assumed that the US 30 Inf. Div., as well as elements of 9 Inf. Div. and of 2 and 3 Armored Divs, were in front of the attack line. Our own attack could no longer make any noticeable progress against this reinforced enemy.

During the night of 7/8 August, 116 Pz. Div., with its left wing, had been able to push forward up to the railway crossing, 500 m northeast of Chérencé, but the attack by the night attack group had been repelled. At the same time, the advanced Kampfgruppe troops of the division were not able to hold their ground, and had to be withdrawn in the face of a strong enemy counterattack. Then the division fought on a line La Foucherie [?] (where street fighting took place) – east of La Mardelle. Enemy tank concentrations led us to expect further counterattacks there.

2 Pz. Div. had also been assaulted in its most advanced attack positions by the US 4 Inf. Div. frontally and, especially, at its flanks. When Le Mesnil-Tôve was captured by the enemy, the Kampfgruppe was cut off in the area of Le Mesnil-Adelée. Its main body was annihilated. The division was thereby forced into defense in the line east of Le Mesnil-Tôve – Hill 280, to the west of St-Barthélemy.

East of Juvigny-le-Tertre, where 1 SS-Pz. Div. had launched an attack from the line 270 (2½ km east of Juvigny) – Hill 273 (2 km northwest of Mortain), no noticeable progress could be made. The division again experienced heavy losses, especially in tanks, through enemy air activity and the increased activity of enemy artillery.

2 SS-Pz. Div. was tied up at a line Hill 285 (1½ km northwest of Mortain) – Romagny against a reinforced enemy, and, furthermore, fought against bravely defended enemy strongpoints, which were in its rear. Reconnaissance secured its southern flank in a line Romagny – Le Masure [?] (4½ km south of Romagny) – St-Jean-du-Corail. As a result, the attack by XLVII Pz. Corps came to a complete stop. The enemy, on his part, launched counterattacks along the entire front line, which had to be defended in battles, causing heavy losses.

LVIII Pz. Corps and 10 SS-Pz. Div. were only just arriving at the area of Beauchêne – east of Mortain. There, they relieved the remnants of 275 Inf. Div., which secured toward the south. The remnants of this division later received orders to move to the Fifteenth

Army, in order to be reactivated there. However, the fragmentary groups (e.g., Kampfgruppe Heinz of 353 Inf. Div.), which were still stationed with LXXXIV Inf. Corps, could not be sent along with it because even a slight weakening of this front line was untenable.

The tactical situation at LXXXI Inf. Corps had continued to develop in a most critical manner. The right wing had been thrown back to Domfront, where a new front line was established in the rear of the [La?] Varenne sector by alarm units, elements of the Reconnaissance Bn of 9 Pz. Div. and Pi Bn of 5 FS Jg. Div. Thereby, the flank of the Seventh Army attack group had become 22 km in depth (Romagny – Domfront) and was threatened accordingly.

In the area around Ambrières, the US 1 Inf. Div. was again present. However, it was possible to repel attacks from this area towards the east and northeast. The tactical situation in the area east and northeast of Mayenne also did not change fundamentally. Two regiments of 708 Inf. Div. were now employed there, while the third regiment in the area of Sillé-le-Guillaume was assigned to Pz. Lehr Div. Air reconnaissance observed three pontoon bridges near Mayenne, one of which was under construction. There, also, the advance of strong forces had to be expected, once the enemy had drawn up from the rear across the river.

On the left Corps wing, only the reinforced Kampfgruppe of Pz. Lehr Div., for the most part, offered resistance on the heights along both sides of Sillé-le-Guillaume, with the front line facing southwest. The entire area between Laval and Le Mans was filled with strong

Men of the US 1st Infantry Division in action. The legend on their helmets—"AAA-0"—is a tribute to the Division's former Commander, MG Terry Allen, and refers to his motto, "Anything, anywhere, anytime, bar nothing." (US National Archives)

enemy forces, pushing forward toward the east (US XV Inf. Corps). At 1530 hrs, the enemy penetrated Le Mans, which was only weakly defended by a battle commander with alarm units (one Luftwaffe battalion and elements of 1 Security Regt). Only during the morning of the same day, the main Seventh Army command post was withdrawn from Le Mans to Bellens [?]. South of Le Mans, the enemy seemed to feel his way forward with only weak reconnaissance forces across the Sarthe to the Loire. At Nantes, Orléans, Blois and Tours, weak bridgeheads had been established by First Army on the north bank of the Loire.

Through fully aware of its existence, LXXXI Inf. Corps now found itself compelled to deliberately ignore the gap at Le Mans, and to restrict itself to preventing an enemy northeastward breakthrough to the Alençon area.

During the day, Army Group had also promised Seventh Army the assignment of two projector brigades. 8 Werfer Bde, which arrived first, was assigned to XLVII Inf. Corps. Contrary to the original plan, LVIII Pz. Corps, in matters of command, had been inserted at the former left wing of XLVIII Pz. Corps. 2 SS-Pz. Div. and the newly brought up 10 SS-Pz. Div. were subordinated to it. The boundary between XLVII and LVIII Pz. Corps was established in a line St-Clément [-Rancoudray?] (XLVII) – road crossing 1 km northward of Hill 307–northeast of Mortain–north slope of Hill 203 (2½ km west of Le Neufbourg) – church of Chasseguey–hairpin curve 1 km northwest of Martigny – road crossing 1 km west of Le Mesnil-Auzenne [Ozenne?] – church of Le Val-St-Père. The boundary to LXXXI Inf. Corps remained at a line Domfront – Barenton. The Corps command post of LVIII Inf. Corps was established at the road of Beauchêne–Ger (2 km northwest of Beauchêne).

At 2115 hrs, the Seventh Army received an order from Genlfdm. von Kluge stating that the attack was not to be continued for the time being, but that preparations for its continuation were to be made. This decision was connected both with the tactical situation at Fifth Panzer Army, where, on 8 August, south of Caen, a deep breakthrough by British troops had occurred, and with the tactical situation at LXXXIV Inf. Corps.

J. 9 August

9 August brought an aggravation of the critical situation on the Seventh Army right wing, as well as in the deep southern flank.

In view of the breakthrough in the area of St-Germain-de-Tallevende, the left wing of II FS Jg. Corps had been withdrawn during the night to Hill 232, northwest of Maisoncelles-la-Jourdan. Nevertheless, the contact with 363 Inf. Div. was only a loose one. Except for strong artillery fire, especially against the left wing of 3 FS Jg. Div., the rest of the Corps front line was calm. Obviously, the British Army had concentrated all its forces on the breakthrough south of Caen, although its right wing remained quiet.

On the other hand, the US First Army continued its attacks against LXXXIV Inf. Corps with unchanged impetus. St-Germain-de-Tallevende and Hill 184 (1½ km southwest of it) had been captured by the enemy. But, meanwhile, Corps had withdrawn somewhat along the entire width of the front line. It had succeeded in reestablishing a continuous and closed front line in the general line Hill 232 – south of St Germain-de-Tallevende – Hill 288 east of Les Monts Bonnel – Perriers-en-Beauficel – 1 km northeast of the church of Chérencé.

Between 0500 and 0600 hrs, enemy artillery had laid down heavy preparatory fire, which was mainly directed on the former MLR; it therefore caused only light damage. Nevertheless, the attacking enemy, whose main effort was now directed against the right wing of 363 Inf. Div., again succeeded in making a deep penetration west and southwest of Maisoncelles-la-Jourdan. Towards evening, the enemy attacking spearheads reached La Lande-Vaumont and La Bercendière [?]. As a result, the danger of a breakthrough was real, and, strategically, this could have a disastrous effect for the entire Seventh Army. Therefore, the Army was forced to take decisive countermeasures.

Meanwhile, the Regt of 331 Inf. Div. (one battalion each form 557 and 558 Gren. Regt, under the command of Oberst Frhr von Bobeneck) had arrived, just in time, at the battle field in the Truttemer area. This regiment, as well as one reserve battalion of 84 Inf. Div. and the remnants of the Kampfgruppen of Pz. Lehr Div. (Commander: Oberst Frhr von Hausser), were at the disposal of Corps, for a counterattack on 10 August. Furthermore, Seventh Army reluctantly decided to bring forward to LXXXIV Inf. Corps one Kampfgruppe of 1 SS-Pz. Div. (composition: one Panzer Grenadier battalion, one artillery battalion, one mortar battalion, and one assault gun company, under the command of Sturmbannfuehrer Schiller) and to temporarily assign it for the counterattack on 10 August. This weakened XLVII Pz. Corps, which was to prepare for the continuation of the attack on Avranches, but there was no other possibility of guaranteeing the restoration of the tactical situation at LXXXIV Inf. Corps, which was absolutely necessary.

On 9 August, the enemy strongly attacked at XLVII Pz. Corps, especially in the 116 Pz. Div. sector around Perriers-en-Beauficel, but, in general, could be repelled. Attacks in the area of Le Mesnil-Tôve against 2 Pz. Div. were also repelled or blocked. Along the entire Corps front line, there was strong enemy artillery fire, and especially strong low-flying airplane activity.

The newly committed LVIII Pz. Corps had taken over command of 2 and 10 SS-Pz. Divs. 2 Pz. Div. was able, by counterattacking, to eliminate a penetration at its right wing west of Le Neufbourg. During the night of 8/9 August, enemy reconnaissance at the widely extended flank front line of 10 SS-Pz. Div. had succeeded in penetrating on both sides of Barenton towards the north, and in advancing with single armored reconnaissance cars (up to the region of Ger and Lonlay-l'Abbaye.) A subsequent attack along the road from Barenton to Ger reached the hill 4 km northeast of Barenton. 10 SS-Pz. Div. was committed, with all its available forces, in order to eliminate this threat to the south flank of the attack group, and to recapture Barenton.

In the course of the reorganization for the continuation of the counterattack on Avranches, Seventh Army had ordered that 116 Pz. Div. be pulled out of the front, while 84 Inf. Div. was simultaneously to retire to a shorter line east of Perriers-en-Beauficel, and the Panzer division was to assemble in the area of St-Sauveur-de-Chaulieu – Sourdeval – Le-Fresne-Poret. Likewise, XLVII Pz. Corps was to withdraw 2 Pz. Div. to the line west of Brouains – Le Mont Morin [?] – Hill 273, and, in this connection, pull 1 SS-Pz. Div. out from the front line and assemble it in the rear of LVIII Pz. Corps.

As a result, the two Panzer units, which were at this time the strongest units, were to be concentrated in the rear of the front line, to give impetus to the new attack. In addition,

Seventh Army expected the arrival of the approaching Panther Bn of 9 Pz. Div. and 2 Mortar Bde (Werfer), both of which were to be brought forward to LVIII Pz. Corps. Furthermore, a regimental group from 6 FS Jg. Div., which had just been activated in the Paris area, was announced. With all these forces, the new attack was to be launched from the area of Mortain – Domfront in the general direction of St-Hilaire – Avranches.

On 9 August, too, the tactical situation at LXXXI Inf. Corps had not yet noticeably changed. The enemy had been able to make progress in the area around Ambrières and Mayenne, and had penetrated opposite 708 Inf. Div. into St-Loup-du-Gast and Montreoil-en-Lassay [Montreuil?]. Thereupon, the Reconnaissance Bn of 9 Pz. Div. pushed forward from the Domfront area towards the south, contrary to orders by Corps and Army, in order to prevent an enemy breakthrough. Enemy attacks against the Pz. Lehr Div. front line in the area of Sillé-le-Guillaume had been repelled. From the Le Mans area, only reconnaissance patrols advanced at first, in an easterly, northeasterly and northerly direction. There, the enemy seemed to draw up from the rear. Even though the enemy attack showed a distinct northeasterly direction before the front line at Ambrières – Mayenne – Sillé, the turning in of enemy armored units from the Le Mans area in the direction of Alençon was not yet clearly recognizable on 9 Aug. Based on current developments, however, the Army had already considered such enemy intentions. Therefore, 9 Pz. Div. received orders to advance into the area on both sides of Beaumont-sur-Sarthe and to prevent an enemy assault towards the north by attacking. On the other hand, Army Group still requested that the division be moved into the Domfront area for the counterattack on Avranches.

Meanwhile, Adolf Hitler had ordered that the command for the new attack be taken over by Gen. Eberbach, CinC Fifth Panzer Army. Therefore, the General handed over his command of Fifth Panzer Army to Oberstgruppenfuehrer Dietrich, and on 10 August took over a staff, Panzer Army Eberbach—not to be mistaken for Panzer Army West, which remained assigned to Seventh Army—which was especially activated from him. The son of the Field Marshal, Oberstlt. i.G. von Kluge, was appointed CinC of the Staff of the Panzer Army. The attack was to be prepared deliberately. First, the stabilization of the tactical situation near Caen had to be awaited. Then the attack was to be executed as described above, and all available forces were to be committed for this purpose, including 9 Pz. Div. Adolf Hitler's order had the following general wording:

"A unique opportunity is offered OB West, by means of a forceful thrust on Avranches, to decisively turn the tide of the entire situation in the west and to gain the initiative. Therefore, the attack is to be launched with all available forces, after a thorough preparation, taking advantage of the enemy situation, which is in our favor. LXXXI Inf. Corps is to participate in this attack. After reaching Avranches, the main body of the forces is to be turned off toward the northeast, regardless of the enemy forces which have broken through towards the south, and the Allied invasion front is to be rolled up by a simultaneous frontal attack by Seventh and Fifth Panzer Armies."

This order did not express anything basically new. Its objective was pure fantasy and was neither in keeping with the actual proportions of strength nor with the situation on the ground, either in the air or in terms of supplies. It failed particularly to consider the tactical situation at the deep southern flank. This represented the apex of conduct by a command ignorant of front-line conditions, taking upon itself the right to judge the situation from East Prussia. Since the time element was of no importance, Army Group and Seventh Army realized that developments on the ground would cause the High Command's orders to be disregarded.

K. 10 August

On 10 August, a decisive change took place in the campaign of northern France, in that, on that date, the main body of the US Third Army unmistakably swerved towards the north and northeast, in the direction of Alençon and Mamers. This move, made in conjunction with the British offensive, revealed the intention of the Allied Supreme Command. A clear decision by the German Command became necessary: they had to decide either to remain within the salient front arc of Vire – Mortain – Domfront and to cling to the idea of an attack on Avranches, or to withdraw to the east and thus evade the enemy's intended encirclement. This was the last chance to carry out the second option.

In an appraisal of the tactical situation which had been transmitted to Army Group B on 10 August, Seventh Army stated that it was to retain the option of attacking, only under certain conditions:

1. Reinforcement of the defensive front line of the Army;
2. Reinforcement of the attack forces, and bringing forward Panzer Ersatz (tank replacement units) for the attacking division;
3. Neutralization of the enemy air forces;
4. Protection of the supply base at Alençon – Chartres by newly brought up forces;
5. Establishing of fuel and ammunition depots.

If these conditions could not be fulfilled, the second possibility had to be considered. Since the Army had no doubt about it, CinC of the General Staff of Seventh Army, at the same time, forwarded to Army Group a detailed and elaborate operational plan for a withdrawal toward the east, However the incomprehensible happened: Supreme Command decided on the first solution, although not one of the necessary conditions could be fulfilled.

At II FS Jg. Corps, the situation at the front line remained quiet. Corps participated with the bulk of its artillery in combating the enemy penetration at the right wing of LXXXIV Inf. Corps. LXXXIV Inf. Corps' counterattack, which had been under way since the early morning, was at first successful. It was executed concentrically from the east, southeast and south against the penetration area. 363 Inf. Div., which was attacking on the right, reached Hill 232 (1 km northwest of Maisoncelles-la-Jourdan) – crossroads 1.7 km west of Maisoncelles-la-Jourdan. However, Hill 232 and the terrain west of Maisoncelles were again lost in a strong enemy counterattack. This counterattack could only be stopped and sealed off south of the locality. 353 Inf. Div., attacking on the left, was particularly successful. 984 Gren Regt pushed forward up to St-Germain-de-Tallevende, while 943 Gren. Regt, on the left, was halted in the river valleys west of Hill 230. Nevertheless, this brought about noticeable relief at this point.

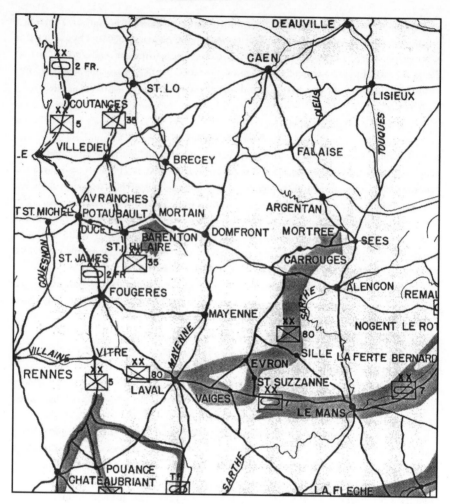

US XX Corps operations during the breakout.

At the left Corps wing, 84 Inf. Div. lost Gathemo in the face of strong enemy attacks. In the evening, the right Army wing (II FS Jg. Corps and LXXXIV Inf. Corps) was located in the line north of Vissoix [?] – Hill 262 – junction of the streams 1 km northeast of Maisoncelles-la-Jourdan – hill north of La Lande-Vaumont – Hill 230 – Hill 305 (2 km southeast of Gathemo).

Now the enemy also launched an attack along the entire width of the front line facing XLVII Pz. Corps. The continuous pressure against 116 Pz. Div. had at first, prevented the pulling out of this division. First it had to clear the situation by a counterattack. This thrust, launched southwest of Perriers-en-Beauficel, succeeded and mopped up the enemy penetration. 2 Pz. Div. was also able to repulse all attacks directed against its front line. On the other hand, the enemy succeeded in making a deep penetration into the left wing of 1

SS-Pz. Div., which extended up to Hill 307 northeast of Mortain and liberated the encircled enemy group, which still held out there. In committing elements of 1 SS-Pz. Div., which had been already pulled out, it was possible to superficially seal off this penetration.

In the LVIII Pz. Corps sector, the front line of 2 SS-Pz. Div., which was threatened at its northern flank by the penetration north of Mortain, was subjected to especially strong artillery fire, which caused heavy losses. On the whole, the enemy pressure against 10 SS-Pz. Div. increased steadily. After the enemy had advanced up to 4 km north of Barenton and had encircled a German Kampfgruppe at Hill 266, our own counterattack became effective. Even though it could not reach the objective, Barenton, the counterattack was nevertheless carried forward up to 1.5 km north of Barenton and thus cleared up the situation. 10 SS-Pz. Div., which, during this operation, had suffered considerable losses, changed over to the defensive. A thrust from St-Georges-de-Rouelley toward the north was repelled.

By this, definite defensive success had been accomplished against the US First Army, which had attacked without interruption using three Army Corps (V, XIX and VII), seven infantry divisions and two armored divisions, which were heavily supported by the air force. The enemy had suffered heavy losses. According to troop information, about 60 enemy tanks were put out of action just during the last two days. But our own troops had also suffered heavy losses during these engagements.

At LXXXI Inf. Corps, the tactical situation had developed in a very threatening manner. In the 708 Inf. Div. sector, Villaines-la-Juhel and Averton were lost against a strong enemy pressure, and the division thus became split into two parts.

In the course of the day, it became apparent that strong enemy forces, including the US 5 Armored Div., had pivotted from the Le Mans area towards the north. In the area of Beaumont-sur-Sarthe, they encountered 9 Pz. Div., two Kampfgruppen of which were engaged in heavy battles on both sides of the Sarthe river. In spite of its utmost commitment, the division could not prevent the superior enemy from pushing beyond it on both sides, especially eastward, and thus reaching the deep flank of Army Group. An enemy armored group attacked, -amongst other targets, both command posts of Pz. Lehr Div. and 9 Pz. Div. at Fresney-sur-Sarthe [?], which had to fall back toward the north. The command of 9 Pz. Div. was not able to concentrate the division for employment as a compact unit.

Meanwhile, Corps had employed the Kampfgruppe of 352 Inf. Div., which was in the process of reorganization, for protection east and northeast of Le Mans, but this was too weak to halt the thrust of the armored forces at all points. On the evening of 10 August, enemy armored spearheads were in Beaumont, Ballon, Marolles-les-Braults, Bonnétable, La Ferté-Bernard and in front of Nogent-le-Rotrou and partly beyond it. 9 Pz. Div. again received orders to attack the enemy in a concentrated thrust, but Corps and Army had realized that the Alençon area was directly endangered at this time. Gen. Kunzen, the Commanding General of LXXXI Inf. Corps, had repeatedly reported that the available forces never would suffice to execute his mission of protecting the flanks. But the only thing the Army was able to achieve was that 9 Pz. Div. at least had been left to him.

A captured enemy map showed further enemy intentions, according to which the US Third Army seemed to advance beyond the line of Bellême – Alençon. Army Group put the Kampfgruppe of 6 FS Jg. Div. at the disposal of LXXXI Inf. Corps for commitment, but it had not yet arrived. The time of its arrival could not be anticipated. In the late afternoon, elements of 9 Pz. Div. still succeeded, by means of a counterattack, in throwing back enemy forces which had pushed forward by way of Rouessé-Fontaine. On 10 August, 9 Pz. Div. and 352 Inf. Div. had put a total of 36 enemy tanks out of action.

During a long evening talk, the Army Chief of Staff reported to Genfldm von Kluge— without disguising any facts—on the dangerous situation, and repeated the request that the Army should at least retire locally, in order to release forces for the protection of the southern flank. The Field Marshal called together the CinCs of Seventh Army and Panzer Army Eberbach for a conference for the early morning of 11 August at Mequillaume [?], east of Argentan, during which final decisions were to be taken.

On 10 August, Gen Eberbach has assumed command of XLVII and LVIII Corps. He had concurred with the opinion of Seventh Army Staff, and, furthermore, had considerably increased the demands as prerequisite for the execution of the attack on Avranches.

L. 11 August

The development of the tactical situation on this day forced us to definitely give up the idea of attacking Avranches.

In front of II FS Jg. Corps, the British forces again became active, and succeeded in penetrating the front line adjacent to the right (II SS-Pz. Corps) in the Chênedollé area. On the other hand, the brave 3 FS Jg. Div. repelled all attacks against its front line, including that by US V Corps, directed against its left wing, putting 32 tanks out of action.

In front of LXXXIV Inf. Corps, the enemy continued his attacks against the new MLR, although not with the same strength as on the preceding days. A penetration made west of La Lande-Vaumont was sealed off. The penetration of stronger enemy armored forces southeast of Gathemo against 84 Inf. Div. was more serious, as this division was already very weakened. The enemy forces, which broke through, tried to roll up the front towards the north and south. Kampfgruppe Schiller of 1 SS-Pz. Div. again had to be committed against them.

Furthermore, elements of 116 Pz. Div. which had been pulled out during the previous night took part in the counterattack. The enemy, who had broken through, had penetrated into their assembly area. The enemy succeeded in taking the important Hills 243 and 305, but it was finally possible to seal off the penetration with the help of the Panzer Kampfgruppen.

At XLVII Pz. Corps, the right boundary of which was formed by the La Sée sector, the main body of 116 Pz. Div. was concentrated in the area of St-Sauveur-de-Chaulieu – Sourdeval – Le Freshe Forêt [?]. The enemy again attacked with strong forces against 2 Pz. Div. and 1 SS-Pz. Div., and was able to make a new penetration southeast of St-Barthélemy and at the seam to the troops adjacent to the left. The pulling out of the concentrated 1 SS-Pz. Div., as intended, was therefore not yet possible. It appeared that the enemy had considerably increased his strength before the Corps front line, so, apart from the general tactical situation, the chances of success for a new attack were very slight.

At LVIII Pz. Corps, the enemy had succeeded in establishing contact with his own elements on the hills east of Mortain, which had been cut off since 7 Aug. Hence these enemy Kampfgruppen, which had been supplied by air, had brought to a successful end a special feat of arms. The intensity of the fighting was characterized by the fact that, on 11 August alone, 2 SS-Pz. Div. put a total of 19 tanks out of action. The tactical situation in front of 10 SS-Pz. Div., subjected to continuous enemy pressure, remained unchanged.

In front of LXXXI Inf. Corps, the enemy continued his thrust into Army Group's south flank on a wide front line. In front of 708 Inf. Div., he especially pressed forward in the direction of Pré-en-Pail, and succeeded in pushing further back the elements of 708 Inf. Div., which were inexperienced in combat and had to fight in an overextended area. Remnants fought their way back to the Domfront–Alençon road.

Pz. Lehr Div., which suffered losses from enemy pressure, had therefore to withdraw to a line Pré-en-Pail – Ormain [?] – St-Denis-sur-Sarthe [?] on account of the tactical situation at both flanks. Although the commitment of 9 Pz. Div. had been able to delay the enemy advance, it had not succeeded in stopping it. The main pressure of the enemy armored forces was at Mamers and along the road of Beaumont-sur-Sarthe – Alençon, where they were able to push forward up to Fyé (11 km south of Alençon). The separated Kampfgruppen of 9 Pz. Div. were engaged in heavy defensive battles against this enemy, and were nearly decimated. The weak Kampfgruppe of 352 Inf. Div. had established a new line of security in rear of the Huisne sector. Thus a gap was formed on both sides of Mamers, into which the enemy armored forces—among them the newly arrived French 2 Armored Div.—pushed, and, meeting only scattered local resistance, these were able to gain ground quickly to the north and northeast.

Another PzKpfw IV of Pz. Regt 3, 2 Panzer Division, knocked out in the fighting near Pont-Farcy in early August.

This situation, owing to which the protection of the supply base at Alençon was no longer assured, induced Genfldm von Kluge, at the conference with the two Commanders-in-Chief, to decide, on his own, to regroup Panzer Army Eberbach, to assemble it north of Alençon, and, with its aid, fight the south flank of Army Group free by means of an attack. First, 116 Pz. Div. and 1 SS-Pz. Div. were to be moved during the night of 11/12 August into the assembly area in the Forêt d'Ecouves – Argentan area. 2 Pz. Div. was to follow the next night, and, if possible, also 2 SS-Pz. Div. For this, the Seventh Army front line had to be moved to the rear, so as to enable it to pull out its forces from a shorter front line. The following line was ordered for this: 4 km east of Viessoix – Coquard [?] – Hill 279, at the road to Tinchebray – Vire – Hill 575 – La Lande-Vaumont – crossroads 1 km east of Vengeons – west of Sourdeval – Hill 314 – Hill 293 (2½ km northeast of Mortain) – southern edge of the Forêt de Mortain.

The Army pointed out that the pulling out of 2 Pz. Div. during the night of 12/13 August would only be possible if an additional evading movement was carried out. But Adolf Hitler, who, in view of the tactical situation at Alençon, subsequently approved of the decision to regroup, ordered as follows: "The idea of attacking Avranches will be adhered to."

This made a further withdrawal towards the east impossible for the time being, because, otherwise, the basis for this attack would have had to be abandoned. However, this was superseded by subsequent events. The counterattack on Avranches, which over eleven days had decisively influenced all German measures of command, was once and for all dropped, owing to the decision to carry out "Operation Alençon."

Chapter 7

1–5 August

by Generaloberst Paul Hausser
Translated by EWS (B-179)

On 31 July 1944, important decisions were made for the days following, at a conference in Seventh Army's advanced CP, near Mortain, during which FM von Kluge was also present.

In the past, and even now, Army Group had undervalued the importance of the actual breakthrough, which occurred on 25–27 July, west of the Vire, near Cerisy-la-Salle – Pont Bocart [?]. The breakthrough at Avranches was the result of the US First Army's direct battle successes, which had nothing to do with the decision made by the Army in breaking out from the pocket, in a southeasterly direction. Breaking Seventh Army into two parts, and thus forcing one of these two into Brittany, would, without doubt, have resulted in the greatest misfortune. But this could not be prevented by the mere isolated commitment of 116 Pz. Div. west of Villedieu [-les-Poêles?]. In his account, Gen. von Gersdorff takes the same one-sided view, as did FM von Kluge.

Only the plugging of the Avranches gap could bring about an easing of the situation. The decision to carry out an advance in this direction had been induced by the Army's directive to assemble all armored units, as quickly as possible, on the southern wing, at least for the time being, for the protection of the left flank. Army Group had planned to bring up all available and additional forces from Fifth Panzer Army (hitherto Panzer Group West)—II SS-Pz. Corps with its 1, 9 and 10 SS-Pz. Divs. However, the events which took place in the Fifth Panzer Army's sector made this possible only to a limited extent.

For strengthening the front, as well as to relieve XLVII Pz. Corps, in addition to 363 Inf. Div., 84 Inf. Div. was scheduled to be added for commitment, and subordinated to LXXXI Army Corps' open flank, along with 9 Pz. Div. and the 708 Inf. Div. The assault group was to be rallied around Mortain, while at the same time the Army front was to be held on the West, as far as possible.

The causeway between the Sée[s] – Salune [?] sector presented itself as the best direction for the thrust. This causeway climbed to a considerable height, from Avranches, via 192–287, to Mortain. The main road had been built along it. It offered tolerably good combat conditions, in spite of hedgerows growing close by the wayside, which made any large-scale employment of tanks impossible.

Any attack north of the La Sée sector was out of the question from the very beginning, because here it would encounter the enemy's major forces and strength. A thrust further south, via St-Hilaire, was taken into consideration and was studied; this thrust would bypass the dominating heights, make the front longer, and lead to time-wasting through detours. So this plan was rejected. It was of the utmost importance that the vital elevated terrain around Mortain should remain in our hands. It was the very importance of this point which forced matters. Each additional day of delay caused the prospect of success in such an attack to recede more and more—an attack deemed by the Army as being quite possible, with favorable chances of success.

In spite of all the frictions and all the stress at the front and in the exposed open southern flank—where the enemy remained not inactive—this fundamental thought was held on to.

1 August

The events of 1 August increased the difficulties for the later execution of these plans. II Para. Jg. Corps was fighting in the high terrain east of Tessy along an approximate line west of the Forest de l'Evêque – the hills north of Guibbeville [Guilberville?] – north of 160 – Domjean. No details are known.

Enemy pressure was increasing against XLVII Pz. Corps. 2 Pz. Div. was fighting along the line Tessy – Beaucoudray. The point of main effort was directed against the right wing, where, during the afternoon, Tessy was lost. 116 Pz. Div. had been withdrawn. The mixed combat groups around Percy were now being commanded by the OC 2 SS-Pz. Div., and they succeeded in holding the hills south of Percy. No direct contact existed to the left.

LXXXIV Army Corps' situation developed more unfavorably. The bow had been stretched too far at this point. With some of its elements, 353 Inf. Div. was still holding on to the section east of Villedieu. The left wing was gaping wide open. Withdrawal movements back to the Forêt de [St-] Sever had been initiated. The bulk of 116 Pz. Div. arrived just in time to help to prevent an enemy penetration between this forest and St-Pois. While some units were engaged in setting up blockading points, between St Laurent-de-Sever [?] and the La Sée sector, another combat group made contact with enemy tanks at the Coulouvray-Boisbenâtre sector, which led to an engagement.

South of the La Sée sector, a combat group from 275 Inf. Div., acting under direct orders from the Army, had set up blockading points around the Reffuveille – Invigny [Juvigny?] area; while remnants of 5 Jg. Div. had set up a blockading line at Chereuse [Chérencé?] and St-Barthélemy. In this area, no contact with the enemy was made. Seventh Army moved its advance up to Flers.

Developments in the situation at Villedieu – Brevey [Brécey?] caused the Army to order, quite early, the withdrawal of its front line to Vire – Pont-Farcy – Montbray – Forêt de Sever – Gives [?], in the La Sée sector, and later on, the commitment of the bulk of 363 Inf. Div., so that 2 Pz. Div. could be relieved, and, at the same time, preparations by 84 Inf. Div. for the relief of 116 Pz. Div., south of the Forêt de Sever. The time set for this action was still uncertain, because the units on the way from the Fifteenth Army were able to cross the Seine only in ferries, and under cover of darkness.

At the coast it seemed—perhaps due to one of our own blows from Pontaubault against Avranches, on 31 July—that the enemy followed up very slowly. Nevertheless, any resistance we put up at Pontaubault could not delay the enemy for very long. Armored enemy patrols were reported active in the vicinity of Rennes, and to the west of there.

On 31 July, the Army's Ia (G-3), proceeded to Le Mans in order to maintain contact with Brittany, and also to inspect all local security measures taken in the open and exposed southern flank. For such security he had only the various combat commanders with their alarm units at his disposal, which in larger towns were being reinforced with antiaircraft artillery forces. It was found that the main point of effort existed in the eastern part of Brittany, near Dol [-de-Bretagne] and Rennes, and further east, along the Mayenne river, along the line Mayenne – Laval. The unit approaching on foot from southern France—708 Inf. Div.—was reported near the Loire.

2 August

The withdrawal of the right wing, during the night of 2 August, was carried out by II Para. Jg. Corps and XLVII Pz. Corps, according to plan. Rearguards, left behind, were posted along the northern bank of the Vire. The front was shortened, and contact with our neighbors was made once more. The armed forces, engaged in prolonged fighting, prevented any enemy success, in spite of the still strong enemy pressure.

East of Villedieu, 353 Inf. Div. succeeded in occupying and in holding all new positions at the western edge of the Forêt de Sever, and on the hills west of Le Gast and further to the south.

Southwest from here, 116 Pz. Div. renewed its attacks in the Coulouvray-Boisbenâtre area, against a strongly armored enemy. The attacks were successful, and in turn prevented an enemy breakthrough to St-Pois. Until the arrival of 84 Inf. Div., the division bolstered up the front, south of 353 Inf. Div. to the La Sée river.

The situation south of the La Sée river was still uncertain. Strong enemy tank forces had crossed through this sector. The area around Mortain caused a certain uneasiness. This sector just *had* to remain in our hands, since it was the point of departure for our planned attack. 116 Pz. Div. had sent its Recon Battalion into this area.

Enemy reconnaissance patrols were feeling their way along the securities set up by 275 Inf. Div. along the Avranches–Tuvigny [Torigni?] road. By now, the enemy had begun to push forward in the exposed, open flank, and to push with strong forces via Pontaubault to west of Rennes, and into Brittany.

3 August

Statements between 2 and 4 August concerning the Army's right wing are not quite exact in every detail, especially since there are no records available. Events taking place on the west wing of Fifth Panzer Army had a marked influence on the orders given. Here, a heavy British attack took place which caused a deep penetration and thus, in turn, forced the commitment of II SS-Pz. Corps. Movements carried out by II Para. Jg. Corps, on the right wing, were due to the evening's successes and were duly influenced by our own counterattack. On 3 August, the movement of retreat might have taken a different turn in the wake of the stiff battles which were fought during that morning, and perhaps might have secured a different front line.

XXXVI Pz. Corps withdrew with 2 Pz. Div. and 2 SS-Pz. Div. behind the Drôme, while at the same time it maintained its contact with the regiment of 363 Inf. Div., northeast of the Forêt de Sever. Some of the units had already been taken to this area, southeast of Sourdeval. In the case of LXXXIV Corps, the reinforced 353 Inf. Div. successfully

GIs walk past an abandoned Flakpanzer 38(t) of Pz. Regt 3, 2 Panzer Division, in Tessy-sur-Vire on 3 August 1944.

defended its positions in the Forêt de Sever. By now, also, 84 Inf. Div. had arrived in the rear of same. It seemed that the enemy's main pressure was directed against the northern wing, where an enemy attack had been met and its force absorbed by a counterthrust on our part on the northern edge of this forest terrain.

The enemy's point of main effort was believed to be south of the La Sée sector, where an attack by him endangered our entire assembly area, which had been selected to serve for our own counterattack, and, indeed, the entire flank.

Meanwhile, an armored enemy attack, supported by fighter-bombers, was launched against our blockading line, along the Avranches–Montain road. The resistance put up by 275 Inf. Div.'s combat groups was overpowered, and the enemy took Le Mesnil-Adelée, St-Barthélemy and Mortain.

Further to the South, the US Third Army's assault gained ground with its eastern units toward Fougères.

4 August

4 August brought renewed commotion in the ranks of Seventh Army, as enemy attacks were stepped up. Events occurring on Fifth Panzer Army's western wing resulted in the issuing of orders for the retreat of II Para. Jg. Corps and XLVII Pz. Corps to the line following the course of the ridges of the St-Allière heights, northeast and north of Vire – St-Sever.

Where II Para. Jg. Corps was located, it had moved forward in conjunction with the Panzer Division's advance on Cheuedelle [?] and, attacking the British at Burey and Forgues

[Fourges?], had wrested these two places from them. Elsewhere, the front could generally be stabilized, in spite of heavy enemy pressure.

In the XLVII Pz. Corps sector, which in the course of the day had been taken over by Corps Headquarters, LXXXIV Corps, the enemy started an attack between Vire and St-Sever. This attack gained ground, and some penetrations were made southwest of Coulouces and the Forest de St-Sever. Units from 2 Pz. Div. and 2 SS-Pz. Div. had been relieved, and were being replaced one by one by the individually arriving sections of 363 Inf. Div.

The day on the western front had ended in an unfavorable manner for LXXXIV Corps. The enemy's main point of effort was near 353 Inf. Div., at Point 289 – Le Gast and south, where, north of Le Mesnil-Gilbert, Hill 211 was lost. Penetration in the Forest de St-Sever could be successfully sealed off. A counterattack by 116 Pz. Div. was unsuccessful, due to the enemy's aerial activity.

Elements from 2 Pz. Div. stood on security duty south of the La Sée river, along a line Chérencé – Me [Le?] Mont Monu [?] – La Graviere [?] – 314; remnants of 275 Inf. Div., reinforced with Pz. Lehr Div. straggler elements which had been rounded up, and antiaircraft forces, secured the forest pass, east of Mortain, to the Barenton–Ger road, and to Barenton and St-Georges [-de-Rouelley?]. Reconnaissance patrols went as far as Barenton. The first elements of 2 SS-Pz. Div. were presumably somewhere east of Mortain.

On the open southern flank, along with the US Third Army's advance into Brittany, a thrust to the south became evident. Enemy advance elements occupied Ernée, coming from Fougères. 77 Inf. Div.'s weak combat group was fighting in coordination with Fortress St-Malo, near Dol.

Headquarters LXXXI Corps (Gen. der Pz. Tr. Kuntzen), was charged with the security of the area along the Loire. All units stationed as far as beyond Mayenne—especially 708 Inf. Div., which, separated from its artillery, crossed the Loire, in single regimental groups—were placed under the command of Gen Kuntzen. These included also Security Regt 1, from Paris, and the departing 9 Pz. Div. (Div. CP at Alençon).

The first thing to be contrived was a blockading line behind the Vereune [?], from west of Domfront as far as Ambrières, to be occupied by forces from Para. Engineer Bn 5, 9 Pz. Division's reconnaissance battalion, and later reinforced by 1 Regt from 708 Inf. Div. Alarm units, later reinforced by one additional regiment from 708 Inf. Div., practiced blockading tactics near Mayenne, as did elements from the Security Regt, along with SS-Pz. Jg. Bn 17 (SS-TD Bn 17, approaching to join its division), near Laval. Additional rear-area blockading points existed in the area around Sillé [?] – Le Mans, as Seventh Army's main CP, and behind the Sarthe. Corps Headquarters had been instructed to cooperate with 13 Flak Div., which had committed a considerable number of units to this sector. It proved possible to assemble 9 Pz. Div. by 6 or 7 August, in the region west of Alençon.

Reference back to FM von Kluge, the Army Group's CinC, in the advanced CP gave an opportunity to talk over the details of the counterattack planned against Mortain – Avranches. Both Army Group and Army were in full agreement as to the importance of this push, as well as the necessity of starting it as soon as possible. According to Army's view, however, it was impractical to launch the attack before the night of 6 August. It was the enemy's aerial superiority which made it necessary to attack during the night. From the reinforcements allotted, Army Group was able to assure the arrival of 1 SS-Pz. Div., owing to the attacks by the British then taking place against Fifth Panzer Army's left wing. 9 Pz. Div.'s withdrawal from the boundary line, between Fifth and Seventh Armies, was, it was learned, being planned. The heavy commitment of our own air arm was urgently demanded.

The course of the fighting on 4 August caused the Army to fall back with its entire defense, during the night, to a line Vire – St-Mauvien [-Manvieu]-Bocage – Champ-du-Boult – the hills west of Gathemo – 211 – west of Lingeard. Corps Headquarters, XXV Corps, in Brittany, was directly subordinated to Army Group.

5 August

For the day when the attack of the left wing would occur, it had been considered important to hold on to the positions in the middle, and at all costs avoid the encirclement of our open left flank then threatening.

The location of II Para. Jg. Corps—in spite of British attacks, and the vagueness of the link at Fifth Panzer Army's boundary line, east of the city of Vire—presented no particular danger. Attacks launched against Burcy were repulsed, and penetrations were sealed off again. A counterattack was carried as far as to the northern edges of Sourdeval.

LXXXIV Corp's withdrawal in the night was successful. On that same day, the evening's main pressure was directed against the entire Corps area, especially against the wings. A strong enemy tank attack west of the Vire met with some success. The enemy advanced to within approximately 3 km west of the city of Vire, and to the hill of St-Martin. A counterattack from our side was only partially successful, owing to heavy enemy fighter-bomber activity.

One penetration, near Champ-du-Boult could be sealed off, and in the south another could be thrown back. Here, 84 Inf. Div. had been committed. On the other hand, the enemy forced his way ahead south of St-Pois, across Hill 211 and from Chérencé on to the north, where he was intercepted and held by 116 Pz. Div., south of Périers.

The situation remained as a whole unchanged in the area of Mortain. Further to the south, reconnaissance verified that strong US forces had turned off in an easterly direction and were pushing ahead with their tanks. After a battle, Mayenne was occupied by the enemy. It seemed that Laval was still holding out. Defensive measures taken by LXXXI Corps were no longer able to bring about a change in this situation, the more so because its forces were not strong enough to prolong any local delaying action.

Chapter 8

6–12 August

by Generaloberst Paul Hausser
Translated by EWS (B-179)

6 August

The heavy attacks continued along the entire front on 6 August. Heavy casualties were the result. The situation in the central sector remained tense. The attacks against II FS Jg. Corps were repulsed.

Heavy penetrations into LXXXIV Army Corps near St-Manvieu (363 Div.) – Bois la Haye, south of Champ-du-Boult (353 Div.), and in the direction of Gathemo (84 Div.), could not be sealed off. The troops were compelled to yield the front at the approximate line of the main road which leads from Vire to Périers; Chérencé remained in enemy hands. The town of Vire—nestling in a hollow—was lost in the evening. A Panzer combat group from Pz. Lehr Div., subordinated to 275 Div., was sent to the region east of Mortain as a security force for LXXXIV Army Corps boundary line. These were the last reserves.

Enemy air activity was particularly heavy in the region assigned to XLVII Pz. Corps. Barenton and St-Georges [-de-Rouelley] were held against enemy attacks.

Preparations for the attack did not proceed according to plan. The transfer of 1 SS-Pz. Div. from Fifth Panzer Army and the task of getting it started off were both notably delayed. Also, friction in other directions caused delay in the preparations for the attack scheduled to commence at 2400 hrs.

XLVII Pz. Corps Headquarters Staff suggested that the attack be postponed for a further 24 hours, as only a night attack could be carried out without interference from enemy aircraft. The grounds for the suggestion were sound, but, despite this, Army ordered the planned attack to be launched at the scheduled time. Any postponement of the attack, when the situation of LXXXI Corps is borne in mind, would notably have diminished its prospects of success.

Here, Laval had also been lost during the day. LXXXI Corps was ordered to take the available sections of 708 Inf. Div. and carry out a push against the flank of the enemy, east of Mayenne, and to join there the flank elements of 9 Pz. Div. arriving from the area west of Domfront and link up with the attack by XLVII Pz. Corps in the general direction of St-Hilaire.

Preparation of XLVII Pz. Corps

a. 116 Pz. Div., without having to give up any troops to 2 Pz. Div., was to assemble north of the River Sée, south of Périers, for an attack against Chérencé in a westerly direction.

149

b. 2 Pz. Div. (in the group to the right), reinforced by personnel transferred from 116 Pz. Div. (Pz. and Gren.) was to assemble south of the River Sée, between Le Mesnil-Tôve and Le Mont-Morin [?], for an attack to the west, along the road from Le Mesnil-Adelée to Le Coudray.

c. Two Panzer divisions (left group), reinforced by a Panzer battalion, 1 SS-Pz. Div., northeast of St-Barthélemy, were to stage an attack against Juvigny via the causeway (described earlier).

d. 2 Pz. Div., divided into two groups, had the goal of recapturing Mortain and pushing forward toward the west.

e. The main body of 1 SS-Pz. Div. which arrived later, was to serve as a second wave in the attack on Juvigny.

The support of 300 fighter-bombers was promised for the morning of 7 August.

The units concerned had been withdrawn from fighting and from other positions. They had been brought to the scene at a hastened tempo, at night—and with difficulty. During their transfer, they were compelled to fight their way through, part of the time, and were in constant danger of being encircled in the process. They had already suffered heavy losses. They possessed a total of 120 Panzers. Despite all, however, the situation, with its possibilities, was judged positive. The weather on 7 August would be the decisive factor. Fog—at least in the morning—surely could be counted on. Advantage had to be taken of

US troops enter a French town that has been, from the appearance of the buildings, liberated without a pitched battle or the use of Allied airpower. (US National Archives)

such weather conditions. The situation of 116 Pz. Div. appeared to be less favorable. The development of events for LXXXIV Corps had prevented the commitment of the former south of the [La] Sée sector; it still remained a question whether the state of affairs on the west wing of this Corps would allow it to expend all its remaining units in combat.

7 August

The pressure against 2 Para. Jg. Corps relaxed to some extent. An attack against the right wing in the afternoon could be repulsed. The MLR was removed farther rearward, in consideration of the neighboring troops, during the night of 8 August, behind the Val sector to Viessoix – Roullours.

In the case of LXXIV Corps, too, the regrouping found necessary by the enemy only allowed for weak reconnaissance pushes on his part. It was only south of Vire that a stronger thrust ensued in the direction of Gathemo against 84 Inf Div—a thrust which gained some ground. The danger of a penetration on the Gathemo – Vengeons strip could only be removed by commiting reserves of 116 Pz. Div.

Attack by XLVII Pz. Corps

North of the sector, 116 Pz. Div was only able to make scant headway; it did, as a matter of fact, make contact with 2 Pz. Div. near Chérencé, but, with the resistance met, it could not get very far across the road from Périers to Chérencé.

South of the River Sée, the attack by the righthand group of 2 Pz Div was launched exactly at the scheduled time (2400 hrs)—surprisingly enough, without any preliminary barrage. It pushed a path for itself, against rather weak resistance, through Le Mesnil-Adelée. The lefthand group had to wait till dawn to start its part of the attack, since 1 Pz Div was late in coming up. They succeeded in taking St-Barthélemy despite strong resistance, and in pushing on to within 2 km east of Juvigny.

In the region around Montain, 2 SS-Pz. Div. pushed forward north and south of the town of that name, taking it in the process, and reached, after fierce fighting, Hill 285 west thereof, as well as Romagny.

Lively defensive artillery fire broke out everywhere after daybreak, and, worse still, heavy bombing raids, in particular, with rocket-carrying planes, which made all further movement impossible. The clear weather favored such tactics. It was only thanks to the superiority of the enemy air force that our own well-prepared attack was checked. This was a danger which could have been foreseen. The promised support of our own fighters never materialized; they were met and dealt with above the fields by the enemy.

Counterattacks on the ground ensued during the course of the day, mainly against the far advanced spearhead of 2 Pz. Div., from north of the Sée river and against Le Mesnil-Tôve, as well as in the region east of the town. They were intentionally left out of consideration by us, so as not to weaken our own strength of attack. The leading sections of 1 SS-Pz. Div. were committed during the course of the day between St Barthélemy, over La Delinière [?].

The state of affairs on the south flank of LXXXI Corps developed highly unfavorably in the meantime. Barenton had been captured by the enemy. Strong tank units were

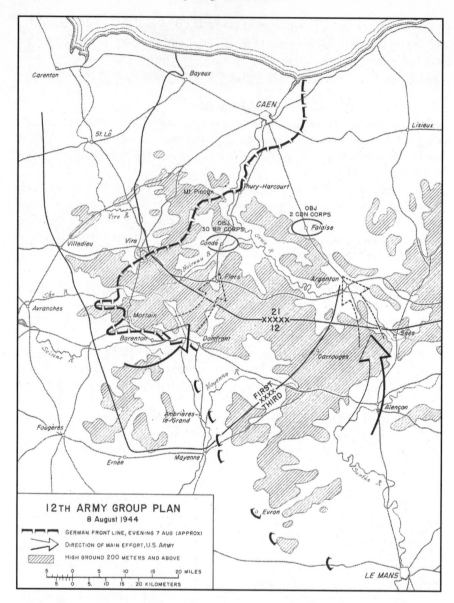

12TH ARMY GROUP PLAN
8 August 1944

⌐ ⌐ ⌐   GERMAN FRONT LINE, EVENING 7 AUG (APPROX)
⟹   DIRECTION OF MAIN EFFORT, U.S. ARMY
▨   HIGH GROUND 200 METERS AND ABOVE

5   0   5   10   15   20 MILES
5   0   5   10   15   20 KILOMETERS

thrusting toward Domfront. Sections of 708 Inf. Div., assigned to Mayenne, yielded and switched northeast. The security regiment at Laval had been overrun. Strong enemy units had reached the Voutre – Ste-Suzanne – Vallon [-sur-Gée?] region. The region of Le Mans, deep within the flanks of the army, was threatened. An assault planned by LXXXI Corps to relieve us of the enemy strain never came off.

Was it possible, considering this development, to continue the attack against Avranches? It had been stopped only by the air force. Perhaps the weather would be more favorable the next day! Parts of 1 SS-Pz. Div. were still available as reinforcements, so there was still another chance, which had to be thoroughly exploited if the entire Heeresgruppe was not to be forced to make a general retreat. The latter idea was turned down flatly by High Command. The attack *was* to be continued, with its main impulse south of the main highway.

8 August

Orders based on this situation issued on the evening of 7 August were, however, altered, to harmonize with Army Group's revised plans. Army Group required one more Panzer division (10 SS), one more mortar brigade, and another Corps Headquarters for Fifth Panzer Army to be brought to the scene ,and to continue the attack with the aid of these new units. 9 Pz. Div. should likewise be sent in. The continuation of the attack was therefore postponed until the reinforcements could arrive, The lines then reached were to be held.

Enemy pressure continued along the entire front, especially against LXXXIV Corps Headquarters in the Vire region. The enemy was making notable advances south of Vire and Gathemo, where detachments of 116 Pz. Div. had to be thrown in.

In the lines already reached, enemy attacks continued against the left flank of the front, now being defended by XLVII Pz. Corps; the advanced wedge of 2 Pz. Div. was compelled to withdraw that evening. Chérencé and Le Mesnil-Tôve were lost to the enemy; St-Barthélemy and the heights south thereof were held. Enemy pressure against the left wing of SS-Pz. Div. took on a threatening aspect.

Two divisions had by now pushed forward in the area of Sillé – Le Mans, in the region assigned to LXXXI Army Corps—east of Mayenne, north thereof, and south of Barenton, where there were now further strong forces. Only the Domfront region appeared to be in immediate danger.

The capture of Le Mans, and a switch by the American forces there to the northeast, brought a threat to the supply base of Alençon. This development tied down all elements of LXXXI Corps, no intervention by 9 Pz. Div. in the battle at Mortain now being possible.

The details which follow on the different commands and orders issued by the Army may contain mistakes, the notes furnished in its War Diary being both incomplete and inexact.

Meanwhile, LVII Pz. Corps Headquarters (Gen. der Pz. Tr Krueger), and 10 SS-Pz. Div., had now arrived. The latter, which had fought within the framework of Fifth Panzer Army since 29 June, had to be sent off immediately in support of the endangered left flank of the attacking forces in the hilly region of the Forêt de Mortain, where it was immediately committed to battle. Both it and 2 SS-Pz. Div. were subordinated to General Krueger's command, while the reinforced 2 Pz. Div. and 1 SS-Pz. Div. remained subordinated to XLVII Pz. Corps Headquarters. In addition, 8 and 9 Mortar Bdes had arrived on the scene.

Orders by Adolf Hitler for all further operations "blamed the failure of the previous attack against Avranches on the fact that one order had been overtaken by the next. The attack was to be tried again after the most thorough preparation, without regard to the safety of our flanks; the outcome of the war would depend on it!" The command was to be taken over by Gen. der Pz. Tr. Eberbach, with both Panzer corps. In contrast to Gen. von Gersdorff, I believe that this Panzer group was meant to be placed under the immediate command of Army Group. But I might be wrong, and in any case it makes no difference.

The visit of General Buhle of the OKW was directed at emphasizing the importance and purpose of this second thrust against Avranches, and at underlining the fact that it was a personal order of Adolf Hitler, rather than exploring the possibilities of putting it into effect. I answered his question more or less in the sense of the estimate of the situation given on 10 August, and did not deny outright the prospects of its succeeding—provided the conditions set forth in that estimate could be met.

9 August

This day brought with it heavy attacks against the LXXXIV Corps front, which led to a deep penetration south of Vire into the La Lande-Vaumont region. Special measures became essential to remove the enemy menace from the rear of our attacking wings. A combat group from 1 SS-Pz. Div. had to be transferred temporarily to support this front.

In the XLVII Pz. Corps sector, the situation remained unchanged, but, in contrast, LVIII Panzer Corps' sector around and east of Mortain grew more tense. Enemy attacks from the south and southwest against Mortain were repulsed; 10 SS-Pz. Div. was compelled to take over the defense of our flank on a broad front up to Barenton. In the adjoining sector, the Domfront front, assigned to the LXXXI Army Corps, was not attacked.

Hard battles took place in the region between Sillé and the Sarthe river near Beaumont and northwest of Ballon (portions of 708 Inf. Div., Pz. Training Div., and 9 Pz. Div.) against superior armored forces of the US Third Army. It appeared, in the evening, that further considerable forces of that Army had captured Le Mans and were switching inward to the northeast. This threatened the permanent supply base of Alençon, and might make all the difference to us.

10 August

This day saw one of the heaviest battles along the entire front. Southeast of Vire, a concentric German counterattack by LXXXIV Corps began against the point of break-through west of Maisoncelles [-la-Jourdan], with portions of 363 and 353 Inf. Divs, supported by combat groups of 1 SS-Pz. Div. and the Armored Instructional Div. It succeeded at first and got as far as Hill 232, St-Germain. Enemy counterattacks checked it later. Further enemy attacks, near Gathemo and Périers, could only be absorbed after they had penetrated our ranks to some considerable depth. South of the [La] Sée sector, east of Le-Mesnil-Tôve, the attacks were repulsed and sealed off northeast of Mortain. The state of affairs around Mortain remained critical.

The counterattack by 10 SS-Pz. Div. on Barenton came to a standstill about 3 km north of this place. The enemy overwhelmed the wing of this division far to the east, where an attack against St-Georges was repulsed. The day was characterized by unusually intense enemy artillery fire and aircraft activity. It cost the enemy heavy casualties, too.

On the unsecured flank, the main thrust appeared to be directed against the defense line Nogent-le-Rotrou – Alençon. The spearheads had already reached La Ferté-Bernard – Bonnétable – Beaumont. 9 Pz. Div. encountered superior enemy forces here, and was attacked and defeated. Further west, those portions at Sillé withdrew to Alençon. No enemy pressure of any importance was felt along the upper reaches of the Varenne.

In an estimate made of the situation, the Army brought out the undermentioned points:

1. *The enemy situation:*

    In the region east of Vire up to the River Sée, there were:

    One British armored and one infantry division.

    American 2, 9, 28, 29 Divisions and armored units.

    On the front between the River Sée and Domfront:

    American 4, 30, 35 Divisions,

    2, 3 Armored Divisions.

    On the south flank:

    1, 79, 80, 90 Divisions; 5 Armored Div.; and French 2 Armored Div.

2. *Our own situation:*

    Continuation of the attack against Avranches is possible only if:

    a. The defense line can be held.

    b. Adequate air support is available on our own side.

    c. The deep Army flank is secured by adequate forces and the supply base of
        Alençon rendered capable of furnishing us with the required amount of
        ammunition and fuel.

If these provisions cannot be fulfilled, then the Army sees itself compelled to yield the front to the enemy and to set up a new front against the flank of Domfront and Alençon.

Heavy American pressure made a withdrawal of the middle as well as of the left flank of the LXXXIV Army Corps imperative. The success of our own attacks on the road to Vire could, therefore, not be exploited.

11 August

The correct conclusions were drawn from this state of affairs on the 11 August in a conference involving Field Marshal von Kluge with the Commander-in-Chief of the Army and Gen. Eberbach. It was now clear to everyone that the conditions stipulated on 10 August could not be met; that another thrust in the direction of Avranches would be impossible; that the Panzer units on the south wing, securing the Army's flanks and the rear, would have to be committed immediately; and that a shortening of the front by a further withdrawal was dictated.

The decision rested with the High Command. Corresponding preparations were made. XLVII Pz. Corps Headquarters, with 2 and 116 Pz. Divs and 1 SS-Pz. Div., were to be extracted from the line in the meantime, to be organized as the Eberbach Panzer Group in the sector north of Alençon. LVIII Pz. Corps Headquarters, with 2 and 10 SS-Pz. Divs, were to follow.

The heavy enemy pressure continued throughout the day. Our combat positions could be held, despite minor penetrations here and there. A deep penetration occurred in the direction of Vengeons and in Mortain. The center of gravity appeared to be concentrated here.

708 Inf. Div., fighting within the framework of LXXXI Corps, yielded and retreated from Sillé to the south-west of Alençon. The enemy followed further east, to the defense

line of Fresnay – Bellême An armored spearhead thrust forward up to Fyé, south of Alençon.

A retreat had been ordered, to be carried out during the night of 11 August. The proposed front was to run as follows: La Lande-Vaumont – Vengeons – the heights west of Sourdeval – 314 and 293 – north of the Forêt de Mortain. The divisions withdrawn— 116 Pz. Div., 1 SS-Pz. Div., and 8 and 9 Mortar Bdes—were set in march in the direction of Carrouges – Argentan. 331 Div. was assigned to the Army. The time when each of these units arrived is not known. The remnants of 275 Div. were withdrawn for reconstitution.

12 August

The decision by the Fuehrer concerning the suggestions made on the previous day reached us on 12 August. It demanded postponement of the planned attack, and the withdrawal of Panzer units, to obviate the danger to our open flank in the Alençon sector. Owing to the fact that the Supreme Command was still obsessed with the thought of an attack on Avranches, it was impossible for Army Group to retreat far enough to the east to escape the threatening encirclement.

To Panzer Group Eberbach—now being placed directly subordinate to Army Group— 2 Pz. Div., along with the portions of units withdrawn, was to be assigned. LXXXI Corps was also placed under its command. The Army gave voice to its point that then the Seventh Army front would have to be maintained only by the remains of four infantry divisions, and insisted that this was impossible without reinforcements. The withdrawal movements during the night of the 12 August went through according to schedule.

The enemy attack continued with undiminished violence, particularly along the Vire– Tinchebray road and the Vengeons–St-Sauveur road, where a deep penetration resulted, and near Sourdeval. Mortain was evacuated. East thereof, the enemy thrust forward north of Barenton.

These happenings, in conjunction with the withdrawal of 2 Pz. Div., made a further retreat necessary during the night of 12 August. For this, the following front line was ordered for the central section of the defense line and the left wing: Coquard [?] – St Sauveur – Placitre [?] – the heights south of Lonlay-l'Abbaye – Domfront.

On the southern front of LXXXI Corps, the west wing around Domfront was swung back to the Forêt d'Andaine; parts of 708 Inf. Div. stood to the west of Alençon. The area extending to Gacé was to be taken over by Eberbach Panzer Group. Reinforcements comprised portions of 708 Inf. Div., while 6 Para. Jg. Div. were on their way to barricade the area of Gacé – [Vitrai-sous-?] Laigle. 352 Inf. Div., which was in the process of reorganization, blocked the area west of Chartres, near Verneuil [?] – Senonches – La Loupe – Courville [-sur-Eure].

The enemy had pushed forward on a wide front against Alençon and Mortagne. His center of gravity lay to the north; the pressure against the eastern section appeared to be less intense.

The Army's supply base had been lost. The consequent difficulties would soon become a reality.

PART FIVE

The Germans had to withdraw to the Seine, their immediate move, Montgomery believed—initially to positions east of the Orne river, generally along a line between Caen and Flers. A (Canadian) drive south from Caen to Falaise would cut behind this first stage of the German withdrawal. The broad Allied intent was to pin the Germans back against the Seine, the immediate mission by the Canadian First Army being to attack toward Falaise.

On 8 August, the Canadian First Army launched Operation "Totalize," a drive on Falaise. The German defensive fighting against the British and Canadian armies was, as in the months before, a masterful display of tactics. While the advance slowed on 9 August, the pressure forced the diversion of reserves sent to the Luettich fighting. General Eberbach was sent along by the High Command from the British front, expecting miracles.

Lt. Gen. Miles C. Dempsey's British Second Army had been attacking southeast from near Caumont since 30 July, was to drive east through Argentan to the Seine. Montgomery believed the Germans had no alternative but to retreat across the Seine.

When the Canadians resumed the attack on 10 August, the US XV Corps was approaching Alençon. On the Allied right, Bradley's 12th Army Group was to make its main effort on the right flank, advancing east and northeast toward the Seine near Paris. The Germans now became aware that the Allied decisions of a week before were giving them the opportunity of a double encirclement, surrounding their forces in Normandy. If the Canadians took Falaise from the north and XV Corps took Alençon from the south, it would create a 35-mile "Falaise gap," and deprive the Germans of two of the three main east–west roads they still controlled.

Montgomery ordered the Canadians to continue their efforts to capture Falaise and proceed from there to Argentan. XV Corps was to advance through Alençon to the Army Group boundary just south of Argentan—a line drawn by Montgomery to separate the zones of operation of the American (12th Army Group) and the British/Canadian forces (21st Army Group).

Chapter 9

Defensive Fighting of the Fifth Panzer Army 25 July–21 August

by Generalmajor Rudolf-Christoph Freiherr von Gersdorff
Translated by Suelzenfuss and edited by Anne Hall (B-726)

1. Introduction

While the imminent start of a strong American offensive against Seventh Army, between the Vire and La Taute [?], became more and more recognizable during the days before 25 July, heavy battles, which had developed in the course of the German counterattacks, had still been taking place in the Orne area, before the front of the Panzer Group, up till 22 July. In spite of heavy commitments on both sides, however, these battles assumed more of a local character, in the form of positional warfare for individual localities and the improvement of positions. The attempted British breakthrough south of Caen had definitely failed.

Nevertheless, the heavy fighting had caused huge losses to the German formations. 16 Lw Field Div. was well-nigh annihilated; the Panzer divisions of I and II SS-Pz. Corps (1, 9, 12 SS-Pz. Divs), as well as 21 Pz. Div., were more or less hard hit. Except for 9 SS-Pz. Div., all the other divisions mentioned were still employed at the front. The infantry divisions which were then arriving (271 and 272 Inf. Divs) were to relieve from the front at least 21 Pz. Div. and the 10 SS-Pz. Div. The foremost elements of the infantry divisions had already been thrown into combat at the endangered front sector on either side of the Orne. With that, 272 Inf. Div. had temporarily taken over the left wing sector of I SS-Pz. Corps between Hubert-Folie and the Orne. Two battalions of 271 Inf. Div. were at first employed in the 10 SS. Pz. Div. sector.

As the German Supreme Command invariably expected a British large-scale attack from the area of Caen in the general direction of Paris, and it assumed that this enemy offensive would advance in the strategically most dangerous direction, it was forced to leave the available Panzer reserves (2 and 116 Pz. Divs, as well as the 9 SS-Pz. Div.) behind the center of Panzer Group West, the more so since it still adhered to the plan to try to resume the offensive against the British.

On 22 July, a period of bad weather started, resulting in a lull in the fighting on 23 and 24 July. Enemy assembly positions were attacked by artillery fire. For the rest, regrouping—which was in progress—was carried on. On that occasion, local reserves, besides the strategic Panzer reserves, were withdrawn from all divisional sectors, and held in readiness.

2. 25–29 July

On 25 July, simultaneously with the decisive American offensive at St-Lô, the expected British assault drive was started south of Caen, which, considering the overall situation, had the significance of a relief attack. After a three-hour preparation by superior enemy artillery,

A Panzer V (Panther) tank knocked out by US fighter-bombers in Normandy. Some pilots are examining their handiwork and discussing air-to-ground cooperation. (US National Archives)

the British Second Army attacked at 0520 hrs across a width of 7 km, between Bourguébus and the Orne in the left sector of I SS-Pz. Corps. Above all, the enemy was successful against 272 Inf. Div.—which as yet had no combat experience—achieving a deep penetration there. St. Martin and May-sur Orne, as well as the village west of Tilly-la-Campagne, were lost. Besides the local reserves, which started to counterattack immediately, the Army decided to send in for a counterattack the bulk of 9 SS-Pz. Div. on either side of the road from Bretteville to Fontenay. Thus, before nightfall, we succeeded in sealing off the enemy penetration tightly, and in recapturing most of the area lost earlier on that day. 1 SS-Pz. Div. recaptured the main resistance line north and northwest of Hill 76 (west of Tilly-la-Campagne) and again occupied the village which had been lost. 272 Inf. Div. recaptured May-sur-Orne and advanced as far as the southern edge of St-Martin. 9 SS-Pz. Div. carried on the counterattack—which was launched at 1730 hrs, as far as Hill 88 (east of May-sur-Orne), where, for the moment, it was halted by the enemy's antitank fire. Additional positions south and southeast of Caen were attacked by our artillery.

Meanwhile, additional elements of 271 Inf. Div. had arrived at II SS-Pz. Corps. At first, the division was employed for the control of the right sector of 10 SS-Pz. Div. The boundary line between these two divisions was ordered as follows: multiple road junction at Fontaine – 500 m northeast of Hill 112 – eastern edge of Amayé-sur-Orne – River Orne.

On 26 July, the counterattack was continued. We succeeded in reestablishing the former main line of resistance to its full extent. New enemy attacks between Tilly-la-Campagne and

St-André could be repelled. The observed moving up of 100 British tanks from the west to the east bank of the Orne indicated that the enemy offensive would be continued. 9 SS-Pz. Div., therefore, was ordered to continue holding the former sector of 272 Inf. Div., whereas all the units of this infantry division were pulled out in order to relieve 21 Pz. Div. during the nights of 27 and 28 July, as had already been provided for previously.

On 27 July quietness prevailed at first. Apparently, the enemy was making new preparations before launching the expected large-scale attack on a broad front. The developments which meanwhile had taken place in the Seventh Army sector compelled the Commander-in-Chief West, Field Marshal von Kluge, to decide on sending off 2 and 116 Pz. Divs to Seventh Army as fast as possible, in order to seal off by counterattack the breakthrough of the US First Army. At about 1200 hrs. Field Marshal von Kluge issued this order at the I SS-Pz. Corps command post, which was located 1½ km east of Poligny [Potigny?] on the road from Falaise to Caen. Thereupon, 2 Pz. Div., that day, left the zone of operations of Panzer Group, whereas 116 Pz. Div. could not start off before 28 July for want of fuel.

Towards evening, the offensive activity of the enemy was resumed. Intensified artillery fire and troop movements south and southeast of Caen also indicated a continuation of the British attempt to break through. On the other hand, we had ascertained that the Canadian 4 and 5 Bdes had been battered considerably—one battalion, for instance, had been completely annihilated—and 41 British tanks had been disabled.

Observed movements of troops and strong enemy artillery fire west of the Orne, at the II SS-Pz. Corps front, made us likewise expect that the British Second Army would extend its attacks against the entire front of the Panzer Group. This was a distinct sign of the enemy's intention to above all contain forces there, so as to keep them away from St-Lô, the decisive point of breakthrough.

The situation did not change on 28 July either. Except for strong artillery fire and fighter-bomber activity, quiet prevailed in general. Meanwhile, 272 Inf. Div.—which had arrived as a compact unit—had relieved 21 Pz. Div. and assumed command of the sector from Troarn to Emiéville. 21 Pz. Div. was kept in readiness as replacement for the Panzer divisions given up to Seventh Army in the Bretteville-sur-Laison [-Laize] – Fresnay [Fresney?] – Les Moutiers-en-Cinglais – Barbery area, so a mobile reserve was again at the disposal of the Panzer Group there. The "Tiger" Pz. Bn 503 was likewise transferred to this area. On account of the new threat against Panzer Group's west wing, Combat Group von Oppeln (Commander of the Panzer Regt of 21 Pz. Div.) was ordered to the area of Coulvain (5 km southwest of Villers-Bocage).

Meanwhile, LXXIV Inf. Corps, which came from Brittany, had, in the meantime, relieved XLVII Pz. Corps in assuming control of the left wing of the Army, whereas XLVII Pz. Corps marched off to Seventh Army in order to assume command of the two Panzer divisions given up to it.

On 29 July, an enemy attack against 276 Inf. Div. along the road from Juvigny to Villers-Bocage—which, at first, seemed to be only a local one—made evident a probable shifting of the enemy's main effort to the west wing of Panzer Group. The attack was repelled, except for one local penetration.

3. 30 July–3 August 1944

On 30 July, the second British relief assault started, and with surprising power hit Panzer Group's left wing. 326 Inf. Div., which was still quite fresh, was employed there. Nevertheless, strategic reserves were lacking, and the division—which occupied a front of about 16 km—had as yet no combat experience. LXXVII Army Corps, which had just assumed command, was attacked along its entire front line, while at the remaining front of Panzer Group, only artillery and assault troop activity took place. The already combat-experienced 276 Inf. Div., which was employed on the right wing, was able to repel all attacks by the enemy. On the other hand, the British VIII Corps was successful against 326 Inf. Div. An attack on the right wing of the division on St-Germain-d'Ectot was repelled after hard fighting. Briquessart [Briqueville?], however, was lost, and the enemy pushed forward on the road leading from Caumont to the southeast, as far as Cahagnes. The left wing of the division was totally defeated at the Army boundary, and could only regain a foothold in the line on either side of St-Quen- [Ouen-] des-Besaces. Enemy tanks, however, had succeeded in penetrating into St-Martin-des-Besaces. The local reserves of 326 Inf. Div., as well as Combat Group von Oppeln of 21 Pz. Div.—which, in the meantime, had arrived in the area of Coulvain—immediately started to launch counterattacks.

On account of the critical developments at the Army boundary, the Panzer Group resolved to transfer the entire 21 Pz. Div. to the area of Le Mesnil-Auzouf (7 km southwest of Coulvain) and to clear up the situation with a counterattack by the compact division. First of all, the LXXIV Army Corps front was withdrawn to a line St-Vaast-sur-Seulles – Orbois [?] – Anctoville – Cahagnes – Dampierre.

On 31 July, the enemy, as expected, continued his attempt to break through. By employing 21 Pz. Div., which had been brought up during the night, a major breakthrough could be prevented. Our counterattack, nevertheless, was not able to prevail against the British VIII Corps, which attacked with superior forces. 21 Pz. Div., as well as elements of 326 Inf. Div., could only gain little ground, and barely fill up the largest gaps. Above all, they did not succeed in holding or recapturing the dominating heights east of St-Martin-des-Besaces. Some enemy tanks which had succeeded in breaking through pushed forward to the south as far as Le Bény-Bocage. From this, we gathered that the direction of the British breakthrough was toward Vire. Panzer Group supposed that Field Marshal Montgomery intended to unite his forces with those of the Americans breaking through in the Vire area, and to push ahead from there in the general direction of Paris. But, in spite of this supposition, Panzer Group also reckoned with further British attempt at a breakthrough from the Caen region towards Falaise. Strong artillery fire and troop assemblies observed in the extensive Caen area pointed to that fact. Therefore, for the time being, a further withdrawal of forces from this area did not seem possible. We had to try to restore the situation at the left wing of the Army solely with 21 Pz. Div.

On 1 August, enemy pressure against the left wing of Panzer Group increased in such measure as to bring about an extremely critical situation. South of Cahagnes, the enemy attacked across the road from Cahagnes to St-Martin against the Coulvain – Jurques line, and could only be stopped at a line from the eastern edge of Coulvain to La Bigne. East of Le Bény-Bocage, the enemy reached Montchamp. In between, 21 Pz. Div. was still fighting on the line La Bigne – Bois de l'Homme – Le Tourneur, north of Montchamp. From there, a broad gap opened as far as the right wing of Seventh Army, where no noteworthy resistance was being offered any longer. 326 Inf. Div. was completely battered, and consisted only of remnants. It had fought heroically. Its Commander, Gen. von Drabich-Waechter, was killed in action at the front line.

The catastrophic situation demanded an immediate decision. In the night of 1/2 August, the Army, therefore, ordered II SS-Pz. Corps, together with 9 and 10 SS-Pz. Divs, to be relieved from the front south of Caen, and to be moved up to the zone of penetration, so as to seal the gap in Seventh Army in a counterattack, and to prevent a new strategic breakthrough by the enemy. Although, considering the continued threatening situation in the area of Caen, this was a difficult decision, it was, however, necessary so as to preserve the continuity of the front. The former sector of 9 SS-Pz. Div. was taken over by I SS-Pz. Corps, which extended its front up to the Orne, and the 10 Pz. Div. sector was likewise taken over by 271 and 277 Inf. Divs. 271 and 277 Inf. Divs were subordinated to LVIII Pz. Corps, which had been newly brought up from southern France.

The relief operations took place according to plan, and without any serious interference by the enemy. At 2200 hrs, the foremost elements of 10 SS-Pz. Div. arrived in the Coulvain area. The Army ordered this division to eliminate the deep penetration at Coulvain – Jurques. II SS-Pz. Corps, together with 9 SS-and 21 Pz. Divs, was to attack on either side of the Souleuvre to the west, close the gap to Seventh Army, and establish contact with the right wing of Seventh Army in the region of the Hill 205 (west of Le Bény-Bocage). Army Group promised Panzer Group the moving up of three infantry divisions of Fifteenth Army (85, 89, and 331 Inf. Divs) for reinforcement of the front south of Caen.

While quietness prevailed, also on 2 August, before the right wing and the center of the Panzer Group—except for weak containing attacks, artillery and fighter-bomber activity—the enemy continued his strong attacks against the left wing of the Army. Some weak attacks were repelled at Coulvain, but, south of it, a group of twenty British tanks, with mounted infantry, succeeded in pushing forward via Sauques Pitot [?] and to Hill 188.

Elements of 10 SS-Pz. Div. and "Panther" tank destroyers of LXXIV Army Corps—which were at our disposal—were sent in against them. The bulk of 10 SS-Pz. Div. was engaged in a counterattack against La Bigne, into which locality the enemy had penetrated. The neighboring 21 Pz. Div. was attacked by superior enemy forces in its salient projecting far to the west, and lost the important Hill 321 and the village of Fremoy [?]. It offered resistance along a line Hill 301 (1½km southwest of La Bigne) – Montamy – Arclais – Le Tourneur, against further enemy attacks, especially on its right wing. 9 SS-Pz. Div. which had moved up by way of Thury-Harcourt, had launched an attack on Le Bény-Bocage at 1800 hrs and slowly gained ground. Some elements of the division had been turned off towards Presles (7 km north of Vire), since the foremost enemy elements had penetrated into that locality in the meantime. Armored reconnaissance pushed forward as far as east and north of the Vire area, thus establishing loose contact with the right wing of Seventh Army. Panzer Army ordered II SS-Pz. Corps to continue the attack on 3 August and to reestablish steady contact with Seventh Army. Vire, which was kept under heavy enemy fire, was to remain in our hands at any cost.

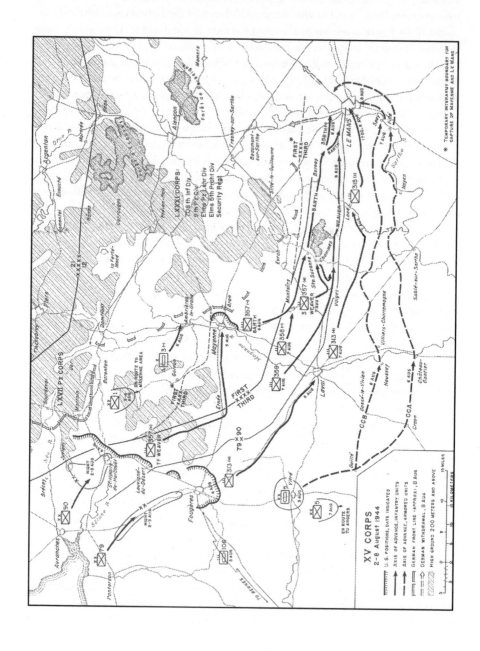

The continuation of the attack on 3 August made it possible to prevent the breakthrough, by way of Vire, of the British right wing. At that time, such a breakthrough would inevitably have brought about the encirclement and annihilation of the German Seventh Army.

10 SS-Pz. Div. had succeeded in recapturing the Hill 188 south of Pitot and in holding it against heavy enemy attacks. Although La Bigne had remained in the hands of the enemy, all attacks from that locality to the east could be repelled. In this area, the fighting had caused heavy casualties on both sides. 21 Pz. Div. had recaptured the dominating Hill 321, and made so much headway at its left wing, too, that the hills west of the road from Villers-Bocage to Le Bény-Bocage remained in our hands.

9 SS-Pz. Div., in an attack, reached the line from a patch of wood 1 km west of Montchauvet – west edge of Courteil[les?] – Le Queillet [?], and then obtained loose contact with 3 FS Div. on the right wing of Seventh Army. In heavy fighting, 50 British tanks were disabled and one armored British battery was destroyed.

After the success of 3 August—which, to be sure, had been very costly—Army Group ordered the withdrawal of the left wing of Panzer Group to a line St-André-sur-Orne – River Orne – Thury-Harcourt – Vire. As a definite point of contact between Panzer Army and Seventh Army, the stream crossing south of Presles was designated. During the withdrawal, 10 SS-Pz. Div. was to be pulled out and placed at the disposal of Army Group in the Vassy area.

4. 4–7 August

The withdrawal, as ordered, first to an intermediate position, concerned only LVIII Pz. Corps and LXXIV Inf. Corps in the first night, and was intended to eliminate the front are north of Villers-Bocage, which was projecting far to the northwest. This was effected according to plan. Until the afternoon of 4 August, the enemy still fired at the former main line of resistance which had been evacuated in the meantime, and above all at Hill 112 and Maltot, on the right wing of LVIII Pz. Corps. Then the enemy followed only slowly with armored reconnaissance.

In the II SS-Pz. Corps sector, during the mobile fighting by 9 SS-Pz. Div., several enemy groups which had been cut off were now seized individually and destroyed. Thus we succeeded, above all, in throwing back strong enemy groups and preventing their escape to the west and north. Contact with the right wing of Seventh Army could be consolidated.

In the night of 4/5 August, the withdrawal to the line as ordered—River Orne as far as to the river bend north of Thury-Harcourt – Roucamps – Estry – north edge of Presles—was effected. It was carried out according to plan, and with the simultaneous pulling out of 10 SS-Pz. Div. On this occasion, the enemy, who had become watchful because of the previous withdrawal, pursued our units more closely, trying again to break up the front. Enemy tank concentrations in front of LXXIV Inf. Corps were attacked by artillery, and reconnaissance thrusts were repelled. In the afternoon, enemy tanks succeeded in penetrating into St-Jean-le-Blanc and in capturing Hill 252 on the northern edge of the village. Elements of 326 Inf. Div. and 21 Pz. Div. were employed in a counterattack against them. Hard fighting developed at 9 SS-Pz. Div. for the domination of the locality of Sourdeval (2 km south of Presles); however, contact with the Seventh Army remained secure.

In the meantime, quiet had prevailed at the LXXVI Inf. Corps and I SS-Pz. Corps front, except for lively artillery and fighter-bomber activity. On 5 August, the enemy for the first time launched a strong attack against Tilly-la-Campagne and St-Martin-de-Fontenay. He succeeded in breaking through with tanks as far as La Hogue[tte?]. Essentially, however, these enemy attacks—which began with brief drum fire—were all repelled in immediate counterattacks, and minor penetrations were sealed off.

Meanwhile, Army Group had ordered Panzer Army to withdraw from the front and send off to Seventh Army the most capable of the Panzer divisions, 1 SS-Pz. Div. Leibstandarte. The division was to be the backbone of the counterattack—decisive for the overall situation—against Avranches. Moreover, Panzer Army was to relieve from the front 12 SS-Pz. Div., which, at first, had also been intended for transfer to the present point of main effort in the Seventh Army sector. Since Army Group and Panzer Army had still to reckon with a British offensive from Falaise in the direction of Paris—trying to bring about a decision—Army Group decided reluctantly to leave 12 SS-Pz. Div. to Panzer Army as an absolutely necessary strategic reserve. In its stead, 10 SS-Pz. Div., which had been relieved from the front at the left Army wing according to plan and was held in readiness in the Vassy area, was later sent off to Seventh Army. For the time being, however, this division, too, had to be left at the boundary between the two Armies, so as to prevent a new disruption of the entire front.

For the relief of 1 SS-Pz. Div., only the reinforced regiment (which had arrived first) of 89 Inf. Div., which was in the process of being brought up, was, for the time being, available. The loss of armor-piercing weapons could be compensated for to some extent by the arrival of 1348 Assault Gun Bn. On account of the delayed arrival of 89 Inf. Div.—caused by the inadequate Seine-crossing facilities—the relief of 1 SS-Pz. Div. could not be carried out according to plan, and, consequently, the division did not arrive, as a compact unit, in time for the attack on Avranches. One Panzer Grenadier regiment, one Panzer battalion and several other units remained south of Caen until 7 August.

On 6 August, Panzer Group West was renamed Fifth Panzer Army. While the situation east of the Orne was calming down after the successful counterattack on 5 August, and only increased artillery and reconnaissance activity was carried on, the disconnected enemy attacks west of the Orne continued. South of Hamars (5 km northwest of Thury-Harcourt), an enemy armored attack was repelled. The main enemy pressure continued to be exerted at the boundary between 326 Inf. Div. and 21 Pz. Div., where the enemy captured Hill 365 (2 km northwest of Le Plessis-Grimoult), and pushed forward over Hill 246, as far as the western edge of Crépigny [?]. 21 Pz. Div., however, was able to recapture Hill 246 by means of an immediate counterattack.

In the II SS-Pz. Corps sector, on the left wing of the Army, all enemy attacks were repelled. Portions of 10 SS-Pz. Div. which were again employed for the consolidation of the situation at the left boundary of the Army, pushed forward from the area of Chênedollé as far as Hill 224 (2 km south of Presles) in a counterattack, inflicting high casualties on the enemy.

On 7 August, enemy attacks increased, most particularly, against Army center, in LXXIV Inf. Corps' sector, where the enemy succeeded in establishing a bridgehead across the Orne near Grimbosq (7 km north of Thury-Harcourt). Besides local reserves, a combat group from 12 SS-Pz. Div. was employed there, and succeeded in limiting that bridgehead considerably. The Army, supposing—evidently on account of the fighting activity of the past days—that the enemy's main effort had shifted to the west bank of the Orne, intended to transfer its now sole remaining Panzer reserve, 12 SS-Pz. Div., entirely to the area north of Condé-sur-Noireau, the more so since the bulk of 89 Inf. Div. had finally arrived, and an additional infantry division of Fifteenth Army, 85 Inf. Div., was already in the process of crossing the Seine.

5. 8–13 August

On 8 August, however, a decisive change took place. The British again launched a large-scale attack east of the Orne on either side of the road from Caen to Falaise. With more than 600 tanks, strongly supported by artillery and fighter-bombers, the British succeeded in breaking through the German front—which had been greatly weakened by the pulling out of the armored units—and by evening they had succeeded in pushing forward as far as Cintheaux and Hautmesnil.

There was no other choice but to establish a blocking position with forces raked up together, and to commit the only reserve still available (to some extent), i.e., 12 SS-Pz. Div. The divisional combat group which was to eliminate the enemy Orne bridgehead at Grimbosq was not available as yet, since it was engaged in heavy fighting. On account of the critical situation, – which, finally, for the first time, clearly revealed the intention of the Allied unified command to bring about a large-scale encirclement—Army Group decided to move Panther Bn of 9 Pz. Div. (which had just arrived at the Seventh Army) up to the Fifth Panzer Army, since at that time it was, above all, important to bring up armor-piercing weapons. Panzer Army itself was compelled to throw into the battle the leading elements of 85 Inf. Div., which was beginning to arrive, and the bulk of which was still crossing the Seine.

However, before the first countermeasures had a chance to become effective, the spearheads of enemy armored forces pushed through as far as [Grainville-] Langannerie (on the road from Caen to Falaise). The left wing of LXXXVI Inf. Corps—272 Inf. Div.—was withdrawn to the general line Bellengreville – crossroads 1 km east of La Hogue – west of Contevi[lle?] – west of Poussy-la-Campagne. From there we tried to establish a new front along a line St-Sylvain – Cauvicourt – south of Hautmesnil – Bretteville, and to cut off from their rear connections the enemy tanks which had broken through, and annihilate them.

On the remaining front, LXXIV Inf. Corps had repelled enemy attacks at Le Plessis-Grimoult, and II SS-Pz. Corps had also been able to eliminate an enemy penetration near Estry. Enemy assemblies and movements—especially in the Hamars – Roucamp area—indicated, however, that the enemy would become more active again also west of the Orne.

The overall situation pointed more and more to the fact that things were coming to a head. Supreme Command had been too late in reaching the decision to finally move up the units of Fifteenth Army to the Battle of Normandy. The difficulties in crossing the Seine and the blasting of a bridge at Hesdin delayed all our movements. Apart from 85 Inf. Div., 331 and 344 Inf. Divs, as well as 17 Lw Field Div., were still in the process of approaching.

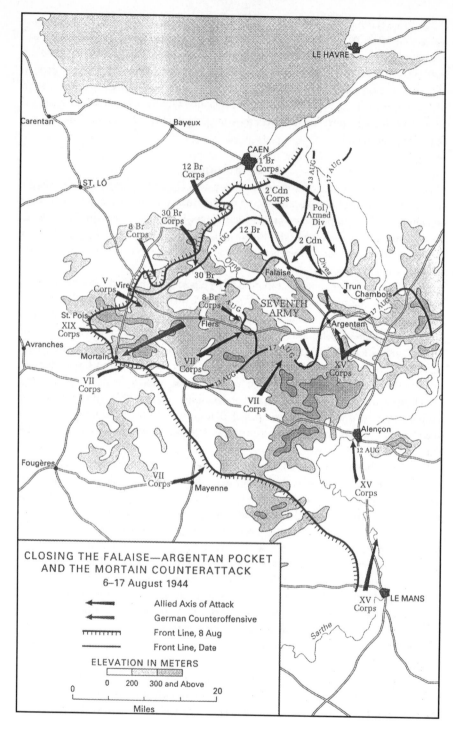

CLOSING THE FALAISE—ARGENTAN POCKET
AND THE MORTAIN COUNTERATTACK
6–17 August 1944

On 9 August, the enemy at first did not seem to continue his major attack against Falaise, but was apparently only drawing up from the rear. Heavy fighting, nevertheless, took place on the entire front of the Panzer Army that day.

In the LXXXVI Inf. Corps sector, the left wing division (272 Inf. Div.) was drawn into the fighting. There, the enemy succeed in penetrating into Benneauville- [Banneville?-] la-Campagne. We did not succeed in building up a blocking position in the area of penetration, as had been intended by I SS-Pz. Corps. German groups which, in places, were still holding out in the penetration area (above all, antiaircraft combat groups and units engaged in disconnected fighting) had been battered by the enemy. The localities of St-Sylvain, Soignolles, Estrées-la-Campagne, Bretteville-le-Rabet, Urville, Couvix [Gouvix] and Bretteville-sur-Laize had—all of them—fallen into the hands of the enemy.

Against Grainville, a counterthrust was launched with Tiger tanks. Although, altogether, 90 British tanks had been destroyed, our own losses were also heavy. Yet there was hope that the enemy would be forced to have a breathing space for a while on account of his high losses of tanks.

In the adjoining LXXIV Inf. Corps sector, the British 43 Inf. Div. and 8 Armored Bde pushed through on either side of Le Plessis-Grimoult as far as Tremblay, thus obtaining a penetration about 4 km in depth there too. In spite of a counterthrust supported by Tiger tanks, the enemy was, by evening, able to widen his penetration by another 2 km as far as St-Pierre-la-Vieille.

In the II SS-Pz. Corps sector, renewed enemy attacks against Estry were repelled. On the evening of 9 August, Panzer Army reported the following forwardmost line, on which an incomplete defensive front could be reestablished: Troarn – Argences – Moult – Airan – Bray [?] -la-Campagne – west edge of the woods south of Fierville-la-Campagne [Fierville-Bray?] – woods 2 km east of Estrées-la-Campagne – south of Grainville – south of Mesnil-Touffre [?] – 1 km south of Fresney-le-Vieux – Espins – Orne bend north of Thury-Harcourt – Thury-Harcourt – south of St-Lambert – St-Pierre-la-Vieille – Lassy.

Considerable movements in the area near the road from Caen to Falaise led us to expect new strong enemy attacks, particularly in this area. It appeared, however, that the enemy had suffered such heavy losses in tanks that on 10 August he was still inactive, except for reconnaissance thrusts and lively artillery activity. However, strong movements in the direction of the front further indicated that he was bringing up fresh forces, with which he would continue his concentrated attacks east of the Orne.

Nevertheless, the lull in the fighting gave us an opportunity to bring up, as quickly as possible, the forces which were in the process of approaching (for, instance 85 Inf. Div.), and to reorganize our forces. On 10 August, a major enemy attack took place only on the left wing of I SS-Pz. Corps, where the enemy achieved a penetration near Croisilles, northeast of Thury-Harcourt, which could be blocked, however, along a line Forges-à-Cambro [?] – south of Croisilles – bend of the Orne. Recognized enemy assembly positions were attacked by artillery especially, before the front of I SS-Pz. Corps, on either side of the road from Caen to Falaise.

On 11 August, the enemy did not continue his large-scale attack either, but confined himself to individual attacks to improve his positions. Yet all the signs indicated that the actual offensive, strategically coordinated with the American offensive, would soon be resumed via Alençon towards Argentan.

In front of the LXXXVI Inf. Corps sector, fighting took place only on the left Corps wing near St-Sylvain. The focal point of combat continued unchanged at the I SS-Pz. Corps front. There, the enemy tried, especially, to push ahead from Grainville along the road to Falaise to the southeast, in the direction of Hill 188, and from Urville to the south. However, this evidently involved only minor forces, while the main body of the enemy troops was still moving into positions of readiness in the area of Fierville – Bretteville-le-Rabet – Estrées la Campagne. On the left wing of Corps, the enemy's penetration at Croisilles had finally been sealed off along a line from Espins to the stream east of Thury-Harcourt. There, too, and particularly north of Thury-Harcourt, lively movements towards the front were observed.

In the sector at the right wing of LXXIV Inf. Corps, the enemy had broken through the line of 277 Inf. Div., and had pushed forward as far as Hill 141, west of Thury-Harcourt. The local critical situation was temporarily cleared up by an immediate counterattack of the division reserves as well as those of Corps which had been raked together. In the II SS-Pz. Corps sector, only local attacks took place on 11 August, from Chênedollé to the east, which were repelled.

On 12 August, the enemy continued his hitherto applied combat tactics of wearing down the German front and containing the German forces by means of individual attacks. But Panzer Army realized that a strong coordinated offensive was still imminent.

Besides continuous reconnaissance thrusts into the area on either side of the boundary between LXXVI Inf. Corps and I SS-Pz. Corps, a British armored group succeeded in breaking through west of the River Laize as far as Moulines, and in bringing about a local crisis there. That day, the main fighting took place in the LXXIV Inf. Corps sector, where the enemy succeeded—in spite of our successful counterattack the day before—in penetrating with tanks, from the north, into Thury-Harcourt. The enemy broke through our front west of Thury-Harcourt after heavy barrage fire in conjunction with phosphorus and smoke. 277 Inf. Div., which had been fighting for many weeks, was almost destroyed in these actions. Even the adjacent 276 Inf. Div. again suffered heavy casualties through a strong enemy attack from St-Pierre-le-Vieille to the east, so , for the moment, it was no longer able to seal off the penetration.

On 13 August, apart from minor enemy reconnaissance thrusts, a lull in the fighting prevailed. The enemy had been successful in his tactics of attrition during the past days. Our front was torn open throughout; the defensive troops were exhausted and the last reserves worn out. For this reason, penetrations and gaps in the front were only superficially sealed off, without the defensive troops being able to dig in properly. Moreover, it was evident that hitherto we had had to deal only with preliminary actions, whereas the major thrust was still to be expected.

On 13 August, Army Group assumed that the American forces—which had advanced via Alençon first to the north—now intended to turn off to the west, so as to thrust against the rear of Seventh Army. If this had been substantially the case, the British main effort would have had to be expected west of the Orne. But, since no strategic reserves were, in any event, available to Fifth Panzer Army to meet this emergency, our considerations were rather immaterial. Due to the overall situation, the opportunity to close the encirclement between Falaise and Argentan presented itself to the Allied command, and it was surprising that the corresponding breakthroughs—by the British by way of Falaise and by American forces by way of Argentan and east of it—had not yet ensued.

Since the German Supreme Command, despite the pressing situation, was still unable to decide on a large-scale withdrawal of Army Group B to the east, it remained for Fifth Panzer Army to protect the north flank of Seventh Army and to prevent the British Army Group from breaking through to the south and southeast. Fifth Panzer Army was compelled to execute this order with the forces available at that time, since, on 12 August, Army Group, because of the overall situation, had had to decide to assemble the divisions of Fifteenth Army which were in the process of approaching (344 Inf. Div. and 17 Lw Field Div.) as a reserve for Army Group west of the Seine, and also to commit 331 Inf. Div., the foremost regiment of which was employed by Seventh Army, for covering the southern flank against the thrust of the US Third Army at Gacé. It was to be expected that all the units which Fifteenth Army could still make available (47, 48, and 49 Inf. Divs, and 18 Lw Field Div.) likewise would have to be employed against Gen. Patton's Third Army. The critical situation on Army Group's southern flank had also caused the pulling out of several GHQ units. On 13 August, Assault Gun Bn 1348 had been given up by Fifth Panzer Army to 331 Inf. Div., so as to lend it the necessary Panzer protection. Panther Bn of 9 Pz. Div., which was to have been brought up to Army, had been stopped on 13 August on its march in the Argentan area, where 116 Pz. Div., which was involved in hard fighting, had to employ it towards the south. All these measures had caused a serious weakening of Fifth Panzer Army, which, on the other hand, could no longer count on getting further reinforcements.

6. The Battle of Falaise, 14–21 August

On 14 August, the long-expected large-scale attack by the British Army Group, with its focal point east of the Orne, began. I SS-Pz. Corps, which in the preceding weeks had been critically weakened through the loss of Panzers and antitank guns, was not able to ward off this attack, which was carried out with the heaviest support from tanks, artillery, and planes.

At the boundary between LXXXVI Inf. Corps and I SS-Pz. Corps, about 80 British tanks broke through, by way of Le Bû-sur-Rouvres, to the southeast. While Condé-sur-Ifs could be held, Ifs-sur-Laison, Ernes and the important Hill 79 (1½ km southeast of Ernes) were lost. The counterthrusts immediately launched by the local reserves, which were held in readiness, did not succeed. In the I SS-Pz. Corps sector, the enemy—who could be stopped only in some localities—reached Olendon by way of Montboint [?] and Sassy via Rouvres. Quilly- [Ouilly-] le-Tesson and Potigny appeared to be lost, although violent tank battles were still raging everywhere. West of the Caen–Falaise road, too, the German defense was battered along the main line of resistance, and the enemy could be superficially blocked only at the line St-Germain-Langot – Le Mesnil – Bonnoeil, with forces which were raked together. However, west of the Orne, too, the left wing of the LXXIV Inf. Corps was affected. Proussy was lost. Weak portions of 21 Pz. Div. were just able to intercept the enemy south of that locality.

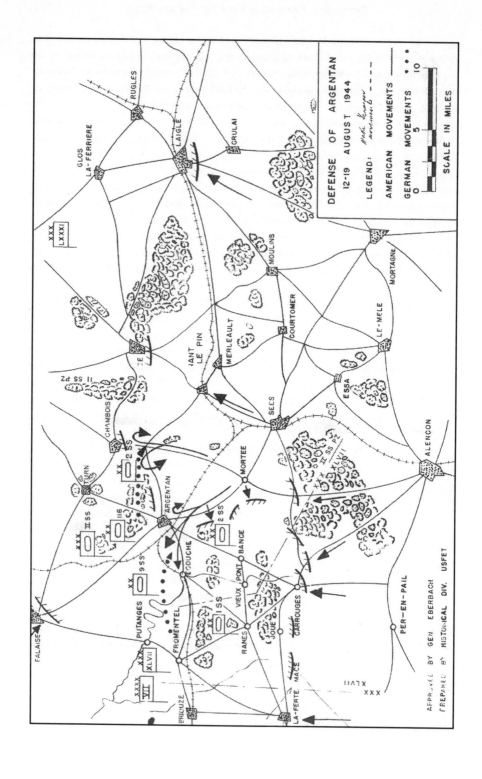

Thus, a wide breach had been made in the German front north of Falaise. It now appeared to be impossible to stop a breakthrough by the British, and thus their linking-up with the American forces. The weak forces of 12 SS-Pz. Div.—which were the only reserves at the disposal of the Army—had to be employed in protecting the main road and the key point of Falaise. Because of the enemy breakthrough, the connection with the left wing of the Army could no longer be kept, so, on 14 August, II SS-Pz. Corps placed itself under the command of Seventh Army, since Fifth Panzer Army had no longer the means of getting its orders through to it.

14 August was also the most critical day for the development of the situation in the Army Group deep flank, where an assault by the US Third Army via Paris to the east, as well as west of the Seine to the north, seemed possible. Army Group, therefore, ordered Panzer Army to clear up the situation immediately by armored reconnaissance in LXXXI Inf. Corps' sector in the Argentan area, south of [Vitrai-sous-] Laigle. The spectre of imminent encirclement became more and more evident.

On 15 August, the enemy continued his offensive with all his might—as was to be expected. On the left wing of LXXXVI Inf. Corps, the enemy pushed forward with about 100 tanks as far as, and across, the Dives near Vendeuvre and Jort. On the right wing of I SS-Pz. Corps, Bernières d'Ailly was lost. From Périers, which was lost during the night, British tanks pushed forward further to the south. But the valiant 12 SS-Pz. Div. succeeded in holding the Falaise area. An enemy assault from Espanzy [?] on Versainville was repelled. Another assault from Soulangy towards Falaise was likewise repelled. Nevertheless, the dominating Hill 168 (4 km north of Falaise) was lost. Northwest of Falaise, we succeeded in stopping the enemy for the time being. An attack upon Trépel was repulsed by 271 Inf. Div. In the LXXIV Inf. Corps sector, no major enemy attacks took place that day.

Although the strategic breakthrough had, so far, been prevented, the front of Panzer Army was split, and they had again suffered heavy casualties, as a result of the enormous use of artillery and airpower by the Allies. A continuous front no longer existed in I SS-Panzer Corps' sector; rather, there were only strongpoints left, which offered tenacious resistance chiefly along the main roads and by making use of defended localities. With regard to the next day, therefore, the situation looked extremely critical. The only measure which could be taken by Fifth Panzer Army consisted in pulling 21 Pz. Div. out from the front of the left wing of the Army and starting it off to the Falaise area. Although Army Group, at the same time, subordinated 344 Inf. Div. and 17 Lw Field Div. to the Army, these two units, which were still in process of crossing the Seine, were absolutely necessary for covering the broad gap between Gacé – [Vitrai-sous-] Laigle and the Seine against the thrust of the US Third Army to the north.

On 16 August, the enemy main effort remained unchanged in the Falaise area. In the LXXXVI Inf. Corps sector, the enemy, who at St-Pierre-sur-Dives had already crossed the river to the east, was thrown back to that locality by 85 Inf. Div. With the intention of widening the penetration area to the east, about 30 British tanks drove via Airan to the north, but they were brought to a stop.

In the I SS-Pz. Corps sector, the enemy had crossed the Dives on a wide front. An attack on Courcy was repelled. On the other hand, the enemy pushed forward in the valley of the river by way of Vicques to Morteaux-Couliboeuf. The strongest pressure was prevailing in the direction of Falaise, where, during the course of the day, the weak remnants of 21 Pz. Div. were able to take a hand in the battle just in time. All day long the enemy, with strong forces, attacked the road crossing at Point 152, 1½ km north of Falaise. Until nightfall, he was repelled by our gallantly fighting troops, but then he succeeded in infiltrating into the northern part of the town of Falaise. On the left wing of Corps, the brave 271 Inf. Div. was engaged in heavy fighting along a line of Bois du Roi – Trépel. However, it could not prevent the enemy tanks from breaking through to Noron-l'Abbaye on its right wing.

In the LXXIV Inf. Corps sector, the enemy also became more active, succeeding in gaining ground sharp east of the Orne, via Quilly to the southeast. Further to the west, where, meanwhile, Corps had withdrawn behind the Noireau sector, a local penetration was made near Cahen [?]. 326 and 276 Inf. Divs, which were fighting there, were entirely worn out, having now only the strength of weak combat groups.

The Army then decided to withdraw the following night to the line Lieury (3 km south of St-Pierre-sur-Dives) – Morteaux-Couliboeuf – Falaise – Noron-l'Abbaye – Les Loges-Saulces – [Condé-sur-?] -Noireau – confluence with the Orne, and to try to establish a new front of resistance along that line, where, for the most part, fighting was going on already.

American armored attacks had been repelled by 331 Inf. Div. on the southern flank, on which occasion 14 American tanks were disabled. 344 Inf. Div. and additional Kampfgruppen (for instance, that of I SS-Pz. Div.) were moving up in order to lengthen the flanking position of Gacé – [Vitrai-sous-] Laigle – River Seine.

Meanwhile, the German Supreme Command had decided to withdraw Seventh Army across the Orne to the east, and to attempt a last-minute escape from the threatening encirclement by way of the narrow loophole still open between Falaise and Argentan. Until this was accomplished—which was possible until about 19 August—Fifth Panzer Army had orders to cover the north flank of this retreat. In order to reinforce the Army for this purpose, at least by forces which were available, Army Group ordered Seventh Army to pull out two infantry divisions in the course of the withdrawal across the Orne to the east, and to bring these up to Fifth Panzer Army in the area south of Falaise. In complying with these orders, Seventh Army assigned 84 and 363 Inf. Div., which, however, in view of the fact that they still had to cross the Orne, could only arrive in the areas as ordered during the night of 17 August at the earliest.

Despite further deep penetrations made by the enemy, we succeeded in keeping open the narrow loophole, even on 17 August—which would hardly have been possible if energetic assaults had been made either by the British or the Americans. Evidently, the boundary between the British and the American Army Groups—running right through the center of the battle zone—had a beneficial effect on the German situation.

Strong enemy attacks against the left wing of LXXXVI Inf. Corps forced it to withdraw behind the Vic[ques?] sector between Cléville and Coupesarte. In the I SS-Pz. Corps sector, we had not succeeded in occupying the intended main line of resistance, which, in the main was to be based on the Ante river. Only the right wing (85 Inf. Div.) put up a defence, along the line Mittois (adjoining here the left wing of LXXXVI Inf. Corps) – Lieury – east of Courcy. From there, a broad gap opened as far as St-Martin-de-Mieux, in which, it is true,

Kampfgruppen were still fighting, but in which the situation was obscure and there was no longer any question of a continuous front. The enemy armored forces broke through there by way of [Les] Moutiers-en-Auge as far as the northern outskirts of Louvières-en-Auge and Fontaine-les-Bassets (northwest of Trun). He had evidently reached the boundary line there, since, fortunately, he did not for the time being, push forward over Trun – Chambois so as to unite with the Americans, from which he hardly could have been prevented by the insignificant opposing forces.

Although elements of II SS-Pz. Corps (2 and 9 SS-Pz. Divs)—which was in the process of withdrawal from the Seventh Army front, and which had been placed at the disposal of Army Group, and ordered to proceed to the Vimoutiers area—had turned off against the enemy, which had penetrated into the Trun area, these elements were not strong enough to close this gap in the front. The left wing of Corps (271 Inf. Div.) was still on the line St-Martin-de-Mieux – Fourneaux-le-Val, adjoining 276 Inf. Div. on the right wing of LXXIV Inf. Corps via Ménil-Vin. It was again intended to establish a new continuous front, planned to run along a line at the Vic sector – Coupesarte – Montviette – Montpinçon [Mont Pinçon?] – Grand-Mesnil – Le[s] Moutier[s]-en-Auge – Beaumais – southwest corner of the Forêt de St-André – Corde[y] – Bilaine [?] river. The two infantry divisions of Seventh Army were subordinated to LXXIV Inf. Corps and ordered to occupy the gap between I SS-Pz. Corps and LXXIV Inf. Corps, and to provide coverage for the remnants of 89 Inf. Div. withdrawing there.

On 18 August, the I SS-Pz. Corps front—which was based on a system of strongpoints— was again broken through, and the ring around the entire Seventh Army and half of Fifth Panzer Army was definitely closed near St. Lambert-sur-Dive (3 km southeast of Trun) With that, LXXIV Inf. Corps automatically became subordinated to Seventh Army.

In LXXVI Inf. Corps' sector, an enemy attack against the Vic position near St-Loup-de-Fribois was repelled. Against the left wing of Corps, between Coupesarte and Montviette, strong enemy attacks were launched continually, and finally it was possible to check along the line Coupesarte – 1 km east of Le Mesnil-Durand – Vic sector, as far as 1 km south of Livarot. However, contact with I SS-Pz. Corps had thereby been lost. The situation at this Corps remained completely obscure. Strong portions of 21 Pz. and 12 SS-Pz. Divs, and the entire 89 and 271 Inf. Divs, were within the pocket, and thus only 85 Inf. Div., together with portions and remnants of all kinds of units, offered local resistance in groups outside of the pocket, without being able to establish any well-connected, unified command and a defensive front.

LXXIV Inf. Corps also informed us by radio messages that, despite its reinforcement, British tanks had broken through its front and had pushed forward as far as Pierrefitte and Ri, so that there, too, a link-up with American forces seemed possible.

Originally, Army Group had kept in readiness II SS-Pz. Corps for the purpose of fighting free the deep south flank facing the American Third Army, in the general direction of Laigle. But the development of the situation made it necessary to employ Corps in an attack in the direction of Trun, so as to split the ring of encirclement and to give Seventh Army a chance of breaking out. For the time being, the battle-weary Corps was still assembling in the Vimoutiers area, and it was doubtful whether it would have enough fuel

A US 4.2-inch mortar in action. These mortars were originally intended to be primarily for firing smoke shell, but they were soon in heavy use for a range of direct support-fire missions. (US National Archives)

for the attack on 19 August. The entire supply situation had increasingly deteriorated on account of the situation in the air and on the land.

Grave anxiety was caused by the situation of the deep southern flank, where the US Third Army was beginning, west of the Seine, to press energetically to the north, and where, therefore, the envelopment even of the remaining portions of Fifth Army seemed imminent.

On 19 August, the enemy was attacking along the whole Army front. In front of LXXXVI Inf. Corps, local reserves succeeded in throwing back the enemy, pushing forward by way of Putot-en-Auge, across the railway line to Houlgate. On the other hand, an enemy penetration into the area of Grandchamp at the Vic front was only blocked along a line St-Loup [-de-] Fribois – Monteille – Lécaude – Lessard-et-le-Chêne. On that account, further withdrawal to the east was ordered for the night following, all the more importantly as heavy fighting had taken place also at the Corps boundary near Livarot, where, again, heavy casualties had ensued. 85 Inf. Div., on the north wing of I SS-Pz. Corps, was able to repel enemy attacks against Montpinçon and Grand-Mesnil.

Although, by this time, II SS-Pz. Corps was fully assembled, it was not able to launch an attack before the early morning of 20 August at the earliest, because of the fuel situation. Only radio communication still existed with Seventh Army. In the afternoon of 19 August, the Army informed us of its intention to break out between Chambois and Trun in the night of 19 August, requesting for that purpose a diversionary attack by II SS-Pz. Corps.

On 20 August, the British intensified their attacks against the right wing of the Army, as a result of which heavy fighting developed at Cabourg and Périers-en-Auge, resulting in heavy losses for 711 Inf. Div. Further to the south, the enemy penetrated into our front as far as Cricqueville-en-Auge and to the line St-Legan-Dubosq – St-Jouin. Northeast of Grandchamp, the enemy expended his penetration of the day before as far as Les Monceaux. In order to give a chance to LXXXVI Inf. Corps to reorganize its forces again, Corps was given the order to withdraw in the night following to the line Villers-sur-Mer – Branville – Annebault – Bonnebosq – St-Ouen-le-Pin – St-Pierre-des-Ifs – Hill 174.

In the I SS-Pz. Corps sector, enemy tanks pushed through east of Livarot, along the road to Orbec. Assembled portions of 21 Pz. Div. were employed in a counterattack against them. Until the breakout by Seventh Army was carried out, contact with II SS-Pz. Corps had to be maintained.

In the morning of 20 August, II SS-Pz. Corps started the attack, sending in 9 SS-Pz. Div., on the right via Camembert – Les Champeaux to Trun, and II SS-Pz. Div. on the left via Goudehard [?] to St-Lambert-sur-Dive – Chambois. The attack by 9 Pz. Div. reached as far as about Les Corniers; the II SS-Pz. Div. was also well able to gain ground, until a heavy tank battle developed north of Goudehard [?]. In this fighting, strong enemy elements which were blocking the east front of the pocket were tied down, and Corps fully accomplished its mission of bringing relief. Thus, early in the morning, Seventh Army succeeded in making a breach in the encircling front between Chambois and St-Lambert-sur-Dive, and in starting the breakout of the fighting elements. From the forenoon, II SS-Pz. Corps was able to cover the portions of Seventh Army which came rushing forward through the breach.

Even on 21 August, this breaking-out of forces from the pocket continued almost all day, so that II SS-Pz. Corps still had to hold the lines reached, for the time being, in order to secure the coverage of the men who were left equipped with only a few combat vehicles and hand weapons.

On the same day, LXXXVI Inf. Corps was attacked along the whole extent of its front, and heavy casualties were inflicted on all three divisions (711, 346 and 272 Inf. Divs). In the new positions, we were able, however, to repel the enemy almost everywhere, for example at St. Vaast, Branville, Annebault, Val-au-Loup [?], and Bonnenosq; the enemy achieved local penetrations only south of St-Vaast and south of Branville.

I SS-Pz. Corps—after the breakthrough at Falaise consisting only of 85 Inf. Div. and the remnants of 21 Panzer 12 SS-Pz. Divs—gave up command of its sector to II SS-Pz. Corps, as ordered by the Army. II SS-Pz. Corps, with 9 SS-Pz. Div. and elements of 21 Pz. Div., now started mobile warfare in the gap facing LXXXVI Inf. Corps. After the successful breakout of Seventh Army, the enemy, for the moment, still seemed to remain inactive at the covering front. He was probably too busy clearing up the battlefield, assembling prisoners and captured material.

The battlefield at Falaise – Argentan offered a spectacle suggestive of battlefields of past wars, which had been confined to a small area. The situation on the south flank of Fifth Panzer Army became extremely critical on 21 August. The far-extended front of 344 Inf. Div. and 17 Luftwaffe-Field-Div., which had just been occupied by the forwardmost elements of the formations, was broken through by American armored forces between

Verneuil [-sur-Avre] and Dreux. There, the enemy pushed through as far as a line Rugles –
Breteuil – Damville – south of Pacy [-sur-Eure]. Fifth Panzer Army, therefore, ordered a
general withdrawal to a line Touques sector – Deauville – Pont l'Evêque, as far as Lisieux –
Glos – Orbec – Rugles – Pacy, to be carried out in the night following, and committed I SS-
Panzer Corps with the assembled armored elements of the I SS, 12 SS, and 2 Pz. Divs, in
the Evreux – Pacy area, so as to secure with these forces the endangered southern flank, in
offensive operations.

7. The Seine Bridgehead (22–25 August)

Early in the morning of 22 August, the withdrawal behind the River Touques had been
successful in general. But now the enemy pursued our troops closely everywhere. Thus, in
LXXXVI Inf. Corps' sector, the pursuing enemy succeeded in crossing the Touques at
Pont-l'Evêque, Brévil and Beuvillers. At various points, our troops, again and again valiantly
putting forth their strength in counterattack, succeeded in throwing the enemy back across the
river. At Coquainvilliers, the enemy crossed the road from Lisieux to Pont-l'Evêque on a
stretch of about 400 m, against which, likewise, an immediate counterattack was launched.

In the II SS-Pz. Corps sector, the enemy pursued our troops closely, especially in the
direction of Orbec, into which locality he penetrated, thus achieving a breach in our new
main line of resistance. Yet Corps succeeded in covering the rearguard troops, which had
been left behind in the former main line of resistance.

The most critical situation remained unchanged in the LXXXI Inf. Corps sector at the
south flank, where the Americans, pushing forward far more energetically, broke through
with 100 tanks to the north at La Benneville [Bonneville?]. Their spearheads reached the
area southeast of Le Neubourg. Against this enemy breakthrough, the forces of I SS-Pz.
Corps—which were still in the process of assembling—were to be employed. But the
strength reports of the units subordinated were extremely low. They were as follows:

1 SS-Pz. Div.: Only weak infantry; no Panzers or artillery.

2 Pz. Div.: One Panzer Grenadier battalion; no Panzers or artillery.

12 SS-Pz. Div.: 300 men; ten Panzers.

116 Pz. Div.: Two battalions, twelve Panzers, two batteries.

21 Pz. Div.: Four battalions, ten Panzers.

It was still to be hoped that these forces would be able to prevent at least the decisive
breakthrough of the American Third Army. Directly west of the Seine, the enemy pushed
forward via Pacy to Evreux. One Kampfgruppe of 17 SS-Pz. Gren. Div., Fick, was still
holding out there along a line La Chapelle – Vernon. Army Group intended to take one
regiment of 49 Inf. Div.—which just had arrived at the east bank of the Seine—across to
the west bank at Notre-Dame-de-l'Isle, in order to establish steady contact between
Kampfgruppe Fick and 17 Lw Field Div. The heavy commitment of the US Third Army
also showed itself in the fact that Conches [-en-Ouche] alone was attacked eight times by
pattern bombing.

On 23 August, the heavy fighting for the Seine bridgeheads was continued. In the
LXXXVI Inf. Corps sector, the fighting which started the day before for regaining the main
line of resistance at Le Breuil and Coquainville [?], was still going on. An enemy group

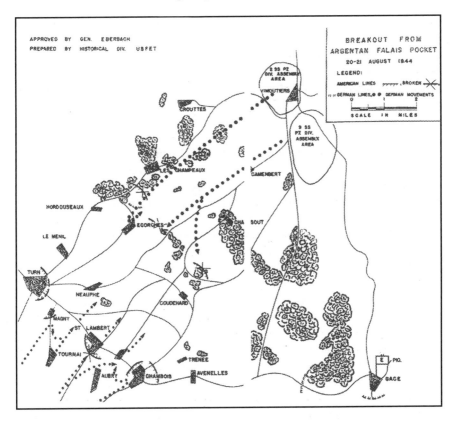

pushing forward from Quilly to the southeast was stopped. In II SS-Panzer Corps' sector, the enemy pressure continued, especially at Orbec and west of La Chapelle-Gauthier.

At the southern flank, a regrouping had taken place, insofar as the Staff of I SS-Pz. Corps had meanwhile assumed command over the infantry divisions committed on the east bank of the Seine (49 Inf. Div. and 18 Lw Field Div.); all of the Panzer units were as a whole subordinated to Generalleutant Gerhard Graf Schwerin. Our counterattack against the far superior enemy at Evreux was not successful; the enemy, on the contrary, was able to penetrate even into Le Neubourg, which was defended by portions of 116 Pz. Div. Finally, the German Panzer units succeeded in stopping the advancing enemy at the line Cresville [Cesseville?] – Surtauville – Crasville – Louviers. It was, for the time being, still possible to hold Louviers against strong attacks from the south and southwest. Kampfgruppe Fick, meanwhile, had withdrawn to the line Louviers – Seine loop north of Heudebouville, since the taking over of one regiment of 49 Inf. Div. had not been effected.

Meanwhile, the remnants of Seventh Army, and the rear elements of the formations which were still fighting in the bridgehead, crossed the Seine by ferries on either side of Rouen. This crossing was continually disrupted by the Allied air force, but not to the expected extent, which would have made it completely impossible to cross in the daytime; the main difficulty was the condition of the utterly inadequate ferries. In most cases, the troops had to shift for themselves the scanty engineer equipment they still had at their disposal.

However, the crossing progressed so well that the Army decided to withdraw to the bridgehead line Honfleur – Cormeilles – Bernay – stream at Serquigny – Cresville [Crasville? Cesseville?]– Acquigny – Heudebouville in the night of 23 August. In the main, this withdrawal, too, was carried out successfully.

On 24 August, the enemy's of main effort was still concentrated against the south wing. In the LXXXVI Inf. Corps sector, British reconnaissance parties only felt their way forward to the new main line of resistance. On the other hand, Kampfgruppe Count Schwerin—which was subordinated to II SS-Pz. Corps—was not given the opportunity of keeping the enemy away from the Seine by mobile offensive action, as had been intended, but it was pressed into active defense. West of the Risle [river], a new defensive front was set up on the line Fiquefleur [-Equainville] – Beuzeville – Brionne, which was heavily attacked by enemy tanks, above all at St-Georges. Near St-Meslain [-du-Bosc] and north of Amfreville, the enemy was repelled. East of Elbeauf [Elbeuf?], however, an enemy armored group succeeded in feeling its way forward to the Seine, and in pushing the security detachments there across to the other bank. At the same time, however, still another Kampfgruppe was fighting at Louviers, with which contact was to be reestablished during the attack.

On 25 August as well, the enemy tried—by a continuous commitment of fighter-bombers and heavy artillery—to crush the Fifth Panzer Army bridgehead and to come up close to the Seine, on which occasion enemy pressure again became most perceptible on the left wing. Yet the attacks generally were repelled. In the LXXXVI Inf. Corps sector, two attacks against Epaignes were repelled. One Kampfgruppe of 9 SS-Pz. Div. was committed against the enemy who had pushed forward across the Risle between Montfort [-sur-Risle?] and St-Philbert [-sur-Risle?]. II SS-Pz. Corps were able to ward off by mobile fighting the heavy enemy attacks against the line of Glos [-sur-Risle?] – Thierville – Bonneville [-Aptot?] – St-Philbert-sur-Boissey, and to throw back the enemy who had pressed forward as far as Elbeuf.

Fighting in the Seine bridgehead still continued with unabated violence on 26 and 27 August. Fifth Panzer Army had, in the main, accomplished its difficult mission of defense during this first phase of the battle in northern France. Considering the inadequate forces and means of combat at its disposal for this purpose, it has indeed carried out a great achievement. It was not surprising that, in the end, it was no longer able to withstand successfully the breakthrough attacks of the British Armies, after almost all of the Panzer formations for the intended counterattack against Avranches had been taken away from it. Their replacement by the infantry divisions of Fifteenth Army, which were unaccustomed to combat, and insufficiently equipped with means of antitank defense, was, in the long run, enough to defeat the British and Canadian attack troops which were fully mechanized and far superior to all GHQ troops.

If we succeeded, in spite of that, in holding the Falaise front until 17 August, and after that, in preventing again and again the complete destruction of Army Group B, which was the aim of the Allied command—it proves how heroically our troops fought against an enemy who was superior in everything.

Chapter 10

Panzer Group Eberbach

by General der Panzertruppen Hans Eberbach
Translated by A. Rosenwald (A-922)

Relations between Seventh Army and
Panzer Group West (later Fifth Panzer Army)

1. In the beginning, Panzer Group West was conceived as a headquarters for a counter-attack by German Panzer divisions in the event of an invasion. It was subordinated to Seventh Army. On 9 June 1944, the Staff was destroyed by a bomber airplane at La Caine, 20 km southwest of Caen. The remnants were withdrawn and supplemented to act as a provisional Army Headquarters. At the end of June, this Headquarters took over the front from the Orne river mouth to Vire. At the end of July it received the designation Fifth Panzer Army.

2. At first, the situation necessitated the commitment of almost all the Panzer divisions in the Caen sector. By the end of June, it was evident that a German counterattack was no longer possible and the centre of gravity of the Panzer forces had to be transferred to the flexible flank, i.e. to Seventh Army. Meanwhile, Seventh Army had only 12 SS-Pz. Div. and 17 SS-Pz. Gren. Div. Goetz von Berlichingen. It further received:

    a. Before the American breakthrough at Avranches: from Panzer Group West—Pz. Lehr Div., 2 Pz. Div. and 116 Pz. Div. ; and from Army Group—9 Pz. Div.

    b. For the counterattack on Avranches: 1 SS-Pz. Div.

    c. After the counterattack on Avranches: 9 and 10 SS-Pz. Divs, with 1 AAA Corps and 2 Proj. Bdes.

    These forces might have sufficed to stop the American advance if they had been transferred to Seventh Army in time. This was never the case. The failure was caused by the fact that the Panzer divisions of Panzer Group West (Fifth Panzer Army), committed at the front, were not relieved by infantry divisions in due time. The Armed Forces High Command is to blame for this. It did not authorise CinC West to act freely, and delayed the transfer of the divisions.

3. There was no friction between Seventh Army and the Panzer Group West (Fifth Panzer Army). Panzer Group West was never opposed to giving away divisions, and has accelerated transfers as much as possible. As a result of giving away 9 and 10 SS-Pz. Divs, Panzer Group West (Fifth Panzer Army) was weakened to such an extent that it could not resist the British breakthrough at Falaise for long. This fact was clearly reported.

4. Since Avranches, the supply of Seventh Army was taken over by the Panzer Group West (Fifth Panzer Army), at first partially and later on completely. The Group was not

181

qualified for this service either by its communication routes or by other factors of the supply service. The possibilities of regular supply were further limited by lack of roads at the bottleneck near Falaise, their condition, and the activity of enemy fighter-bombers. These circumstances, despite the excellent work of the Chief Supply Officers of Fifth Panzer Army (Panzer Group West), are chiefly to be blamed for the catastrophe. The Armed Forces High Command had no understanding of require-ments necessary for the supply of several Panzer divisions. Also, CinC West probably did not always fully appreciate the difficulties of this service.

I no longer remember the exact roads the divisions which were given by Panzer Group West (Fifth Panzer Army) to Seventh Army occasionally used for these displacements. The decisions were always made by telephone calls between the two chiefs. A different road was assigned to each division. Whenever possible, the march was fixed to take place at night. Armed Forces High Command sometimes ordered that the march take place in the daytime. The losses to enemy aeroplanes were then very high (up to 30%), depending on weather conditions.

I cannot recollect the telephone order to me on 6 August Probably it dealt with taking back the front by several attacks, maybe from the Odon sector to the region of Thury-Harcourt on the Orne.

I. Visit of Lt. Gen. Warlimont and Lt. Gen. Buhle from Armed Forces High Command to Fifth Panzer Army (Panzer Group West)

1. On about 1 August, Lt. Gen. Warlimont from the OKW arrived at my Staff in order to get a closer view of the situation and to report this to Hitler's headquarters. He was informed in detail of all difficulties, of the whole situation, and of our particular wishes, and was supplied with all documents concerned, which he took with him. A wave of optimism flowed from him. Among other things, he hinted at the arrival of aeroplanes in big numbers, and at a sufficient supply of tanks and men to arrive very soon. He asked me what I thought of Seventh Army's counterattack on Avranches. I said I considered it hopeless because:

    a) the enemy air forces would soon stop it, if not crush it,

    b) the ground forces that stand at our disposal are too weak,

    c) even in case the breakthrough, contrary to the expectations, should succeed, our forces would not suffice to keep the new front against an attack with massed material,

    d) the supply of 4 Pz. Divisions through the narrow channel and during the few night hours would not be possible.

    Warlimont retorted that I was looking too darkly on the situation. He knew of no other solution. I said that in my opinion the only possible solution was an immediate retreat to the Seine–Yonne line. Warlimont characterized this as politically unbearable and tactically impracticable. The enemy, thanks to its full motorization, would overtake us and destroy our units, which were equipped with horse-drawn vehicles. I pointed out that a retreat, covered by our still intact Panzer divisions, would be feasible without a catastrophe. Warlimont stuck to his opinion. My Chief of Staff, Maj. Gen. Gousse, and my G-3 were present at this conference.

2. About 7 August, Lt. Gen. Buhle came to my Staff (Fifth Panzer Army). Being detained at the front by fighter-bombers, I did not see him personally. My CofS was instructed by me to tell Buhle the same as I had told Warlimont. According to his report, he did that, and especially pointed out the impossibility of winning back Avranches by repeating the attack after the first one had failed. He had also pointed to the necessity of drawing the consequences from this immediately. Buhle had been impressed by this, but still wanted to hear the opinion of Seventh Army before forming his own.

3. To Field Marshal von Kluge and his CofS Maj. Gen. Speidel, my CofS, and myself have uttered the same statements, pointing out, especially, the necessity to decide upon a retreat to the Seine immediately. I had the impression that they agreed with my point of view, and that, however, the Armed Forces High Command did not agree with their proposals.

II. Dismissal as Army Commander

On the 8 or 9 August, Field Marshal von Kluge gave me, over the phone, the order to give Fifth Panzer Army over to General of the SS-Sepp Dietrich. The attack on Avranches, according to an order from Hitler, would be repeated. With an emergency Staff, I have to take over the command of the Panzer divisions provided for this attack, and will be subordinated to the CinC of Seventh Army, SS-Gen. Hausser.

I again immediately say that I consider the attack hopeless, and that my assignments to this post would therefore be very unpleasant to me. It did not help; the order stood. I had to go to Seventh Army on the same day.

Seventh Army was obviously not very pleased with my turning up there. The insertion of my Staff between the Army Staff and the Corps Staff was unnecessary, and meant, in the prevailing situation, a very unpleasant lengthening of the command channel.

I think that the distrust against the army generals after the 20 July was decisive in my dismissal as army commander. Otherwise, it would have been unaccountable:

1. to take the Army away from me after a faultless command for seven weeks;
2. to give it to SS-Gen. Sepp Dietrich, who was unable to fulfil this task; and
3. to subordinate me to the CinC of the neighboring Army, SS-General Hausser;
4. to carry out an attack which I had repeatedly declared as hopeless; and
5. for which, moreover, I was not needed.

III. Organization of Staff Panzer Group Eberbach.

My Staff received the designation Panzer Group Eberbach. The initial organization was made by CinC West. Owing to the swift events and repeated shifts, parts of the Staff never did reach me. I never had more than three radio stations, of which very often only one was in order. The Staff was, therefore, able to function only with the aid of the Staff of Seventh Army or one of the Corps staffs. It was a burden for these staffs. During the commitment, I had repeatedly reported this fact and requested the dissolution of this Staff as worthless and without any meaning. CinC West agreed to this. The Armed Forces High Command admitted this point of view only when, after the battle of Falaise, the Staff consisted only of one truck, one special-missions staff officer, the driver, and myself.

As Chief of Staff, I asked the Field Marshal to appoint his son Lt. Col. G. Kluge.

IV. Situation at Seventh Army

Time: The Pz. Divisions which had taken part at the first offensive on Avranches (1 SS-Pz, 2 SS-Pz, 3 Pz, 116 Pz) had in the meantime fallen back to practically the starting positions and were there engaged by the pursuing enemy. First after disengagement they were available for the second attack. The infantry was numerically absolutely insufficient to relieve them. A shortening of the front had to be made in order to make the relief possible at all. This shortening also benefitted the enemy. First of all, all these measures took much time. For five days (14) we could not even think of the 2nd attack on Avranches. What did, however, the enemy do in the meantime? Nothing stood in his way to close the trap in which the *7. Army* already stood. It was unaccountable that the Armed Forces High Command could not see this, after Stalingrad, Tunis, etc. During all that time, the Armed Forces High Command formed its decisions on the present situation without taking into account the possible actions of the enemy.

Area: The blow against Avranches did not this time have to take place directly towards the west, in which case the surprise moment would have been entirely lacking. The Army had to start from the district of Barenton to St-Hilaire, and from there to Avranches and Pontaubault. It had consequently to make an advance of 65 km, instead of 40 km, and afterwards to hold a comparatively longer front. The appropriate forces for this were not available.

Forces: Without the aid of strong air forces, this longer attack had even less prospect for success than the first one. Our air forces were now weaker than ever before. Of course, they promised to add the 9 and 10 SS-Pz. Divs to those already present, but all these divisions were so worn out and battle-weary that only one-third of the tanks that took part in the first, shorter, unsuccessful attack were now available—at best, 120 Panzers. Besides, it was clear that the drawing away of 9 and 10 SS-Pz. Divs from Fifth Panzer Army (Panzer Group West) would inevitably lead to a British breakthrough on Falaise.

Supply: The ammunition and fuel situation at Seventh Army was bad. Le Mans stood to fall. Alençon was threatened. Accordingly, the situation of the supply services also did not promise success after a second attack on Avranches.

At first, I reported this estimate of the situation to the Seventh Army. On the next day, I made it out in writing, and repeated again that I considered that the attack would be unsuccessful. At the same time, I pointed to the necessity of throwing back the enemy at Alençon in order to keep open the necessary supply and retreat routes, and so avoid a catastrophe. Besides the Army, my report went also to the Army Groups. On the same day (10 August), the report was read in my presence to Field Marshal von Kluge at his Headquarters. Seventh Army agreed with my point of view.

In order to secure even the minimum amount of freedom of action, it was imperative to prop up, if possible by an offensive, the deep flank of Seventh Army and to evacuate the "finger" of the Seventh Army at Mortain. These necessities were clear. Armed Forces High Command (OKH) had, by its unrealistic illusions of an attack on Avranches, prevented the accomplishment of these objectives until now. Now, even the Armed Forces High Command could not close its ears to the necessity of making an immediate attack on the flank of the enemy advancing towards Alençon and Laigle and throw him back, and in this part, agreed with Kluge's proposal. On the contrary, it did not authorise quitting the "finger," but, as if hypnotized, kept to the thought of an assault on Avranches. Thereby, Hitler made it impossible for Seventh Army to put immediately at my disposal the Panzer divisions necessary. These half-measures had necessarily to lead to cstastrophe in case the enemy was acting the right way, i.e., quickly. He was. Overall measures taken at that time were "two days too late!"

Perhaps this would have been the right time for Field Marshal Kluge to act against Hitler's order to save the two armies (Seventh and Fifth Panzer). But after the 20 July Plot he was watched in such a sharp way that it would have been especially difficult for him. The result would simply have been his substitution by a more manageable tool.

V. Preparation for the Counterattack at Alençon.

1. *Time and forces:* For the counterattack at Alençon, the following units were allotted:
    a. LXXXI Corps (Kuntzen) with the remainder of 9 Pz. Div, the remnants of 708 Inf Div, one heavily battered security regiment, and parts of a parachute antitank regiment, the time of arrival of which could, however, not be awaited.

       These units could, therefore, not be taken into account for an attack. Excepting the parachute men, who were not yet at hand, nothing could be expected of these units even for defense.
    b. Beginning on 12 August, XLVII Pz. Corps (Funk), with 116. Pz. Div, which, with its front parts, was to arrive at Argentan on the 12 August; 1 SS-Pz. Div., or Leibstandarte, the foremost parts of which were to move into assembly position in the forest area north of Alençon; and 2. Pz. Div., assembly time and place as with the Leibstandarte.
    c. Beginning on 15 August, II SS-Pz. Corps (Bittrich), with 6 SS-Pz. Div and 9 SS-Pz. Div.

2. *Intention:* It was to be foreseen that the arrival of 11 SS-Pz. Corps could not be awaited. My intention was, therefore, to assemble XLVII Pz. Corps (Funk) in the forest north of Alençon. The movement was to be covered by 8 Pz. Div, and as soon as possible, probably in the evening on 14 August. The Pz. Corps had to attack the enemy flank either south or north of Alençon, depending on the development of the situation.

3. *Development of the situation at LXXXI Army Corps on 11 August. Loss of Alençon:* On 11 August, at about noon, my CofS and I arrived at the Headquarters of Corps Kuntzen (LXXXI) northeast of Alençon. Our Staff, so far as already formed, was also expected to arrive there. Kuntzen informed us that, since this morning, the weak 9 Pz. Div was being attacked by at least one armored division. He expected bad news also from his weak security detachments.

   Late in the afternoon, 9 Pz. Div reported that superior enemy forces had broken through. The remainder of the division was assembling itself at the edge of woods north of Alençon, and tried to keep the position there. The strength of the division was only about one battalion, one artillery battalion, and half a dozen tanks.

According to this, the enemy could be expected to arrive any moment at Corps Headquarters. Kuntzen gave orders for an immediate departure for the region east of Argentan. At the same time, tank artillery fire was heard at a very short distance, and enemy airplanes made any movement impossible. Enemy shell fire hit. Round about us smoke clouds were rising from burning cars. My Staff did not arrive.

At first, in the evening, we could break camp. A bakery company was taking defense position at Sées. On all streets, rear services flooded northwards.

I sent an officer to 116 Pz. Div. with orders to push to Sées at night and keep its position there. To the commander of an AAA regiment, who reported to me in order to get permission to retreat from Argentan, I gave the order to arrange defensive positions there and to hold them.

4. *Enemy attack on Argentan on 12 August:* As the center of gravity of my Panzer Group for the next few days lay at XLVII Pz. Corps, on the next morning we drove to Corps Headquarters Funk, which, having no information about the new situation, had established itself near Vieux Pont, 14 km southwest of Argentan. Funk had, however, already made contact with the remnants of 9 Pz. Div., and taken command over them in the morning. Parts of a reconnaissance detachment and parts of his signal battalion were covering the Headquarters at a distance. No report had yet arrived from 116 Pz. Div. Whether Sées was still in our hands was not known. The whole day enemy fire was heard from a short distance. Every moment the enemy might appear at the headquarters. Fighter-bombers, however, made the transfer of the headquarters impossible.

In the afternoon, at last, the report arrived. Parts of the 116 Pz. Div, without tanks (two battalions, two artillery battalion) were advancing towards Sées, but, owing to a tough resistance from the enemy, they made but slow progress. In the evening, another report reached Headquarters. According to this, parts of 116 Pz. Div had been destroyed by heavy artillery fire from massed enemy tanks. The enemy was forcing his way toward Argentan.

On the night, both of the Headquarters made a shift to the region of Chanedouil, 20 km west of Argentan. Notwithstanding the short distance (30 km), this move took six hours. It could be felt that the whole supply service for 1½ Armies was congested on the few roads between Falaise and Argentan. As the weather was good, for the most part, the columns were able to move only during the eight night hours. The large number of burned-out motor vehicles created many bottlenecks. In consequence, all the streets were congested, and the traffic was moving merely at a walking pace. The shifting of troops took several times longer than under normal conditions. The supply service was endangered.

The loss of Alençon deprived Seventh Army of its supply bases. It was now entirely dependent on Fifth Panzer Army. I instructed their QM on the 11 August to deliver gasoline and ammunition to the district south of Argentan for the Panzer attack.

At night, the remnants of 116 Pz. Div reached the outskirts of Argentan. They, together with the Antiaircraft Regiment, in a thin line on both sides of the town, held their positions, and the town, against heavy attacks by the enemy, and put several enemy tanks out of action.

A disabled and abandoned PzKpfw IV is inspected by US troops.

5. Fights in the Forest Area North of Alençon on 12 August

On 13 August, at noon, weak elements of 1 SS-Pz. Div. (Leibstandarte) had reached the forested area north of Alençon. Difficulties with the release and congestion of the roads led to the artillery arriving first without infantry protection, then the signal battalion, and, much later, the tanks, while the mass of the infantry did not arrive until the next day. Besides, most of the units were cut to pieces on the march because of traffic congestion during air raids. 2. Pz. Div arrived in better condition, but had at first only half of its forces. In spite of different routes, both divisions got mixed up at night. The commanders, pursued by the fighter-bombers, tried to get their units together. Many companies had not nearly reached their march objectives, but, on account of the incessant air attacks, had sought the nearest shelter. The news about the destruction of 9 Pz. Div had not gotten through to the lower units yet, and therefore they considered themselves more or less secure in the woods north of Alençon.

The enemy was now forcing his way right into this confusion. He went around the remnants of 9 Pz. Div. A crisis arose, and units of 2 Pz. Div. had to rescue units of 1 SS-Pz. Div., and vice-versa. The forest area north of Alençon was lost. From the region southeast of Argentan, the enemy was pressing westwards over the Orne. We succeeded in stopping him at the Cance brook. In the evening, 9 Pz. Div had but the strength of one company.

VI. Going Over to Defense (14 August)

At night from 13 to 14 [August], further units of the two divisions arrived, and we succeeded in building up a thin front. 1 SS-Pz. Div defended the line La Fête-Maci (exclusively) – Carrouges – Chahains, the 2 Pz. Div from there the west bank of Cance brook up to

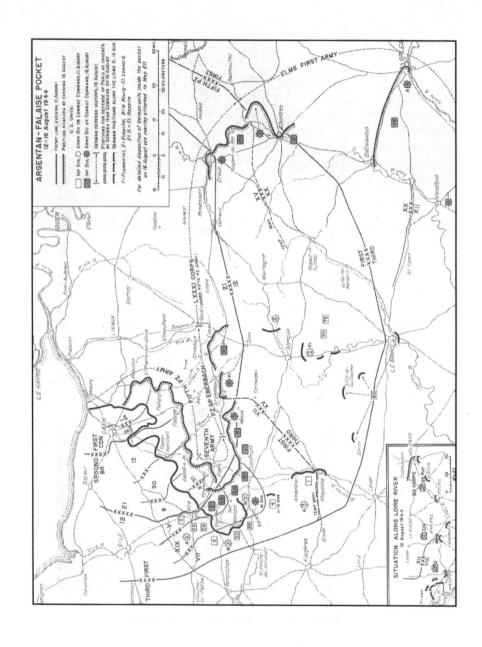

ARGENTAN–FALAISE POCKET
12–16 August 1944

Ecouché. There, it contacted 116 Pz. Div as before. II SS-Pz. Corps succeeded in arriving with stronger units on 16 August.

With the loss of Alençon and Sées, the situation had changed entirely. As the enemy stood close to Falaise in the north, the mouth of the encirclement had a width of only 30 km. The ammunition and fuel situation was dreadfully serious: for the supply of the 1½ Armies, only three roads were available at night time. In consequence of the lack of fuel, a number of tanks of I SS-Pz. Div had to be blown up. 9 Pz. Div was annihilated. In view of this situation, which I fully described in my report to Army Group, I stressed once again the necessity of an immediate and quick retreat on a large scale; otherwise, a complete collapse was unavoidable. Just at that time Panzer Group received by wireless an order from Hitler which, in broad terms, read as follows: "The attack ordered by me, southwardly past Alençon towards the east is to be effected under all conditions immediately as a preparation for an attack on Avranches." Thereupon, on 14 August, I sent my last special-missions staff officer to Army Group with the following report:

"Enemy attack with a presumed strength of two armored divisions and one infantry division. He has surprised 2 Pz. Div. and I SS-Pz. Div. (Leibstandarte) while assembling in the forest north of Alençon, and thrown them back to the line La Ferte – Carrouges – Cance brook, causing heavy losses to them. Parts of 116. Pz. Div. annihilated at Sées. Rest holds against heavy enemy attacks both sides Argentan. Panzer strengths: 1. SS-Pz. Div.—30; 2. Pz. Div.—25; 116 Pz. Div.—15. 9. Pz. Div still has company strength. Owing to fighter-bombers at day time and traffic congestion at night, fuel and ammunition situation very serious. Lack of fuel caused 1. SS-Pz. Div to blow up a number of tanks. Under flank protection, a quick withdrawal from encirclement of Seventh Army imperative in order to avoid catastrophe. Execution of order of Supreme Command first after bringing up II. SS-Pz. Corps as well as fuel and ammunition; this not possible before the 16 August. Success improbable."

At the same time, the officer had to report the condition of my Staff, and propose centralized command by Seventh Army. He arrived at the headquarters of Army Group B on 14 August, wounded, and delivered the report.

On 14 August, 1 SS-Pz. Div. (Leibstandarte) was attacked the whole day. Its parts were not all organized, and in the course of that day and 15 August it was slowly driven back. 2 Pz. Div held its sector. On both sides of Argentan, however, the enemy succeeded in penetrating in places along the thin line of the bleeding 116. Pz. Division. West of Argentan, the enemy pushed 2 km over the Orne and took Ecouché. East of Argentan, he penetrated into the Forêt de Gouffern and endangered Chambois.

The morale of the German troops in the west suffered at that time a blow from which it did not recover. The Atlantic Wall was for too long a period described by our propaganda as unconquerable, the invasion as a sure defeat for the enemy. For a long time, the soldier had been told of the coming of new arms, masses of new German aircraft, and submarines. And, instead of all this, he had now to wage a war of the poor man against an enemy who had everything in abundance, who was fresh, while the German soldier had already been engaged in hard fighting for five years, and, moreover, during the last two years had suffered only defeats. And at the shore he saw hundreds of enemy vessels; every day he saw hundreds of enemy aeroplanes flying to Germany, entirely undisturbed, and coming back again as from a parade, apparently without any losses; and he received from home news of towns destroyed. A glance at the map was sure to suggest doubt, even to the common soldier, as to whether he was commanded in a reasonable way. He had no time for thinking, but his feeling told him that this war could no longer be won. He felt himself betrayed. He no longer fought with a belief in victory and a reliance on his command, but only from a soldier's pride and for fear of defeat.

But not all of the soldiers had this sense for duty and this kind of pride. For the first time, not only Poles and Alsatians but even single Germans deserted to the enemy. The sinking of the soldier's spirit was even more evident in the "morale of the arms." Some tanks were left standing without being blown up, MGs were thrown away, guns were left lying, stragglers without arms were numerous. "Catch lines" in the rear of the front had to be inaugurated. Even the SS-was no exception to this rule. 1 SS-Pz. Division (Leibstandarte) has never before fought so miserably as at this time.

The fighting morale of German troops had cracked. I openly reported this to Field Marshal Model on 18 August at a meeting in Fontaine-l'Abbé (which Lt. Gen. von Gersdorff mentions in his work), just as I had done face to face with Kluge, because I considered this fact an important basis for all the decisions made by the High Command. Achievements like breaking out of the encirclement, and the counterattack by II SS-Pz. Corps on Trun, are therefore to be ranked very highly.

A US 81 mm mortar in action. This weapon was the US infantry battalion's "vest-pocket artillery." (US National Archives)

On 14 and 15 August, the situation as to fuel and ammunition remained equally bad as the fighter-bombers blew up the majority of fuel tank vehicles.

VII. Commitment of II SS-Pz. Corps near Argentan, 15– 16 August

As soon as the arrival of II SS-Pz. Corps was completed on 15 and 16 August, together with fuel for 20 to 50 km, Corps was immediately committed to relieve the desperate situation on both sides of Argentan. Despite the fact that the number of tanks of each division lay below 20, they succeeded in cleaning out the forest area east of Argentan. At that time, also, two projector brigades were allotted to me. They however, had almost no ammunition for their projectors, and could therefore be used as infantry forces. All divisions subordinated to me could at best be considered as regiments at that time. Also, their artillery had often only the strength of an artillery battalion. Officers and men were extremely tired and hungry.

Since 15 August, the Seventh Army CP lay in the immediate vicinity of my Staff. We were in personal contact daily. Our views on the situation coincided. The Seventh Army CP did much to keep traffic on the supply roads moving by segregating the horse-drawn vehicles, and by establishing one way traffic to and from the front. The results were poor. The orders could not get through in such a situation.

VIII. Field Marshal von Kluge's Last Visit (15–16 August)

On 15 August, I was visiting 116 Pz. Div in Pommainville [?]. There I received a wireless order to meet Field Marshal Kluge in Nécy. I waited three hours for him. He did not come.

In the evening, I received an order by radio from Army Group B, asking what I knew of the fate of Field Marshal von Kluge. Soon after that another radio inquiry came from Hitler's headquarters, with the same text. In reply to my answer, I received a second message from Hitler's HQ:

"Ascertain whereabouts Kluge. Report results hourly." The matter gave us much anxiety, but at midnight Kluge arrived at my CP. The fighter-bombers had shot up his car and his two radio stations. Afterwards, he got mixed up in the chaotic night traffic. Thus he had personally experienced the desperate situation of the rear service routes.

Only in the PW camp did I hear that these inquiries of Supreme Command were not prompted by an anxiety for the personal fate of Kluge, but by the suspicion he might have had a meeting with American officers in order to capitulate or surrender personally. Through investigations Hitler had made in the meantime, he had ascertained that Kluge had previous knowledge of the 20 July Bomb Plot.

Kluge discussed the situation with SS-General Hausser, Lt. Gen. Funk, and me, each in turn. Each of us told him that an attack with divisions now bled white, without air forces, and without a safe supply service, was unthinkable. Only a quick withdrawal from the encirclement could, perhaps, avoid a catastrophe. Kluge was now ready to give all orders for evacuation of the "finger," as we had proposed, but only after having communicated with Hitler's headquarters. Without its approval, he did not dare to make such a far-reaching decision. The people there, he said, lived in another world, without any idea of the actual situation here, as he knew from our reports and what he himself had experienced in the last 24 hours.

If and when, on 16 August, the order from CP Seventh Army for a quick withdrawal from the front was made, I do not remember now. Fifth Panzer Army was fighting at Falaise on that day. On the left flank of Seventh Army, we lost La Fête-Maci. The front had to be pushed back approximately to the line Le Grais – Rânes – Boucé.

In the night, I transferred my CP to the Staff of II SS-Pz. Corps in Montabard, north of Argentan. Staff of Seventh Army shifted to Nécy. The work of the Staff was disturbed by heavy artillery fire and air raids. The troops suffered hunger. Also, my Staff had had no bread for two days.

IX. Transfer of II SS-Pz. Corps
to Vimoutiers to Set as Army Group Reserve (17 August)

In the morning of the 17th, II. SS-Pz. Corps and the projector brigades received the order to proceed immediately to Lisieux as a reserve for Army Group. The fuel necessary for this move had arrived at night. The front gaps on both sides of Argentan, which had just been filled, were more than open again through the removal of Corps. I had nothing to close them.

After a few hours, new orders arrived for II SS-Pz. Corps. The enemy had taken Falaise, and Corps had, as soon as possible, to go into battle position near Vimoutiers, and to march by day, despite losses. As II SS-Pz. Div had lost all its big radio stations, it was difficult for Bittrich (Commanding General II SS-Pz. Corps) to transmit the new orders to his divisions. At last, he succeeded in doing so, and Corps was set to march to Vimoutiers at day time suffering heavy losses from fighter-bombers.

Late in the afternoon, when the whole Corps was on the way, and the Commanding General alone was still present, a third order came: "Enemy has broken through southeast of Falaise, pushing on Trun. II SS-Pz. Corps throws enemy back and holds Trun."

Can Bittrich still reach his divisional COs? The radio stations had been dismantled, and it was difficult to drive on the totally congested roads. Bittrich immediately set out personally in order to try to reach his divisional COs. At the same time, 116 Pz. Div reported that the enemy had overthrown the weak security detachments east of Argentan, which had replaced II SS-Pz. Div. and taken Le Bourg-St-Léonard, and that Chambois was impassable owing to heavy enemy artillery fire. The story was that Trun had been taken by British troops.

The gap for the Army's retreat had a breadth of only 10 km!

X. Conference with Field Marshal Model, 18 August

During the night, I received a wireless message stating that Field Marshal Model, who had relieved Kluge, would like to meet the Commanding Generals of both Armies and me next morning at 0900 hrs at Fifth Panzer Army headquarters in Fontaine-l'Abbé. The distance was 75 km. I needed from 1500 hrs until 2300 hrs for the trip, primarily because I got caught up in II SS-Panzer Corps' movements. We saw grievous pictures. Bittrich's attempt to reach his divisions and to lead them against Trun failed.

Every day I had, as often as possible, visited the divisions subordinated to me. I could, therefore, give Model a true picture of the situation – strengths, supply, morale—and did so.

Model's order was: "My intention is withdrawal behind the Seine. For this purpose, first we need a stiffening of the bottleneck at Trun and Argentan with Panzer divisions, in order to enable Seventh Army's infantry divisions to retreat." Subordinated to Seventh Army, I was to lead the Pz. Corps to the bottleneck. In the course of our conference, a report reached us that Trun was in the hands of British troops. Thereby the encirclement was practically completed.

Breaking Out of the Encirclement
I. Preparations for the Counterattack
by II SS-Pz. Corps on 18 and 19 August

Instead of SS-General Hausser, CofS of Seventh Army, Col. von Gersdorff was present at the conference. With him, we came to an agreement that I should immediately leave for the Staff of II SS-Pz. Corps near Meulles, in order to lead Corps to the combat area near Trun. The distance to Meulles was 35 km. I was, however, so often attacked by fighter-bombers and my car pierced through by bullets that I contrived to arrive at the Staff of II. SS-Pz. Corps at 2200 hrs. There I was informed that the British and American troops had met southeast of Trun, and had thus completed the encirclement of Seventh Army.

At the same time, Bittrich reported that his Corps was utterly torn asunder in consequence of night marches and air attacks. Until now, he could not contact any of his divisional staffs, but he knew that his troops had neither fuel, ammunition, food, nor signal equipment. He could not tell when Corps would again be ready for action.

I gave Bittrich the order to lead his Corps, as soon as possible, to the combat zone on both sides of Vimoutiers, and to be ready to attack the area southeast of Trun, in order to support the operations for breaking out of the encirclement. I then immediately proceeded at night to the Staff of Fifth Panzer Army, in order to have my decision confirmed, and to coordinate the attack of Corps with that of Seventh Army, and also in order to secure from Fifth Panzer Army, as soon as possible, the necessary supplies for II SS-Pz. Corps.

My decision was confirmed. The attack by II SS-Pz. Corps had to begin at night on 19/20 August. Seventh Army was, accordingly, informed by me through wireless, as were all Corps in the encirclement—insofar as they could be reached by radio.

On 19 August, in the afternoon, I visited Bittrich again. He still had no fuel, and had received very insufficient quantities of ammunition. Despite this, he expected to be ready for action in the evening. The fuel arrived only near morning. It took some hours before it was distributed and tanked. Army Group made haste, and on 20 August, at about 10 o'clock, the two divisions were ready to fall in. They were able to do it as a consequence of the bad weather, which hindered the actions of enemy air forces.

II. The Counterattack (20 August)

Both divisions had together only 20 tanks. One of the divisions possessed only one infantry battalion, the other had two. One road of advance was packed with burned-out vehicles to such an extent that the tanks had first to clear an alley before passing.

As far as I can remember, one combat group of the division advanced along the route from Vimoutiers to Trun, the other one along the Cam[em?]bert – St-Lambert road. At first, the advance made good progress. It came to a stop, however, in front of a range of hills (258 south of Les Champeaux, 240 at Ecorches, 262 north of Coudehard). In the afternoon, the range of hills was taken. After that, the advance made practically no more progress. In spite of this, a gap was forced in the encirclement, and the first 2,000 men joined the division, getting out of the encirclement.

III. The Result

During the rest of the day, and the whole night, soldiers with and without arms were streaming out of the encirclement. Altogether, about 50 guns and 25 tanks might also have got out.

The achievement of the units forcing the "breakthrough" was a big one. Nevertheless, as a unit, they could be used no more. Commander Seventh Army, Commander 1 SS-Pz. Div. (Leibstandarte), and other generals were wounded. A number of generals were killed in action; others were captured as PWs. Almost the whole armament of the Army—tanks, guns, radio stations, motor vehicles, substantial parts of trains and supplies—was lost. Even the number of rescued machine guns was insignificant.

The number of men who got out of the encirclement, after it was closed, can be estimated at about 20,000, although the Allied forces reported the number of prisoners taken at 50,000. It is very difficult to estimate the number of men killed in action. Having no actual data at hand, I should estimate their number for the period of 10–22 August at 20,000.

Rallying points for all encirclement divisions were fixed, where potatoes and most supplies were kept ready. Bread could not be procured. These points, however, did not correspond with those assigned by Seventh Army, so nothing remained but to arrange new rallying points behind the Seine, and, at the Seine, points for guiding, ration supplies, making payments, and distributing clothing.

On 21 August, at noon, when the arrival of soldiers from the encirclement had stopped entirely, and when the pressure of the American-British troops on II SS-Pz. Corps became stronger, I considered the task of Corps fulfilled.

The retreat to and over the Seine commenced.

PART SIX

The US XV Corps moved on Alençon and Argentan on the 12–13 August. Its spearhead, the French 2nd Armored Division, seized the bridges over the Sarthe in a night attack on 12 August. Hitler still wanted a counterattack, but the movement was putting more forces into potential encirclement. The British Second Army, driving from the northwest, accelerated German movement eastward. The Germans were building up the shoulders of the emerging Falaise Gap by 13 August, not fleeing east. Fifth Panzer Army first started to look towards escape early on 13 August. The Germans had started on 11 August to withdraw, to some extent, their salient at Mortain, but Hitler was still insisting on another attack toward Avranches.

XV Corps (Third Army) was committed to action near Avranches, between VIII Corps (Third Army, clearing Brittany) and VII Corps (First Army, expecting orders to advance east from Avranches). XV Corps, already around the German left flank, started the the encircling maneuver eastward to the Seine. With the Canadians attacking toward Falaise, XV Corps secured Alençon on 12 August. Patton had set the Corps objective at the Army Group boundary north of Alençon and just south of Argentan. XV Corps wanted to continue its advance to Alençon and the north of Argentan. The Canadians were advancing slowly, while XV Corps had moved rapidly. At first, Patton sent orders to reach Falaise and make contact with the Canadians.

On 12 August, terrain and roadspace concerns hindered XV Corps' chance to exploit its tactical success gained by a rapid advance. The Forêt d'Ecouves, a large wooded area just south of Argentan, was to be bypassed by both of that Corps' spearhead armored divisions, the French 2 Armored Division to bypass the forest on the left (west), and the US 5 Armored Division to drive around the eastern edge. Fearing ambushes by tank-killer teams in the woods, the French changed routes and blocked 5 Armored's advance for six hours during the afternoon of 12 August. Eberbach used that time to hastily assemble a coherent defense by the morning of 13 August. Then XV Corps got a taste of what the British and Canadians had been fighting since D-Day.

Attacking toward Argentan on the morning of 13 August, XV Corps struck skillful resistance and was halted. It then received a still-controversial order: the advance halted temporarily, Bradley having forbidden further movement north to Falaise. Hitler had ordered an attack against the deep left flank of XV Corps. Bradley, wth "Ultra" decrypts, was concerned about their potential for a counterattack. The counterattack never took place, and US VII Corps came up and filled the gap on XV Corps' flank. Bradley was "less interested in encirclement than in destruction," in the words of historian Martin Blumenson. The destruction would be carried out by artillery and airpower.

XV Corps was to hold in place, 25 miles south of the Canadian spearheads. Montgomery believed that the Canadians would close the gap first, but they did not take Falaise until 16 August, and a fifteen-mile gap still remained between it and the US XV Corps, through which the Germans were withdrawing. Allied intelligence thought that most German forces had already withdrawn, but this was not the case.

To the south, the US XII and XX Corps (Third Army) were assembling near Le Mans, preparing to advance on Chartres and Orléans and threatening Paris and its key river crossings. They moved east on 14 August, followed by XIX Corps, heading to the Seine. There was little resistance. Orléans and Dreux were liberated on 16 August, and Chartres saw fighting before being liberated on 18 August.

On 14 August, Hitler conceded that withdrawal from the Mortain salient was necessary, and that the renewed attack toward Avranches was impossible. The invasion of southern France occurred on 15 August, and Hitler now realized that the German position in France was indefensible. On 16 August, the Germans began to organize a withdrawal through the "Falaise Gap." Hitler was told by von Kluge that withdrawal was the only option. He raged, sent Model to replace von Kluge, and suspected von Kluge of seeking to negotiate with the Allies; von Kluge committed suicide rather than face a Nazi "people's court." The withdrawal, started that evening, increased pressure on US forces around Argentan, and the German maneuver through the Falaise Gap and out of the pocket proved to be well-organized and well-executed.

On 14 August, as Montgomery had had a full day to order XV Corps across the Army Group boundary and had not done so, Bradley, at Patton's urgings (and without consulting Montgomery), held part of XV Corps at Argentan and sent part east toward Dreux and the Seine, crossing it at Mantes-Gassicourt during the night of 19 August. An XV Corps armored division moved downstream from Mantes-Gassicourt on the left bank of the Seine, to drive the Germans from crossing sites. First Army's XIX Corps joined this effort to deny the Germans easy crossings over the Seine.

A final attack to close the Gap did not get under way until 18 August, with US and Polish forces (the latter fighting as part of the Canadian First Army) linking up the next day. The US V Corps took over the XV Corps divisions that had been held at Argentan and used these to drive north.

On 20 August, the Gap was closed, with US forces already crossing the Seine. By not closing the Gap earlier, the Allies were able to reach the Seine more quickly and encircle the Germans at less cost. On 21 August the Falaise pocket was finally sealed. Over 50,000 German troops had been captured, 10,000 had been killed, and 313 tanks had been lost.

Chapter 11

The Battle of the Falaise – Argentan Pocket 12–21 August

by Generalmajor Rudolf-Christoph Freiherr von Gersdorff
Translated by H. Heitman (B-727)

A. Original Situation

The battles commencing on 12 August in which Army Group B was involved were dictated by the efforts to escape encirclement by the Allied armies, or to fight free the threatened flanks. To this end, Fifth Panzer Army fought a purely defensive battle to frustrate the efforts of the British to effect a breakthrough, while Seventh Army simultaneously fought on the defensive against the US First Army and, employing its Panzer units, attempted to defeat the US Third Army in mobile combat. Both attempts failed as a result of technical inferiority on the ground and in the air, deficient supply services, and the effects of tactical errors of the German Command. Even while this battle was in progress, the High Command could not decide to initiate a retirement to at least behind the Seine river, and therefore a battle of extermination developed west of the Seine which decisively affected the entire battle for France and the outcome of the whole war.

The decision taken on 11 August by OB West (Generalfeldmarschall von Kluge) to send the newly constituted Panzer Group Eberbach into offensive action against the American Army under Gen. Patton, advancing on Alençon and to the east, was subsequently approved by Adolf Hitler, but with the following rider (in verbatim): "The idea of the attack on Avranches is to be adhered to!" This command precluded any voluntary abandonment of the envisaged attack basis—the area between Sourdeval, Mortain and Domfront—and consequently made it impossible to contract the line of defense against the British Second and US First Armies. The Falaise Pocket was the direct outcome of this decision.

In the course of the discussion which took place on 11 August between Generalfeldmarschall von Kluge, Generaloberst Hausser and General der Panzertruppen Eberbach, the decisive importance of the supply basis in the Alençon – Chartres area for the conduct of battle by Seventh Army and Panzer Group had again been stressed. The loss of the stockpiles in this area set a seal on all that happened in the ensuing period. The shortage of ammunition and fuel was so acute that its effect on the conduct of battle was momentous.

On 11 August, Generalfeldmarschall von Kluge had given orders that the now independent Panzer Group Eberbach was to assemble in all haste in the area northwest and north of Alençon (Forest d'Ecouves), in order to drive into the west flank of the enemy, who was advancing north, to beat him, and thereby to fight free the deep southern flank of Army Group B. For this purpose, Seventh Army was to assign Panzer Group (Panzer Army) the following forces: XLVII Pz. Corps with 2, 116, and 1 SS-Pz. Divs, Panther Bn of

9 Pz. Div., Mortar Bdes (Werferbrigaden) 8 and 9 immediately, and, further, LXXXI Inf. Corps with 9 Pz. Div., Pz. Lehr Div., and 708 Inf. Div. Further forces from LVIII Pz. Corps and from II SS-Pz. Corps were also later to pass under the command of Panzer Group, as circumstances permitted. Of the XLVII Pz. Corps forces, to begin with only 116 Pz. Div., which had already been pulled out of the front, was available; only elements of the Artillery Regt and of the Panzer Regt of this division had to remain in position to maintain coverage to the north until early morning on 12 August. All other units had as yet to be pulled out of the front; this was only possible if a partial retirement took place. Such retirement was also essential in order to restore a connected front on the right wing of Seventh Army, and in order to take on what had hitherto been the attack front, a line in the terrain more suited to the defense. Apart from the command to adhere to the idea of an attack on Avranches, the rear and flank of the new Operation "Alençon" had to be protected against heavy attacks by the British and by the US First Army.

Seventh Army therefore ordered a withdrawal during the night 11/12 August to the line Hill 275 – La Lande-Vaumont – Hill 338 (1 km east of Vengeons) – west of Sourdeval – road bend 2 km south by southwest of Sourdeval – Hill 314 – Hill 293 – southern fringe of the de Mortain forest. In the course of this movement, 1 SS-Pz. Div. and the Mortar Bde were to be pulled out to begin with, and preparations made to pull out the two Panzer divisions. Fifth Panzer Army at the same time ordered the withdrawal of II SS-Pz. Corps, which formed its left wing, in order to straighten out the front. The road junction 4 km east of Viessoix was the new point of contact between the two armies. 116 Pz. Div. ordered that all available elements were to move into the eastern section of the d'Ecouves forest, north of Alençon, during the night 11/12 August, for employment by Panzer Group Eberbach.

B. Assessment of Enemy Situation

As compared with their strengths at the commencement of the campaign in northern France, on 25 July 1944 the British invasion army had been increased by two armored task forces, and the American by one infantry and four armored divisions.

Army Group B, on the other hand, had received one Panzer division (the 9th) and eight infantry divisions (84, 85, 89, 271, 272 331, 363, and 708). Since 24 July however, four infantry divisions (91, 243, 275, and 352), 5 Fallschirm Jaeger (Parachute Infantry) Div., and 17 SS-Pz. Gren. Div. had been totally annihilated, while three Panzer divisions (Pz. Lehr, 9, and 21) and three infantry divisions (326, 353, and 708) had been shattered so much that they could scarcely be reckoned with as units. The increase by nine major units was thus offset by the loss of 10–12 major units.

Hence, in making comparisons, one must consider that the Allies had been reinforced by seven divisions, of which five were armored divisions, while the strength of the Germans had diminished by two to three units. In actual fact, the strength ratio was in even greater measure unfavorable, as all German units had suffered heavy losses which could not be replaced from reserves, whereas the Allies' superiority had increased considerably. This comparison made it clear that the ratio of strength had changed materially to the disadvantage of the Germans, which fact would necessarily make itself more acutely felt in the battles now commencing in open terrain. Even the arrival of the units moving forward could bring about no material change in this unfavorable ratio of strengths. These units were 6 Para. Inf., 17 and 18 Lw Field Divs, and 48, 49, and 344 Inf. Divs.

On the British front, there were two defined points of main effort, on the Caen–Falaise road and on the right wing, both of which points were recognizable by the presence at each of them of two armored task forces. Strategically seen, the most dangerous sector was still that southeast of Caen. Even though comparatively fresh divisions (including 85 and 89 Inf. Divs) had been sent into position here, the inferiority of these purely infantry divisions as compared with the highly mobile British and Canadian forces was clearly obvious. The breakthrough aimed at by the Allied Command toward Falaise menaced the main body of Army Group B, and without doubt was coordinated with the offensive launched by the US Third Army toward the north.

On the front held by Seventh Army, the American point of main effort had shifted gradually to the south flank. Nevertheless, the US 7 Inf. and 2 Armored Divs, attacking on the bend in the German line, had a crushing superiority over the four battle-worn German infantry divisions which, practically speaking, were to hold this front alone. It therefore seemed impossible to make *all* Panzer units available to Panzer Group Eberbach for Operation "Alençon."

Without the US divisions tied up in Brittany and on the Loire, four enemy infantry divisions (1, 79, 80, and 90) and two armored divisions (French 2 Div, and 5 Div.) had to be reckoned with on Army Group's south flank. At the time, the US 7 Armored Div. had

One of the advantages enjoyed by the Allied armies in Normandy was the direct air evacuation of casualties—as here, in a C-47 of the US Army Air Forces. (US National Archives)

not yet been identified. Against these six enemy units, to begin with six German units (1 SS, 2 SS, 2, 116, and remnants of 9, and Pz. Lehr Div.) could be committed, and it was hoped that, later, further forces (II SS-Pz. Corps, 6 Para. Inf., 17 Lw Field, 344, and remnants of 331 Inf. Divs) could be brought forward to Panzer Group Eberbach, in order to gain a superiority of strength in the open battlefield to be expected on the south flank.

However, these calculations were based on the assumption that time would be gained through the enemy Command acting too hesitantly—in other words, not enough allowance being made for the inferior mobility of the German units. Whereas the chief objective of the American command was clearly defined as the thrust to the north, aiming at the envelopment of considerable German forces, the continued advance of enemy forces to the east was regarded as the lesser strategic threat. It seemed that the rapid capture of Paris, by surprise, was the immediate and restricted objective of the enemy Command,—which would, naturally, have been of essential importance from a psychological and political point of view. As Seventh Army and Panzer Group Eberbach could not possibly control this area strategically, Headquarters First Army were set up there on the left wing of Army Group B.

C. Seventh Army 12 August Situation Report

Resulting from these deliberations, Army on 12 August submitted the following assessment of the situation to Army Group:*

"In terms of the new directive, Seventh Army has the mission of holding an assembly area for the future thrust to the coast. Apart from this, the execution of its mission by Panzer Group Eberbach—namely to fight to free the rear and flank of the Army—depends upon the front of Fifth Panzer Army and Seventh Army being held. As further Panzer units are to be pulled out, this task is to be accomplished by Seventh Army with four battered infantry divisions. Opposing this thinly manned front, there are five enemy infantry divisions and three and one-half enemy armored divisions.† Owing to continuous attacks by these enemy forces, our own forces are becoming weaker and weaker day by day. Furthermore, there are at least three enemy infantry divisions on our weakly protected south flank, which must be expected to attack if the operation conducted by Panzer Group Eberbach should take effect.

"In these circumstances, it appears essential that either Seventh Army be reinforced with infantry units and antitank weapons for its mission, on which the successful execution of the entire operation hinges, or the salient in the front jutting to the west be abandoned and a new front established in the area southwest of Falaise. The reduction of length on the front which would be achieved by this measure would make it possible to reduce the width of sectors and to reinforce the weak covering forces south of Domfront. In comparison, the disadvantages resulting from the abandonment of valuable terrain would appear of less importance. Until such time as the Panzer Group shall be ready to launch a thrust toward the coast, it appears of greater importance to maintain a final and secure front in the general

---

* From *War Diary* of the Seventh Army, Document VI: Phone Calls and Conversations (re-translated from English).
† "This includes the British units on the extreme right wing of the Army."—Remark by author.

line of Falaise to Flers to Domfront and southward for the purposes of assembly, than to hold the present front and constantly have to reckon with its collapse and to expect a new breakthrough in the Domfront area and south thereof."

It was quite clear to Seventh Army that even this proposed partial withdrawal only represented a half-measure, as compared with the operational proposal unofficially submitted to Army Group suggesting a retirement across the Seine river. However, the Army had to take into consideration the order given by Supreme Command that the idea (or plan) of attack be adhered to.

D. Seventh Army, 12–13 August

II FS Jg. Corps had manned its new MLR according to schedule, but had only been able to establish loose contact with adjacent units. Contact at the seam with Army, particularly, gave rise to difficulties daily. The boundary was always fixed by Army Group, and directly between the armies, but in practice it was never maintained. Heavy artillery fire and intense activity by low-flying planes was kept up on the Corps front during 12 August, without the enemy launching any major attacks.

On the other hand, he continued his attacks against the new front of LXXXIV Inf. Corps with undiminished vigor. Again, the main pressure was southeast of Vire, where the enemy attacked on the front held by 363 Inf. Div. along the road to Tinchebray and on either side of La Lande-Vaumont after several hours of preparatory artillery fire. The enemy succeeded in effecting a penetration 4 km deep in the direction of Truttemer-la-Grand. All Corps reserves were made available to 363 Inf. Div. to seal off this penetration, but they remained too weak for a possible counterattack for the purpose of clearing up the penetration.

353 Inf. Div. also failed to prevent a number of penetrations. There, the enemy attacked in the area [Trouville-?] La Haule – Vengeons and was able to gain terrain locally, which was retaken in part in counterattacks.

Enemy attacks were less vigorous on the 84 Infantry Div. front. It now became increasingly clear that the US First Army was attempting to break into the German front salient on its flanks southeast of Vire, and in the Domfront area, while refraining from frontal action. During the afternoon of 12 August, XLVII Pz. Corps handed over its sector to 2 Pz. Div. and moved to its new area north of Alençon. The entire 1 SS-Pz. Div. had been pulled out during the night and was ready for departure. Its departure was delayed owing to the lack of fuel. Though enemy pressure was relaxing in this sector, it was evident that only a renewed contraction of the front could make it possible to pull out 2 Pz. Div. in the following night.

The enemy had been quick to follow up the retirement of LVIII Pz. Corps to the hills east of Mortain, but did not attack 2 SS-Pz. Div. on that day, restricting himself, rather, to artillery fire. However, starting at 0730 hrs, he resumed his heavy attacks against 10 SS-Pz. Div., but these attacks were successfully repulsed. It was of interest to note that the enemy blasted the bridge spanning the La Varenne, on the Barenton–Domfort road, 800 meters west of Rouelle. This proved that the US First Army apparently had no further major attack objectives direct to the east. Apparently by means of attacks against the flanks of the German salient in the front, it intended cutting out slices, much as one would cut a cake. The Army therefore proposed withdrawal to the line Mont de Cerisy (7 km northwest of Flers) – Mont Crespin – Hill 313 – Hill 304 – Larchamp – Hill 328 – Hill 251 – Hill 212 (northwest of Domfront), whereby it could escape the pincer movement of the enemy and pull out further Panzer forces for Panzer Group Eberbach.

However, these proposals of Seventh Army were rejected, or a decision was deferred. In this connection, the enormous distance separating Supreme Command in East Prussia from what was happening in Normandy proved fatal, as all decisions arrived too late in spite of modern means of communication.

Withdrawal during the night of 12/13 August to the line Coquard [?] (course of line to this point to remain as hitherto) – St-Sauveur-de-Chaulieu [?] – St Martin-de-Chaulieu [?] – Placitre [?] – ridge south of Lonlay-l'Abbaye – Domfront was approved, and orders given that, in the course of this withdrawal, 2 Pz. Div. be pulled out. The boundary between LXXXIV Inf. Corps and LVIII Pz. Corps was extended in the line Ger – Chanu (LVIII responsible for the localities). Army Group ordered the boundary between Seventh Army and Panzer Group Eberbach be fixed in a line La Ferté-Macé – Lassay [Lessay? Lassy?] (Seventh Army responsible for the localities). Thus, those elements positioned in the Domfront area (Reconnaissance Bn of 9 Pz. Div., Engineer Bn of 5 Para. Inf. Div. and one alarm battalion), and also 708 Inf. Div., again came under the command of Seventh Army, which in turn assigned them to LVIII Pz. Corps.

As from 12 August two factors made themselves increasingly felt:

1. *Signal Communication*, which in ever-increasing measure failed. The majority of the telegraph and telephone lines to the rear followed the course via Le Mans and Alençon. Following the loss of these localities, only a few lines remained available, which were heavily overloaded. The lines to the front were continuously interrupted by artillery fire and low-flying planes. Radio communication suffered from the fact that, in the meanwhile, numerous radio stations had failed (a result of low-level air attacks, and technical deficiencies).

2. *Supplies* constituted the great problem following the loss of the Alençon area. For supply servicing, Seventh Army and Panzer Group Eberbach were assigned to Fifth Panzer Army. Supply Administration Staff Group of Seventh Army assigned a liaison staff to Fifth Panzer Army.

However, the limited supplies of the Fifth Panzer Army could by no means meet the demands of all three armies, and, quite naturally, it first satisfied its own needs before passing on anything to the other Armies. Furthermore, supply lines did not function smoothly, and the supply routes were far longer, so that the supply columns were no longer able to complete the supply trips in one night; sometimes these columns, not having been informed in time about rapid developments in the situation, wandered around in the rear area or ran up against the enemy. High losses in both vehicles and supplies resulted, and such losses were further aggravated by the increasing activity of low-flying planes.

So far as food supplies were concerned, these circumstances were not so significant, as the troops had adequate supplies, but the lack of fuel and ammunition often led to serious crises. When it became apparent that the loss of the Alençon area could not be averted, Seventh Army employed all available transport space to ship the greatest possible quantity of supplies to the troops before the enemy captured the dumps, but this measure had only been partially successful owing to the general confusion brought about by developments in the situation, as well as by low-flying planes and the rapid advance of enemy tanks.

On 13 August, the US First Army had resumed its offensive, by which II Para. Inf. Corps was only affected on its extreme left wing.

On the other hand, the situation on the right wing of LXXXIV Inf. Corps became exceedingly critical. In the sector held by 363 Inf. Div., the Field Replacement Battalion which had perforce to be employed as a full battalion was overrun in its positions northeast of Truttemer-le-Grand. The enemy penetrated deeply, and succeeded in taking Truttemer-le-Petit. Using all reserves, counterattacks were launched which led to bitter fighting. The small village of Le Fay changed hands three times, and finally remained occupied by the enemy. In the evening, it was possible to seal off the enemy at the line Gd. Beursigny [?] (on the Vire–Tinchebray road) – Truttemer-le-Petit – Hill 367. 353 Inf. Div. had, meanwhile, been reinforced by 331 Inf. Div., and, broadly speaking, was again able to hold the MLR on this day.

During the lull on the left wing of Corps, 2 Pz. Div. had been pulled out and relieved by 84 Inf. Div. in the course of the withdrawal to the east, and during the night elements of it had moved off to their new sphere under Panzer Group Eberbach.

West of Domfront, on LVIII Panzer Corps' front, the enemy continued to attack at his point of main effort. Elements of the US 30 Inf. Div. and 3 Armored Div. had been identified there. 10 SS-Pz. Div., which had only had the strength of a Kampfgruppe (combat group) since it was first sent into action here, was unable to prevent a deep penetration on a front 1 km wide south and southwest of Lonlay-l'Abbaye.

Seventh Army was unable to remedy the situation, having no further reserves available. By a local withdrawal, it was possible to seal off the penetration. In agreement with the right wing of LXXXI Inf. Corps, the left wing of Corps had on 12 August been withdrawn to the Domfront–Alençon road. The enemy penetration beyond this road, effected by elements of the US 1 Inf. Div. at Chapelle Moche [?] and Couterne, rendered the situation most critical for the southern flank of the Army, which was vainly waiting for the effects of the attack launched by Panzer Group Eberbach to make themselves felt. It was not possible to establish contact with 708 Inf. Div., which had returned to the command of the Army. Evidently the division, which was almost completely immobile, had been scattered in the struggle against the numerically superior and highly mobile enemy.

To begin with, the Reconnaissance Bn of 9 Pz. Div. alone had to take over the protection of the south flank of the Army in mobile action. Army Group demanded of Seventh Army that 2 and 10 SS-Pz. Divs be pulled out in the following night, but was not able to sanction any substantial withdrawals. In view of the situation at the left wing, Seventh Army had to refuse detaching both divisions simultaneously. Even the pulling out of only one division— 2 SS-Pz. Div.—was only possible if a limited withdrawal movement be carried out on the left wing. Owing to the deficient communication system, which permitted only radio messages, Seventh Army therefore, on its own initiative, ordered LVIII Pz. Corps to withdraw behind the Egrenne sector, at the same time pulling out 2 SS-Pz. Div. LXXXIV Inf. Corps had to remain in its MLR, which had been established in combat.

No communication existed with Panzer Group Eberbach, so Seventh Army was not informed as to the situation there. Actually, there had since 12 August been a wide gap in the area of La Ferté-Macé, which was practically without any protection. Here, the enemy missed a great opportunity by only advancing hesitatingly to the north on 14 August, instead of quickly exploiting the gap in the front.

E. Panzer Group Eberbach, 12–13 August

Marching in two groups, 116 Pz. Div. (new Commander: Oberst Gerhard Mueller) during the night 11/12 August had been the first unit of the Panzer Group to move into the new zone of action. The northern group (reinforced Gren. Regt 60) had been sent in via Sourdeval – Tinchebray – Flers – Briouze – Ecouché – Mortrée to Sées, the southern group (reinforced Pz. Gren. Regt 156) moving along the southern parallel road via Flers – Messei – St-Gervais – La Ferté-Macé – Carrouges to La Ferrière-Béchet. The other units committed, Pz. Regt 16 and one artillery battalion, were to follow up the northern group by day, moving in loose formation. Orders for the first movements were issued by Gen. Eberbach from the new command post of LXXXI Inf. Corps in Château d'Almeneches, 9 km southeast of Argentan.

Meanwhile, LXXXI Inf. Corps' position had become extremely critical. On the right wing, 708 Inf. Div., which had in the meantime been heavily battered, had become so inferior to the enemy that one could no longer speak of any defense existing there. Separate Kampfgruppen (combat groups) of the division were fighting or their own, and endeavoring to fight their way through to the north. In the course of these actions, the bulk of the division was captured. In the fulfillment of the particularly difficult mission assigned this division, the lack of experience and the poor condition of the division had naturally made themselves particularly felt. Remnants of the division assembled on 14 August in the Faverolles area, 8 km north-northeast of La Ferté-Macé.*

On 12 August, the Pz. Lehr Div. was in the line Pré-en-Pail – Ormain [?] – St-Denis-sur-Sarthon along the south fringes of the Forêt de Multonne. 9 Pz. Div., adjacent to the left, had been completely annihilated by the superior enemy. Remnants fought their way back northward, and some to the northeast. Alençon was lost, as no forces were available to hold it. Contact with the security detachments of 352 Inf. Div. had been lost; they were now fighting in the zone of the First Army, newly committed by Army Group in the area west of Paris.

East of Alençon, the enemy continued his irresistible advance to the north, and reached Sées on 12 August, there running into the elements of 116 Pz. Div., ordered to that area by Gen. Eberbach. Whereas the northern group from this division was still to the rear on account of the air situation and bad road conditions, the southern group had already reached the forest 3 km west of Sées at 0900 hrs, and had been committed from there to defend Sées. Having no antitank weapons—and no adequate artillery support could be provided on

---

* Details are lacking as no reports on 708 Inf. Div. are available.

account of the hasty commitment—the combat group was beaten by the enemy and scattered to such an extent that it could not be employed in combat for the next few days.

Meanwhile, LXXXI Inf. Corps had sent in the divisional reserve of Pz. Lehr Div., consisting of one engineer battalion and eight tanks, to attack the east flank of the enemy armored forces which were continuing their advance on Argentan via Mortrée. Taken in conjunction with the delaying actions fought by the elements of 116 Pz. Div. along the road Mortrée–Argentan road, this thrust successfully brought the enemy advance on Argentan to a standstill. Chiefly, 116 Pz. Div., in the course of this action, committed one artillery battalion and a number of tanks just returned from repair. As a result of the French 2 Armored Div. being thus delayed, the time required for assembly of 116 Pz. Div. was gained. The Panzer Regiment arrived in the afternoon, having lost 40% of its strength while moving forward in daylight, as a result of action by enemy low-flying planes. Pz. Gren. Regt 60 did not reach the Loucé area (2 km southeast of Ecouché) before nearly 1400 hrs. The foremost battalion was already committed west of the Argentan–Mortrée road, but had to withdraw to Ecouché in the face of heavy enemy pressure. Owing to the turbulent course of events, the division had become thoroughly mixed up and was fighting in separate groups.

In the evening, the division reassembled on either side of Argentan. Ecouché seemed to have been lost. An advance by the enemy on Montgaroult (3 km north of Ecouché) was repelled by a motorcycle platoon from Pz. Gren. Regt 60. Argentan itself was held by weak security detachments, including three Panzer and one Panzer infantry detachment, which, however, it was possible to reinforce considerably during the night. Here, evidently, the enemy had lost the opportunity on 12 August of taking the important center, Argentan, in a dashing surprise attack.

Advance elements of 1 SS-Pz. Div. having arrived on 12 August in the area of Carrouges, Pz. Lehr Div. was ordered to hand over its sector to 708 Inf. Div., and to move via Putanges [-Pont-Ecrepin] to the area east of Argentan, in order to position itself adjacent to 116 Pz. Div., to protect Army Group's deep flank against the enemy advancing to the north from Mamers. The division left I Pz. Gren. Bn of Pz. Gren. Regt 906 and six tanks in the positions west of Alençon, there to await the arrival of sizable units of 1 SS-Pz. Div. Assuming wrongly that the assembly area would be secured, this division had placed at the head of its marching column units that were not combat-efficient, such as the Reconnaissance Battalion. The main body of the division did not reach the Fromentel [?] area on the Flers–Argentan road before early morning on 13 August. Panzer Group Eberbach had set up its command post 2 km south of Vieux [-Pont?] (9 km north of Carrouges).

In the evening of 12 August, the Commander of 2 Pz. Div. had reached Les Noes [Noës?] (3 km northeast of Carrouges), traveling ahead of his division, which was pulled out in the same night. The advance units (Reconnaissance Bn) could be expected early on 13 August, the main body of the division only during the day or early on 14 August. Thus, in the evening of 12 August, Panzer Group was in a tight spot. Under enemy observation, it had to assemble and concentrate, and therefore had, perforce, to take up defensive positions to start with.

Developments in the situation on 13 August definitely put an end to all ideas of an offensive operation by Panzer Group Eberbach.

On the inadequately protected Alençon–Carrouges road, the enemy advanced, and, after overcoming weak resistance, was able to penetrate into Carrouges. Simultaneously, the remnants of 708 Inf. Div. were utterly beaten by the US 1 Inf. Div. so that the entire Carrouges–La Ferté area lacked cover. On a broad front, the enemy crossed the Domfront–Alençon road. Even though it be true that shortage of fuel had delayed its movements, the actual reason for the failure of 1 SS-Pz. Div. (with its main body not yet being ready for action) must be sought in the inadequate and inexperienced commander.

2 Pz. Div., pulled out 24 hours later, had concentrated in its new area almost at the same time as 1 SS-Pz. Div. As the first unit, the Reconnaissance Bn of 2 Pz. Div. had arrived early on 13 August at St-Martin-des-Landes (2 km southeast of Carrouges), but had been too weak alone to hold up the thrust on Carrouges, the more so as the enemy had advanced simultaneously from Sées and Montrée, strongly supported by low-flying planes. At 1600 hrs, Le Menil-Soulleur [Le Ménil-Scelleur?], La Drutière [?], Les Loges and St-Sauveur-de-Carrouges were reported occupied by the enemy. Hence, the Staff of 2 Pz. Div. was encircled in Les Noës. A number of unit commanders of the division, who had gone on ahead there, drove right into the enemy. At 2000 hrs, Radio Calais reported the capture of Gen. Frhr von Luettwitz, the Commander of the division; nevertheless, during the night, he, together with his entire Staff, was able to make his way back during the night to Ranes through Le Menil-Soulleur, which, surprisingly enough, was again clear of the enemy.

In these circumstances, Panzer Group had no choice other than to first establish a defense front adjacent to 116 Pz. Div. Therefore, 2 Pz. Div. was ordered to fight through to Ecouché in order to establish contact with 116 Pz. Div., and to man a defense line along L'Udon creek south of Ecouché. Adjacent to them, 1 SS-Pz. Div., swinging south of Rânes to the southwest, was to establish a front and seek contact with the left wing of Seventh Army. On 13 August, XLVII Pz. Corps assumed command over the three Panzer divisions. Both Corps and Panzer Group had set up command posts in the vicinity of Fromentel.

During the night, 116 Pz. Div. had been able to bring up quite sizeable reinforcements. There were the newly assigned II/Pz. Regt 33 of 9 Pz. Div., together with 35 Panzers (Mark V), which happened to be on their way through Argentan, and one flak (antiaircraft) assault regiment (Commander: Oberst Roehler), with three light 20 mm and one heavy 88 mm battalions. What was most important was that, with the use of the Panzer battalion and one light flak battalion, it was possible to provide adequate protection for Argentan, and thus to save this important center from the enemy at the last moment. On 13 August, the division succeeded in reorganizing its units, which had become mixed up. The enemy launched reconnaissance attacks on the division front, and these attacks were repelled. It seemed that he was closing up from the rear, and concentrating for a renewed attack on Falaise. The flak regiment went into action against the particularly vigorous activity of low-flying planes on both sides of the Orne. In the afternoon, Gen. Eberbach, from the divisional command post at Pommainville [?], gave orders to stage an attack on 14 August with the restricted objective of preparing to expand the Argentan bridgehead.

In the meantime, Pz. Lehr Div., with its forward elements, had reached the area east of Argentan, and, in the forenoon on 13 August, had taken up positions in a front facing south at Le Bourg-St-Léonard and at Nonant-le-Pin. The divisional combat group (Pz. Gren. Regt

901), hitherto committed with LXXXIV Inf. Corps, had in the meantime been transferred back to the division, and was sent into the defensive positions facing south on either side of Gacé.

Here again, in an energetic and determined thrust to the north, the enemy could have succeeded on 13 August in penetrating via Chambois toward Trun – Falaise, thereby enveloping Seventh Army and considerable parts of Fifth Panzer Army. Evidently, the demarcation line separating the British from the American Army Group had a retarding effect, or the provision of coverage for the operation in the north, directed at Paris, had absorbed too many forces.

In that area, to the west and northwest of Paris, the weak combat group of 352 Inf. Div. was still providing coverage alone in the line Verneuil [-sur-Avre?] – Senonches – La Loupe – Courville [-sur-Eure?]. On 13 August, this combat group had not as yet contacted the enemy. LXXXI Inf. Corps, now available after XLVII Pz. Corps had been committed in the Argentan area, was inserted and placed in command in the gap between 352 Inf. Div. and the left wing of Panzer Group Eberbach, under the direct control of Army Group. At the outset, Corps had only alarm units, elements of 331 Inf. Div., and a combat group of 6 Para. Inf. Div. at its disposal. This latter consisted of one parachute infantry battalion and one light mortar battalion commanded by Hptmn Rappraeger. It was pushed ahead, with its forward elements as far advanced as [Villiers-sous-?] Mortagne, where, however, it was thrown back by the US 5 Armored Div. on 12 August. It then put up a defense south of [Vitrai-sous-?] Laigle. while adjacent to it. in the west, elements of 331 Inf. Div. endeavored to establish contact with Pz. Lehr Div. in the direction of Gacé. It was obvious, however, that these measures only provided protection for the main localities, roads and road junctions, which the enemy could bypass at his pleasure. Later, LXXXI Inf. Corps and 344 Inf. Div. and 17 Lw Field Div. were brought forward and subordinated.

F. 14–16 August

14 August was a turning point in the battle for France. in that. on this day. it became clear that further offensive intentions were entirely out of the question, and that the only possibility was a withdrawal to the east. However, Supreme Command probably only accepted this after all efforts to repel Allied landings on the Mediterranean coast had failed.

Also on 14 August, the points of main pressure on the Seventh Army front remained in the same sectors as heretofore. On the front held by II Para. Inf. Corps, the enemy penetrated to St-Quentin-les-Chardonnets. This penetration was successfully cleared up in a counterattack by evening, but 3 Para. Inf. Div. had suffered such heavy casualties in the fighting of the past few days that the combat efficiency of this excellent unit also decreased to a critical degree. In addition, Corps had to pay particular attention to its right flank once more, as the British had again become active and penetrated deeply toward Condé-sur-Noireau, in the sector of the adjacent unit. It was, therefore, no longer possible to pull out II SS-Pz. Corps (21 Pz. Div. and 9 SS-Pz. Div.) at this point, a process which had already begun. II SS-Pz. Corps had no contact whatever with Fifth Panzer Army, and therefore received no directives whatever from that headquarters. For this reason, Seventh Army assumed command over Corps.

Fierce defensive actions were fought on the right wing and in the center of the front held by the LXXXIV Inf. Corps. 363 Inf. Div. was heavily attacked on its right wing, and was

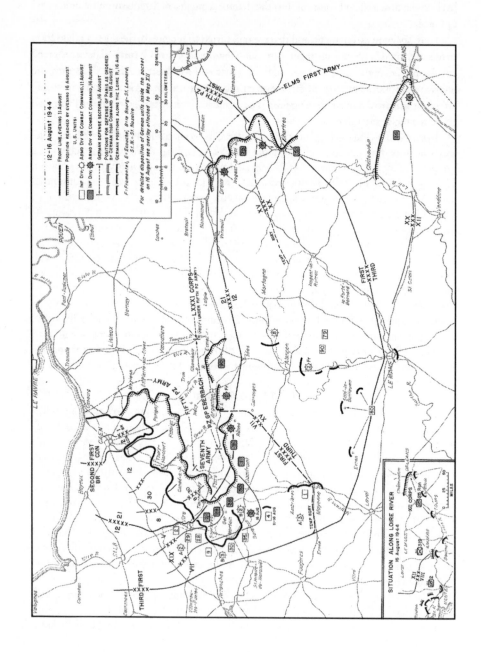

only able to restore the situation by the use of the divisional reserves. On the 353 Inf. Div. front, the commanding heights east of St-Sauveur were lost. The enemy penetrated as far as the St-Christophe-de-Chaulieu area. Here also, to replace the heavy losses incurred, the last reserves were thrown in; these reserves consisted of a newly arrived March Battalion of men who had been on leave from their units stationed in Norway, and had been collected in the interior zone and moved to France as replacements. There was only slight pressure on the 84 Inf. Div. front. On the whole, the Corps front, engaged for weeks past in heavy defensive action, was strained to breaking point. A withdrawal was the only thing that could prevent a collapse of the defense.

In the course of the withdrawal by LVIII Pz. Corps across the Egrenne, 2 SS-Pz. Div. had been pulled out of the front, as planned, and sent to the Ranes – Fromentel area. Corps was in most critical position, owing to the threatening situation at LXXXIV Inf. Corps, and, particularly, on account of the unclear situation in the La Ferté-Macé area. It was to be expected that enemy would spare no effort, and would use all available means, to take the important junction of Domfront, which constituted the southern cornerpost of Seventh Army. The enemy air force had been in action since early morning, and the enemy commenced the expected attack on the Domfront around midday. Though tenaciously opposed by the defenders, he penetrated the locality at 1510 hrs. In the late afternoon, the enemy gained further ground in a new attack, reaching Hill 201 and the "La Chapelle" hill north and northwest of Domfront, respectively. Corps ordered 10 SS-Pz. Div. to retake Domfront in a counterattack, using all reserves. Even though the objective of this attack was not gained, nevertheless the important hills north of the locality were retaken in the counterattack, and therewith the enemy penetration was sealed off. At about the same time as the enemy thrust to Domfront took place, the security line held by Pz. Reconnaissance Bn 9 at Perrou, 7 km southeast of Domfront, was penetrated. By evening, the following situation had developed on the left flank of Seventh Army:

The enemy apparently had bypassed La Ferté-Macé. La Sauvagère, 7 km northwest of La Ferté-Macé, was in enemy hands. Only a weak group, approximately 100 men strong, had been found left of the 708th Inf. Div. in the Faverolles area. Together with Pz. Reconnaissance Bn 9, this group was ordered to set up a new security line in the general direction of the north bank of L'Andainette [?] – south of Champsecret – La Coulonche – Lonlay [-l'Abbaye?]. Seventh Army called upon Panzer Group to use its mobile forces in establishing contact with this security line. This no longer took place, as the reconnaissance unit sent out by 1 SS-Pz. Div., the extreme right unit of the Panzer Group, were only able to reach the area northeast of La Ferté-Macé. Thus the gap remained. As Seventh Army had no forces available, it requested that 2 SS-Pz. Div., which it had detached, be employed in the La Ferté-Macé area.

Panzer Group Eberbach had, admittedly, succeeded in establishing a connected front on 14 August, held by (from right to left) 1 SS-Pz. Div., 2 Pz. Div., 116 Pz. Div., and Pz. Lehr Div., but it seemed impossible to stage a new attack with any hope of success while in such a widespread, defense formation.

1 SS-Pz. Div. was holding the sector south and east of Rânes, and found itself compelled to commit strong forces to protect its west flank. 2 Pz. Div. was on the defensive on the

banks of the L'Udon Bach (no doubt this should read L'Udon creek) between Vieux-Pont and to the southwest of Ecouché. In an attack, its left wing successfully established contact with 116 Pz. Div. General Eberbach rescinded his order to 116 Pz. Div. for an attack with a restricted objective south of Argentan, and now ordered that the division take up defensive positions along the line Ecouché – Argentan – Le Bourg-St-Léonard.

The critical situation in the area between the Forêt de Gouffern and Forêt de St-Evroult, which was only weakly held, and which was crossed by a number of good roads, made it essential to shift Pz. Lehr Div. eastward. The overall situation was highly critical for Panzer Group on 14 August, even though the only heavy attacks which took place were on the 116 Pz. Div. front, where a penetration effected by the enemy was cleared up in a counterattack. Spread out over a wide front, Panzer Group was responsible for the protection of the entire flank of Army Group. The very existence of Fifth Panzer Army and of Seventh Army hinged upon this flank. However, even after the arrival of 2 SS-Pz. Div., Panzer Group was not yet strong enough to fulfill its mission by offensive action. In view of the situation at Condé and Domfront, 10 Pz. Div. and II SS-Pz. Corps could not be expected to arrive for a few days yet,, at the earliest. In addition, Panzer Group was experiencing the same difficulties as Seventh Army with respect to ammunition and supply shortages in ever increasing measure. Therefore, both Panzer Group Eberbach and Seventh Army demanded that the salient in the front jutting out to the west be withdrawn. Army Group approved this withdrawal, on condition that by doing so, to begin with, 9 SS-Pz. Div. and, later, 10 SS-Pz. Div. and 21 Pz. Div. be made available for use elsewhere.

Thereupon, Seventh Army ordered a withdrawal during the night 14 to 15 August to the line south of Condé – Mont de Cerisy – Mont Crespin – Larchamp – St-Bômer-les Forges – northeast of Domfort [Domfront] – Champsecret – La Coulonche. In the course of this movement, 9 SS-Pz. Div. was to be pulled out and set on the move to the area north of Argentan, at the disposal of Panzer Group Eberbach. A decision having now been giving by the higher command authority, it was possible in advance to brief the troops on the next line to which they were to retire: Vere [?] – Bach [?] – east of Flers – northeast section of the Forêt d'Andaine. During the movement, LVIII Pz. Corps and 10 SS-Pz. Div. were to be pulled out. The advantage of thus prudently giving the order in advance was that the troops were able, at least in modest measure, to prepare the next line of defense, and, furthermore, that the movements could be conducted systematically.

The withdrawal movement was carried out as planned during the night, and 9 SS-Pz. Div. was successfully pulled out, but it was not possible for the division to move off immediately, owing to the lack of fuel. Seventh Army did all within its power to remedy this shortage, which was unfavorably affecting the movements of the entire Army. All supply columns were escorted by officers, who were provided with special authority giving them road priority. Traffic regulation was organized, military police employed, and a blocking system introduced to speed up supplies for the troops as much as possible. However, only very limited success was achieved. Above all, the toll taken by low-flying planes increased heavily, particularly in the terrain toward the west, where it became ever more open. Shortage of transport space, overcrowded roads, and lack of organization were the other causes which led to only a fraction of the requirements in all types of commodities reaching

German PWs line up, guarded by a US Military Policeman, to be shipped to camps in Britain. (US National Archives)

the troops. For this reason, Army ordered the destruction of all such vehicles as could possibly be spared, and that, apart from combat vehicles such as tanks, antitank guns, radio vehicles, etc., only an absolutely essential complement of vehicles be taken along.

The enemy had only hesitatingly followed up on the II Para. Inf. Corps front on 15 August. Combat outposts left behind were able to hold up the advance in the Tinchebray area for a long while, and to keep the enemy in the dark about the withdrawal movement. 3 Para. Inf. Div. had been separated into two groups of each two regiments, which relieved each other in rotation in the several lines during the withdrawal.

On the LXXXIV Inf. Corps front, the enemy followed up more quickly on the left wing. There, he attacked 84 Inf. Div. in strength, and was able to penetrate to as far as Hill 255, 2.5 km west of St-Clair-de-Halouse. On the whole, however, the pressure was progressively relieved on the western front of Seventh Army. On the other hand, attacks increased in intensity on the south front of LVIII Pz. Corps. Along the Domfront– [Le] Châtellier road, the enemy attacked in the morning on 15 August in a northerly direction. The enemy, being superior, was able to take the elevated terrain north of Domfront, and then also St-Bômer-les-Forges, as well as Les Forges. Champsecret remained in our hands. A counterattack by a combat group from 10 SS-Pz. Div. brought about some temporary relief, but failed to retake the lost terrain. The main body of Pz. Reconnaissance Bn 9 was in the La Coulonche area, its primary task being to provide coverage for the road to Bellou. Adjacent to these troops were the remnants of 706 Inf. Div., covering the La Ferté-Macé – Briouze road in the east, south and southwest of Lonlay-le-Tesson.

On Panzer Group Eberbach's front, the enemy's point of main effort appeared to be east of Argentan, which clearly indicated the his intention of carrying out a pincer movement toward Trun – Falaise. 2 SS-Pz. Div. was therefore sent into position in the eastern sector of the Forêt de Gouffern, and 9 SS-Pz. Div. was also transferred there. Both divisions passed under the command of II SS-Pz. Corps, after that Corps had been pulled out of the Condé area. The enemy had, however, also attacked 1 SS-Pz. Div., and succeeded in capturing Rânes and in forcing back the right wing of Panzer Group. The gap between Seventh Army and Panzer Group was still open. Both headquarters placed their hopes in the hesitation the enemy displayed in this sector.

On the 2 Pz. Div. front, things were comparatively quiet. On the 116 Pz. Div. front, the enemy felt along the entire front with strong scout patrols, and attacked in strength on the left wing, where he was able to penetrate into Le Bourg-St-Léonard, which was only weakly held by the Reconnaissance Battalion. Further eastward, Pz. Lehr Div., which had meanwhile been reinforced by the Panzer Infantry Battalion of 344 Inf. Div. sent on ahead, succeeded in beating off an enemy tank attack. Our own security detachments were also still fighting enemy armored spearheads in the Boulaine-la-Marche [Moulins-la-Marche?] area.

On 15 August, for the first time again, 352 Inf. Div., in strongpoint positions on a wide front northwest of Paris, came into contact with the enemy. In this action, the US 7 Armored Div. was identified for the first time. From papers captured in a destroyed tank at Courville [-sur-Eure?], it was discovered that the objectives to be reached by this division were as follows:

First objective: the line St-Arnoult, 5 km northwest of Courville – Senonches;
Second objective: the Eure river, on both sides of Dreux;
Third objective: the Seine river, on both sides of Houdan.

Thus the intentions of the enemy were in large measure revealed. While the enemy was successfully repelled, with the loss of one tank, south of Courville, the weakly held strongpoints held by 352 Inf. Div. at Senonches, La Loupe, and Belhomer[t-Guéhouville?] fought a delaying action against the enemy, who was feeling his way ahead along all roads toward the north and east. The Combat Commandant of Chartres reported Brou occupied by the enemy. Under enemy pressure, 352 Inf. Div. intended withdrawing to the line Dreux – Le Boullay-Thierry – Berchéres, 9 km north of Chartres. Dreux itself was held by an assault gun battalion commanded by Messerschmidt. The Eure crossings were readied for demolition.

Seventh Army had planned a withdrawal during the night 15/16 August to the line Vere creek – north of Aubusson – east of Flers – western fringes of Bois de Messey [?] – northeast of Forêt d'Andaine, in the course of which movement 21 Pz. Div. and 10 SS-Pz. Div. were to be pulled out of the right and left wing, respectively. 21 Pz. Div. was to move to the area north of Falaise and be at the disposal of Panzer Group, while 10 SS-Pz. Div. had orders to assemble in the Saires-la-Verrerie area. By reason of the menacing situation in the area northwest of Domfront and in the La Ferté-Macé area, it did not seem possible for the division to move to the east. Contact was taken up with the adjacent unit, LXXIV Inf. Corps (Commander: General der Infanterie Straube), controlled by Seventh Army. At this point, the following units were in position on either side of the Orne, but still north of Noireau, reading from the right: 277, 276 and 326 Inf. Divs, with the front facing north. All these units, particularly 326 Inf. Div., were badly battered, and their combat efficiency was only slight. In the new line taken up by Seventh Army, the right wing, behind the Vere creek, had been slightly improved by field fortifications by II SS-Pz. Corps and II Para. Inf. Corps.

Seventh Army ordered that, as from 26 August, 363 Inf. Div. be assigned to II Para. Inf. Corps. The new demarcation line ordered between II Para. Inf. Corps and LXXXIV Inf. Corps took the course: south of Flers – Chênedouit (II Para.) – Putanges [-Pont-Ecrepin?] (LXXXIV). Seventh Army's command post was moved to Chênedouit. The command post of II Para. Inf. Corps was moved to southwest of Ste-Honorine, that of LXXXIV Inf. Corps to La Morandière, 2.5 km southeast of Echalou, and that of LVIII Pz. Corps to La Raigière [?], 4 km northwest of Briouze. The latter Corps was to be held at the disposal of the Army after 10 SS-Pz. Div. had been pulled out.

In late afternoon, it was observed that the enemy, who had now followed up, was concentrating on the front ahead of the right wing of LXXXIV Inf. Corps, in the region north of Montsecret, north of Tinchebray. However, by carrying out the ordered withdrawal during the night 15/16 August according to plan, the troops escaped the expected attack.

Also on 16 August, the enemy again followed up slowly, ahead of the west front. 21 Pz. Div. had to be left with units of LXXIV Inf. Corps for employment at this point in mobile antitank action. The main body had moved off to the east. On the II Para. Inf. Corps front, the day passed quietly. On the other hand, the enemy had now discovered the gap north of La Ferté-Macé, and had penetrated as deeply as Le Ménil-de-Briouze and to Lignou in the north. Thus a serious menace to the entire front of Seventh Army had developed. As a countermeasure, and particularly because the enemy had also penetrated into La Ferrière-aux-Etangs, LXXXIV Inf. Corps bent back its left wing from Mesney [?] St-Gervais via Saires-la-Verrerie to Bellou-en-Houlme. 10 SS-Pz. Div. received orders to attack the enemy who had broken through from the west in the direction of Le Ménil-de-Briouze, and to force him back toward the south. Briouze was covered by elements of Pz. Reconnaissance Bn 9 and of 708 Inf. Div., which had switched to the east. Panzer Group Eberbach was requested to support, on the east, the attack by 10 SS-Pz. Div.

The attack by 10 SS-Pz. Div., which was staged by LVIII Pz. Corps, was a complete success. To begin with, the division retook Bellou, which had been taken by the enemy, and pressed the enemy so far back to the south that the danger of Seventh Army being enveloped northwest of the Orne was once more dispelled at the last moment.

The front held by Panzer Group Eberbach and XLVII Pz. Corps had withdrawn to the line running generally from Briouze to Ecouché in the face of growing enemy pressure. Ahead of 116 Pz. Div., an enemy attack along the Ecouché – Argentan railroad at Goulet was repelled, with the enemy losing a number of tanks. Argentan was under continuous heavy artillery fire, but was successfully held against all enemy attacks.

On the left wing of 116 Pz. Div., strong elements of 2 SS-Pz. Div. had now been committed. SS-Panzer Regiment Deutschland had orders to retake Le Bourg-St-Léonard, in which action it was to be supported by tanks and artillery of 116 Pz. Div. This attack also succeeded, but the enemy was able to penetrate into the locality again in a counterattack, so that it was now partly in German and partly in American hands.

On 16 August, the entire situation was decisively influenced by British armored forces penetrating the Fifth Panzer Army front in the vicinity of Falaise. In this action, the enemy had also advanced west of Falaise to as far as Le Mesnil-Villement, so the eastward withdrawal of Seventh Army and of Panzer Group Eberbach across the Orne appeared endangered. In these circumstances, Army Group ordered as follows:

1. Commencing during the night of 16/17 August, the armies will withdraw across the Orne in two or three night movements;

2. Combat is to be conducted in such a manner that two divisions of Seventh Army can forthwith be made available and be transferred to the Falaise region to Fifth Panzer Army. Arrangements were to be made directly between the two armies;

3. Panzer Group Eberbach will cover the withdrawal in the Argentan area by offensive action. Two Panzer divisions will be held at the disposal of Army Group, under the command of II SS-Pz. Corps, and transferred to the Vimoutiers region;

4. Following direct communication with Panzer Group Eberbach, Seventh Army will submit proposals for the boundary line from the Orne to the east.

On special orders by Generalfeldmarschall von Kluge, HQ LVIII Pz. Corps was committed on the Orne to regulate traffic. Only four bridges were available to the two armies for the crossing:

1.   At Le Mesnil-Hermei [Herman?];

2.   At Ste-Croix-sur-Orne;

3.   At Putanges;

4.   West of Montgaroult.

Bridge No 2 was earmarked for supply traffic, mainly east to west direction. Bridge No 1 was to be used by II Para. Inf. Corps, Bridge No 3 by LXXXIV Inf. Corps, and Bridge No. 4 by Panzer Group Eberbach. On these three bridges, the traffic would move mainly from west to east.

10 SS-Pz. Div. passed temporarily under the command of the LXXXIV Inf. Corps. Withdrawal was ordered for the night 16/17 August to the line Bréel – N.D. [Notre-Dame-] du-Rocher – west of Ste-Opportune – hills northwest of Briouze – Briouze. During this movement, II Para. Inf. Corps was to pull out 363 Inf. Div., and LXXXIV Inf. Corps was to pull 84 Inf. Div. out of the front, both of which divisions were to be moved to Fifth Panzer Army in the Neuvy – Bazoches area.

Since the British breakthrough toward Falaise, LXXXIV Inf. Corps also no longer had contact with Fifth Panzer Army, and Seventh Army assumed command over it, ordering it to withdraw on the right wing of the Army and cover the north flank of Seventh Army.

G. 17–18 August

While the withdrawal across the Orne to the east was taking place according to plan, the overall situation was becoming increasingly critical owing to the developments at Fifth Panzer Army. There, the connecting line of defense had collapsed at some points. East of Falaise, the enemy had succeeded in penetrating the front held by I SS-Pz. Corps, and had managed to cross the Ante creek at Damblainville. At this point, the 4th Canadian Armored Div. and the Polish 1 Armored Div. continued their advance toward Trun. Falaise itself had been taken by the Canadian 2 Inf. Div.

In spite of their having been in action for only a comparatively short time, the infantry units controlled by Fifth Panzer Army were severely battered and worn. The main body of

85 Inf. Div. had been forced eastward across the Dives, while to the southwest of this division there was a wide gap in the front. The combat efficiency of 12 SS-Pz. Div. was extremely low, and the remnants of 89 Inf. Div. south of Falaise were attempting to establish a new defense line based on the hills and wooded sections, and concentrating their efforts mainly on blocking the large road from Falaise to Argentan. The divisions under LXXIV Inf. Corps by now had been reduced to weak combat groups, which were putting up localized resistance but could no longer hold a connecting line. In coordination with the movement of Seventh Army, they broke loose from the left wing and also crossed to the east bank of the Orne.

At Seventh Army, the withdrawal to the next line of defense west of the Orne had been carried out according to plan, without the enemy following up in force. The bulk of 363 and 84 Inf. Divs had been pulled out of the front, and set on the march to the Orne. These divisions had not yet reached their assembly areas south of Falaise, however, as the mounting activity of the low-flying planes and the few roads and bridges available did not allow rapid movement. A combat group of 84 Inf. Div. in the Briouze region remained as yet under the command of 353 Inf. Div., and was only to be pulled out during the following night. While the day passed quietly, Seventh Army, having removed the command post to Nécy as from 17 August, issued the following orders:

1. Intense enemy pressure east of Falaise. Only slight enemy pressure on the front held by this Army.

2. During the night 17/18 August, Seventh Army will withdraw with the main body behind the Orne, leaving strong security detachments in a line generally: Val d'Orne (1.7 km east of La Forêt-Auvray) – St-Aubert-sur-Orne – Launay – Ménil-Gondouin – La Fresnaye-au-Sauvage.

3. The following units will be detached from the Army command: 363 Inf. Div. from the command of II Para. Inf. Corps; 84 Inf. Div. and 10 SS-Pz. Div. from the command of LXXXIV Inf. Corps.

   These divisions are to be moved to the Fifth Panzer Army:

   363 Inf. Div. to the Bazoches – Champcerie – Neuvy area;

   84 Inf. Div. to the Vignats – Ronay [Rônai?] – Nécy area;

   10 SS-Pz. Div. to assemble in the Monceaux [-au-Perche] – Giel [-Courteilles] – Habloville – Noirville [?] area.

4. Missions for the II Para. Inf. Corps (3 Para. Inf. Div.) and LXXXIV Inf. Corps (353 Inf. Div.): defense of the Orne.

   Mission for the security: Withdrawal to behind the Orne only if heavily pressed by the enemy.

5 Boundaries:

   Right boundary between II Para. Inf. Corps and Fifth Panzer Army: La Forêt-Auvray (Seventh Army) – Bazoches (Seventh Army – Neuvy (Seventh Army – Nécy (Fifth Panzer Army) – Trun (Seventh Army).

   Boundary between II Para. Inf. Corps and LXXXIV Inf. Corps: Launay – St-Croix (LXXXIV Inf. Corps) – Ronay (II Para. Inf. Corps).

   Left army boundary between LXXXIV Inf. Corps and Panzer Group Eberbach: Le

Fresnaye-au-Sauvage – Giel (Seventh Army) – Occagnes (Panzer Group Eberbach) – Bailleul (Seventh Army).

Points of Contact:

Between Fifth Panzer Army and II Para. Inf. Corps: Val d'Orne, 1.7 km east of La Forêt-Auvray; between II Para. Inf. Corps and LXXXIV Inf. Corps: Launay, 1 km southwest of St-Croix; between LXXXIV Inf. Corps and Panzer Group Eberbach: La Fresnaye-au-Sauvage.

6. Localities of new command posts are to be reported. The advanced Army command post will be transferred on the morning of 18 August to the region south of Vimoutiers.

84 and 363 Inf. Divs passed under the command of the LXXIV Inf. Corps; their respective commanders were to report at the Corps command post in Noireville, 2 km northwest of Habloville. Corps considered it possible that the enemy might advance to as far as the line Nécy – Bazoches during the night 17/18 August.

Gen. Heinrich, Commander of 89 Inf. Div., reported at the Army command post in Nécy with the information that the remnants of his division—several hundred strong, with few weapons—were still holding out on the hills east of Corday.

Only one enemy attack took place on the western front—against Pointel, east of Briouze, where a combat group from 84 Inf. Div. was hard pressed locally on account of deficient contact with Panzer Group. Action taken by the reserves of 353 Inf. Div. succeeded in restoring the situation, and also in extricating the 84 Inf. Div. combat group.

As the first unit, Panzer Group Eberbach had withdrawn 1 SS-Pz. Div. across the Orne, and concentrated it in the northern section of the Forêt de Goeffern, while 2 Pz. Div. covered the other forces crossing the Orne. Enemy pressure was not heavy ahead of 116 Pz. Div., nor at any point on the Army Group B southern front, which in fact surprised the German Command. Had the American forces systematically attacked the thin, drawn-out front of Panzer Group, they could easily have broken through it, and advanced toward the British forces. In such a case, the Falaise – Argentan pocket would have been closed on 16 or 17 August.

In terms of the Army Group order, II SS-Pz. Corps (2 and 9 SS-Pz. Divs) was to move to the region east of Vimoutiers. On receipt of reports about the British breakthrough toward Trun, both Panzer Group and Seventh Army requested that Corps be halted for commitment on either side of the Trun–Falaise road in counterattack against the British. This was refused, but elements of 9 SS-Pz. Div. had already been dispatched to the Trun area to cover the rear. Elements of 116 Pz. Div.—namely, a small combat group, including three to four tanks—was now also sent to the Trun area, further weakening the southern front. The same division sent another combat group consisting of Panzer Jaeger (antitank) and engineers into position on both sides of Occagnes to cover the Falaise–Argentan road. The Flak Assault Regt, in position on the hills around Montabard, was also made available for this purpose, but the majority of its forces were engaged as antiaircraft protection at the Orne bridges.

The threat of encirclement had by now become so apparent that a mass flight of trains, rear services and dispersed personnel towards the east set in. Nevertheless, on 17 August, one could not as yet talk of any panic. Although the roads were [chaotic?], signs of dissolution [breakdown] had only become noticeable to enforce marching discipline—at least by daylight.

In the evening on 17 August, the impression was gained that the British penetrations south and east of Falaise had at least been superficially sealed off. Surprisingly enough, pressure exerted by the Americans had relaxed, so Seventh Army and Panzer Group Eberbach believed that they could carry out the withdrawal across the Orne, and later across the Dives, within two or three nights, as planned. In order to counteract the tendency to retreat headlong, Seventh Army decided to keep its advance command post at Nécy for the time being.

Disengaging movements were carried out successfully, and according to plan, during the night 17/18 August. The Commanders of Seventh Army and Panzer Group Eberbach were ordered to the Fifth Panzer Army command post in Fontaine-l'Abbé early on 18 August, there to report on the situation to Generalfeldmarschall Model, who was to relieve Generalfeldmarschall von Kluge as Commander-in-Chief. Generaloberst Hausser, unwilling to leave his Army at such a critical juncture, sent his Chief of Staff, Oberst i.G. Freiherr von Gersdorff [the author]. Although Trun had meanwhile been lost to the enemy, the trip out of the defined pocket by way of St-Lambert was by no means difficult, apart from the sudden concentrations of artillery fire on the St Lambert – Chambois area.

On the basis of the reports by Gen. Eberbach and Oberst i.G. Freiherr von Gersdorff, Generalfeldmarschall Model had ordered both armies to withdraw behind the Dives in two night movements, in order to withdraw further from there to the Touques sector, where they were to establish a new line. Simultaneously, he intended sending II SS-Pz. Corps in to attack from the Vimoutiers region toward Trun, in order to relieve the pressure on the northern flank of Seventh Army, and to render possible the withdrawal to the east. However, this order, which accorded with the measures already adopted, was overtaken by the course of events. The counterattack on Trun, carried out with forces from 116 Pz. Div. and the 9th SS-Pz. Div. that were too weak, had failed, and attempts to contact II SS-Pz. Corps in order to halt it and launch it in an immediate attempt to fight free the north flank of Seventh Army were also unsuccessful. On 18 August, the main body of Corps reached the Vimoutiers region, to where they had been ordered.

In the Trun area, the enemy had been noticeably reinforced, and some of his forces now pushed toward St-Lambert. To meet the British, the Americans (from whom the withdrawal of II SS-Pz. Corps could not for long remain concealed) now also became more active, and attacked along both sides of the Le Bourg-St-Léonard–Chambois road, where only weak security detachments of 116 Pz. Div.'s Reconnaissance Bn were in position. Action by the artillery, by 116 Pz. Div., and by strong elements of 8 Werfer (Projector) Bde made it possible at least to halt the enemy, who was trying to sweep ever farther east, in the Chambois region. An evening attack on Chambois was repelled by weak elements of 116 Pz. Div., supported by two tanks, under the command of Maj. Graf Bruehl, Acting Commander of the Panzer Regt. At this point, Oberst i.G. Freiherr von Gersdorff [the author], Chief of Staff of Seventh Army, succeeded during the evening of 18 August in making his way back on foot into the pocket. In spite of the small "opening" at Chambois, practically speaking the pocket was closed.

In the meantime, the British had also renewed their attack both along and to the east of the Falaise–Argentan road. When Canadian tanks penetrated as far as Nécy, the Seventh Army command post was forced out of that locality under fire. It was transferred to an old stone quarry on the outskirts of Villedieu-lès-Bailleul. Seventh Army Staff suffered losses in personnel besides losing the bulk of its vehicles and radio equipment.

LXXIV Inf. Corps had intended committing 363 Inf. Div. along the ridge north of the Bilaine creek in a line from Hill 248, north of Rônai, to Corday, and 84 Inf. Div. east of that point. In the afternoon, 363 Inf. Div. had taken up the assigned positions, and those elements of 89 Inf. Div. still in position there were subordinated to it. They successfully held their positions against light attacks. 84 Inf. Div., on the other hand, only arrived later in its assembly area, as a consequence of its long approach march. The advance elements of this division had to be employed in sealing off the penetration at Nécy. The remaining divisions of Corps (combat groups from 271, 277, 276, and 326 Inf. Divs) were still fighting in forward positions on the Orne, and between the Orne and the Corday. Some of them retreated eastward, south of this line.

353 Inf. Div. now also was placed under the command of II Para. Inf. Corps. By order of Army Group, LXXXIV Inf. Corps, which thereby became available for other uses, was to be detached to the Paris region at the disposal of First Army. Since this was no longer possible after the pocket had been closed, Seventh Army ordered that Corps assume control of those forces that were fighting on the north front of the pocket (namely, units of divisions of I SS-Pz. Corps), and of 84 Inf. Div. Hence, Corps was in command in the sector extending from Trun to north of Rônai. Meanwhile, 10 SS-Pz. Div. had concentrated east of the Orne, and Army also assigned this division to Corps, ordering that the breakthrough effected by the British in the direction of, and northeast of, Nécy be cleared up in a counterattack, and a connected front be established between the Dives and the Falaise–Argentan road.

However, Corps considered this attack impossible by day, on account of conditions in the air. Instead, Corps entered full vigor upon the task of ordering the units that had become mixed, as well as of establishing a connected line generally from southwest of Trun – Ommoy – Brieux – north of Rônai. In spite of intense activity by the artillery and low-flying planes, LXXXIV Inf. Corps succeeded in establishing this front by 18 August.

II Para. Inf. Corps, having transferred the command post from the Nécy region to La Lande [-Vaumont?], 1.5 km northwest of Villedieu, still had considerable elements of 3 Para. Inf. Div. in advance positions on the Orne, where the enemy pressure had ceased altogether. As yet, division combat outposts had no contact with the enemy on the west bank of the Orne. Withdrawal had been ordered for the evening to the Caen–Argentan railroad in the Nécy – Occagnes sector. Enemy pressure was more severe on the front of the newly assigned 353 Inf. Div., particularly so on that division's left wing, for which reason the main body of the division, during the day, retreated eastward to the railroad. It was possible to do so because low-flying enemy planes were mainly concentrated over the Trun – Chambois – Vimoutiers area and, furthermore, as the enemy did not follow up very vigorously from the west.

Panzer Group Eberbach was again subordinated to Seventh Army, which was due in particular to the fact that Gen. Eberbach, on his way from Fifth Panzer Army, had not succeeded in reentering the pocket. He had driven on to the command post of II SS-Pz. Corps, immediately east of Vimoutiers, in order to coordinate his own measures with the intended attack by that Corps toward Trun. He remained with that Corps.

Maintaining contact with the 353 Inf. Div., 2 Pz. Div. withdrew to a line Occagnes – northern outskirts of Argentan, where it went into defensive positions. Adjacent to the east was 116 Pz. Div., covering Argentan and the Forêt de Gouffern toward the south in strongpoint positions, while sizeable elements of the division had moved eastward in the area Le Bourg-St-Léonard – Chambois – west of Trun. In contrast with the front held by II Para. Inf. Corps, enemy pressure was heavier here. Le Bourg-St-Léonard, the northern part of which had still been held, was lost in the morning. By evening, the enemy had succeeded in closing the pocket, as has been previously described.

Elements of 116 Pz. Div., supported by units of 9 SS-Pz. Div., had attacked Trun, but had not succeeded in entirely clearing the locality of enemy forces. The British, on the other hand, had succeeded in taking Magny [-le-Désert?], southeast of Trun, and in advancing as far as Hill 107, south of Magny. The weak security detachment attached to the divisional command post (Tournai-sur-Dive), consisting of three tanks and a few riflemen of the divisional Staff, succeeded in retaking the commanding hill, which then repeatedly changed hands. After the security detachments had been reinforced with a number of tanks, the enemy eventually sealed off the line from Hill 107 to Hill 113 (1.5 km southwest of Trun). The right wing of the division had been seriously weakened by units being pulled out for the Trun – Chambois area, and here the enemy succeeded in penetrating into the southern part of Argentan, the northern part of which town was still successfully held.

In the Forêt de Gouffern, the enemy managed to bypass the strongpoints held by Pz. Gren. Regt 60, and so also succeeded in infiltrating into the northern sections of the forest. To strengthen this threatened front, 1 SS-Pz. Div., which had meanwhile concentrated in the northern part of the Forêt de Gouffern, was committed with the front facing south. However, considerable forces of this division had already driven eastward out of the forming pocket, unknown to the Army, probably acting on orders received through SS-channels. In the evening of 18 August, 116 Pz. Div. still succeeded in conducting trains, artillery elements and elements of Projector Bde 36, which unit had no more ammunition, out of the pocket, via Chambois. In like manner, the Staff of LVIII Pz. Corps just managed to escape from the pocket, after having fulfilled its mission on the Orne, in the execution of which it suffered losses in personnel and matériel. Hence, the pocket, even now, had not yet been firmly closed at the southeast corner.

18 August had been characterized by intensive activity by enemy low-flying planes. Ceaselessly, the enemy air force had attacked the columns crowded together in the congested area, all hurrying eastward via Chambois – St-Lambert, besides screening off the entire area of Vimoutiers – Trun – Gacé. Considerable numbers of German vehicles were destroyed here, the countless fighter-bombers even pursuing individuals and single vehicles.

During the night of 18/19 August, the most intense artillery fire was suddenly brought down on the entire area in the pocket, causing further heavy losses; fire continued throughout 19 August. In spite of this, the withdrawal movements ordered were successfully carried out during the night. LXXIV Inf. Corps. with 363 Inf. Div. took up the line from north of Rônai – Neuvy-au-Houlme – Habloville, while the remnants of the other division retreated eastward beyond this line. Through the line held by 353 Inf. Div., already in position on the railroad, II Para. Inf. Corps withdrew 3 Para. Inf. Div. to the hills of Montabard.

Outside the pocket, Fifth Panzer Army still had its right wing anchored on the Dives, whereas the left wing of LXXXIV Inf. Corps had been pushed back far to the east. Only elements of 85 Inf. Div. were still fighting in the St-Pierre-sur-Dives region, but the withdrawal of the entire front to the Touques sector could not be delayed for long.

II SS-Pz. Corps arrived in the Vimoutiers area and west thereof, but was only able to complete assembly in time to start its diversionary attack during the night 19/20 August at the earliest. Weeks of heavy fighting had weakened the Corps' two divisions—2 and 9 SS-Pz. Divs. Their combat strength was only equal to that of weak combat groups. They could only be employed for a circumscribed mission commensurate with their strength and combat efficiency.

The forces committed east of the pocket were now under the command of LXXXI Inf. Corps. Simultaneously with the arrival of parts of 344 Inf. Div., the combat group of Pz. Lehr Div. in the area (on both sides of Gacé) had been pulled out on 17 August; it had to leave one Panzer Grenadier battalion, one company of engineers, ten tanks and one battery in position at the front, which would otherwise have been too seriously weakened. The remainder of Pz. Lehr Div. was sent off to the Senlis area for rehabilitation.

In the meantime, the enemy had advanced further on a broad front to the east and northeast, and had forced back the strongpoints of 352 Inf. Div., which were only able to delay him at restricted points. Whereas, in the easterly direction, the enemy had reached a line approximately from Orléans to Chartres, in a northeasterly direction he had already reached the Seine in the Nantes sector. At this point, 18 Air Force Field Div. (commanded by Gen. von Treskow), 49 Inf. Div. (commanded by Gen. Macholz), and 6 Para. Inf. Div. (commanded by Gen. von Heyking) had been committed for defense of the north bank of the Seine just in time. Elements of 331 Inf. Div., the small combat group Rappraeger of 6 Para. Inf. Div., 344 Inf. Div., and the approaching 17 Air Force Field Div. were between the pocket and the Seine. The last-named division had been relieved from its positions on the coastal front at Le Havre on 12 August by 226 Inf. Div. (commanded by Generalleutnant von Kluge), and reached the new area to which it had been assigned (Verneuil – St-Georges-Motel) by 17 August.

SS-Pz. Kampfgruppe (combat group) Mohnke (elements of 1 SS-Pz. Div.), which had hitherto held security positions here, was subordinated to 17 Air Force Field Div. On the other hand, this division had been compelled to leave Jg. Regt 39, one battalion of artillery, and one company of engineers behind in the Le Havre coastal sector, as 226 Inf. Div., which relieved 17 Air Force Field Div., was not strong enough to relieve the entire division. In its new sector, 17 Air Force Field Div. assigned Jg. Regt 47 to the right and Jg. Regt 34 to the left, holding SS-Pz. Kampfgruppe Mohnke as reserve behind the right wing. As cover for the exposed left flank, division placed the Fusilier Bn in a bridgehead on the east bank of the Eure river at Pacy-sur-Eure. The boundary line between 344 Inf. Div. and 17 Air Force Field Div. ran in a line from Verneuil to Conches (both localities to 344 Inf. Div.).

On 17 and 18 August, the enemy had only pressed forward northeastward via Dreux, which was lost on 17 August. 17 Air Force Field Div. therefore transferred the SS-Panzer Kampfgruppe to the left wing, with orders to seal off the region between the Seine and Pacy-sur-Eure. It was surprising that the enemy did not advance with stronger forces in a northerly direction west of the Seine on 17 and 18 August. Had he done so, he would have met no serious opposition, and, by quickly gaining possession of the Seine crossings southeast of Rouen, could have rendered it impossible for even a single man of the entire Army Group to escape eastward across the river. Here, once again, the seam between the British 21 and US 12 Army Groups seems to have played the part of guardian angel to us.

H. Escape from the Pocket, 19–21 August

Early on 19 August, Seventh Army was encircled in the area of Trun (exclusive) – Brieux – Rônai (LXXXIV Inf. Corps) – Neuvy-au-Houlme – Habloville (LXXIV Inf. Corps) – Pierrefitte – Occagnes (II Para. Inf. Corps) – northern outskirts of Argentan – Chambois – hills south of Trun (XLVII Pz. Corps). Inside the pocket were two Army staffs (Seventh Army and Panzer Group Eberbach), four Corps staffs, remnants of five Panzer divisions (1 SS, 10 SS, 12 SS, 2, and 116) besides nine infantry divisions (3 Para., 84, 89, 271, 276, 277, 326, 353, and 363).

In the morning on 19 August, once Seventh Army had gained the impression that the night withdrawal had been carried out according to plan, and, furthermore, that on the northeastern front of the pocket the enemy still had only weak forces and no connecting front, Army considered it still possible, in an attack, to carry out the intended withdrawal across the Dives during the night 19/20 August. Army therefore ordered that the following units should attack to the east at the following points: Panzer Group Eberbach, with elements of XLVII Pz. Corps, at Chambois; II Para. Inf. Corps, with 3 Para. Inf. Div., at St-Lambert; LXXXIV Inf. Corps, with 12 SS-Pz. Div. and 277 Inf. Div. (to be newly assigned), at Trun. The objective was, in the evening on 19 August, to fight the Dives position free, to occupy that position with the front facing southwest, and then to take up the other forces of the Army. These forces—namely, 84 Inf. Div., LXXIV Inf. Corps, 353 Inf. Div., and remnants of XLVI Pz. Corps—were to remain in their present positions for the time being, and provide coverage from there for the flanks and rear of the attacking forces, and then be pulled out eastward through the new line of resistance. A simultaneous diversionary attack by II SS-Pz. Corps, with its left wing based on Trun, in the general direction of Falaise was to cover the north flank of the attacking forces, and at the same time to establish contact with Fifth Panzer Army. Panzer Group Eberbach was to take up contact with elements Pz. Lehr Div. and 331 Inf. Div. in the Gacé area. The intention was, then, to withdraw from the Dives front to the Vis [?] sector south of Vimoutiers, while pulling out the bulk of the Panzer forces from the front for use elsewhere.

Developments in the situation did not allow of these intentions to be carried out, however. Whereas the enemy pressure on the northeast front of the pocket was only slight on 19 August, the enemy had continued attacking from the north and south. Thus, the British advanced southward on Ri via Rônai, held by only weak security detachments of 10th SS-Pz. Div. Here, together with tanks of 10th SS-Pz. Div., the artillery of 363 Inf. Div.

repelled the enemy armored attacks, accounting for a number of enemy tanks. The Americans also attempted to advance on Conneaux [Commeaux?] from the south. In spite of this critical position, the gallant 363 Inf. Div. held out in its advanced, bastion-like position in order to make it possible for all units of LXXIV Inf. Corps [to complete] the withdrawal eastward. Not before 1600 hrs did the division withdraw in the direction toward Montabard. Contrary to expectations, this movement succeeded. Had coordination been better between the British and American armored spearheads, this division could easily have been totally annihilated.

353 Inf. Div. had withdrawn strong forces to the west fringes of the Bois de Feuille and the Forêt de Gouffern during the night 18/19 August, leaving only advanced combat outposts at the railroad line.

At XLVII Pz. Corps, the enemy had meanwhile succeeded in taking Ste-Eugénie [St-Eugéne?] and Fougy (northwest and north, respectively, of Le Bourg-St-Léonard). From Hills 156 and 149, to the north of these two places, the enemy had such favorable observation points that he was able, with directed artillery fire, to combat any movement inside the pocket. In the northeastern parts of the pocket, enemy artillery fire was therefore particularly effective. In a heavy attack by the enemy, Chambois was finally lost. Similarly, the enemy also now advanced with strong forces from Polish 1 Armored Div. from the Trun area toward St-Lambert – Chambois.

When, after dodging intense artillery fire, the Commander-in-Chief and the Chief of Staff [the author] of Seventh Army in the morning on 19 August reached the command post of Panzer Group Eberbach and 116 Pz. Div.—located in the group of houses south of Tounai-sur-Dive—they were able to gain a personal impression of the critical developments of the situation on the south front of the pocket. Generalleutnant Elfeldt, Commander of LXXXIV Inf. Corps, arriving at the same command post, reported on the situation on the north and northeast front, explaining that he could hold out no promise of success for the attack on a broad front across the Dives, as ordered by the Army. Enemy forces in the Trun area were too strong, he said, and also he considered the terrain particularly unfavorable for an attack across the Dives. The Commander-in-Chief had already consulted with the Commanding General of II Para. Inf. Corps, Gen. der Flieger Meindl, and the Ia (Operations Officer) of LXXIV Inf. Corps, Maj. i.G. Prinz Holstein. On the basis of this personal appreciation, Army Command was able to obtain a clear picture of the situation inside the pocket.

Above all, the condition of the troops had been so adversely affected by low-flying planes and artillery fire during the past two days that a systematic conduct of battle no longer seemed possible. The troops had scarcely any more artillery and heavy weapons, and only very little ammunition left. The fuel supply would be at best sufficient for the few vehicles still available. On 18 August, Seventh Army had requested that ammunition and fuel supplies be flown into the pocket, designating an area east of the Bois de Feuille as a spot for them to be dropped. However, this aerial supply service was never carried out, or, where it was carried out, only in inadequate measure. Lack of fuel and prime movers had already made it imperative to destroy numerous guns; thus, for instance, all guns of 84 Inf. Div. had to be destroyed.

The morale and fighting skills of the individual German soldier remained of a generally high level throughout the campaign in Normandy—one reason why so many of them were able to escape through the Falaise Gap. (US National Archives)

It was possible neither to stage a planned attack nor subsequently to establish a line of resistance on the Dives. The Commander-in-Chief therefore decided to order a breakthrough from the pocket at the weakest spot in the enemy's enveloping ring, namely on both sides of St-Lambert-sur-Dive. The plan of establishing a line of resistance on the Dives had to be abandoned under existing circumstances. Army assumed that, at St-Lambert, it would strike the seam between the American and the British forces and hence a soft spot.

Army ordered that, during the following night, XLVII Pz. Corps and II Para. Inf. Corps launch a sudden surprise breakthrough attack on a narrow front to break the encircling ring, the former to attack at Chambois, the latter at, and northwest of, St-Lambert, and that all other units be conducted northeastward out of the pocket through the gap thus torn. Seventh Army reported its intentions by radio to Army Group and Fifth Panzer Army, and requested that the diversionary attack by II SS-Pz. Corps be launched in the direction of Trun – Chambois simultaneously with the breakthrough attack, in order to take up the forces breaking out of the pocket, and to contain and delay the enemy. Seventh Army was able to send out the order to break out, as well as information regarding the attack by II SS-Pz. Corps, to all units within the pocket, but had no guarantee that the messages were received by the addressees, as no confirmation was received.

Areas were determined on the hills on both sides of Goudehard as the assembly area for all units, once they had succeeded in breaking out. Castle Travers, 2 km southwest of Le Sap, was envisaged as the next command post for the Army.

At LXXIV Inf. Corps, 277 Inf. Div. was withdrawn as the first unit, and assigned to LXXXIV Inf. Corps, for the purpose of relieving 12 SS-Pz. Div. in the Trun – Ommoy section; 12 SS-Pz. Div. was to take part in the breakthrough by II Para. Inf. Corps. However, the Army ordered that both divisions be assigned to II Para. Inf. Corps, so as to insure unified command in both defense and breakthrough operations on the east front of the pocket.

For the greater part, the combat groups of LXXIV Inf. Corps had been assembled in the northwest sector of the pocket, without the enemy having followed up in force from the west and northwest. Ahead of 353 Inf. Div., the south flank of the division in particular was threatened. The division therefore employed its engineer company as protection at this point; the engineer company was later absorbed by XLVII Pz. Corps. Further, the division left only weak rearguard detachments on the southwest fringes of the wooded area, and concentrated the main body of the remaining forces in the Tournai-sur-Dive region.

At XLVII Pz. Corps, in the afternoon on 19 August, the north part of Argentan was finally lost, after having been hotly contested for eight days by elements of 116 Pz. Div. In a follow-up thrust to the northeast, the enemy reached Bon-Menil [?], and forced the remnants of Pz. Gren. Regiment 60 (still about 60 men), committed to positions there, further back. Corps, from the command post still in the woods east of the road bend south of Bailleu[l?], ordered 1 SS-Pz. Div. to break through on the right and 2 Pz. Div. on the left along the line Chambois – St-Lambert while, in a line southwest and north of [Urou-et-?] Crennes – south of Tournai, 116 Pz. Div. was to cover the rear and the south flank of the breakthrough attack.

II Para. Inf. Corps ordered that 353 Inf. Div. should break through on the right via St-Lambert-sur-Dive, and 3 Para. Inf. Div. on the left via a mill 2 km southeast of Trun. The forces were to break through the enemy encirclement in wedge formation, using Indian tactics, without firing, and setting their course by compass. The entire movement was to be conducted as a surprise attack, and the hills of Goudehard [Coudehard?] were be gained without delay, and new positions taken up there. Both divisions were to detail rearguards. At 353 Inf. Div., Gren. Regt 984 was detailed to the right, Gren. Regt 941 to the left. Regt von Dobeneck, of 331 Inf. Div., was to follow behind the right wing. Gren. Regt 942 was

An artist's impression of a German troop column on the move. In Normandy, such movement usually took place at night. (US National Archives)

detailed as rearguard. The attack objective for 353 Inf. Div. was the western slope of Mont Ormel, south of Goudehard. Similarly, 3 Para. Inf. Div. ordered the formation of two wedges, namely Para. Inf. Regt 5 on the right, via the mill immediately northwest of St-Lambert, and Para. Inf. Regts 9 and 15 on the left, via the mill 1 km east of Hill 107. Para. Inf. Regt 8 was detailed as rearguard.

Together with all officers, NCOs, and enlisted men of the Army Staff, the Commander-in-Chief of Seventh Army proceeded to 3 Para. Inf. Div. in order to take part in the breakthrough there. The Chief of Staff, who had been wounded in the morning, attached himself to Headquarters Panzer Group Eberbach, together with officers and men of the Army Staff. Activity by enemy low-flying planes had decreased in intensity over the pocket on 19 August, and their main effort shifted farther northeast to the Vimoutiers area. In contrast, extremely heavy shelling went on throughout the entire day from all directions. Enemy pressure had subsided and, incomprehensibly, had even ceased altogether at some points. Had the enemy attacked in force on all sides on 19 August, the regroupings and other preparations necessary for the breakthrough out of the pocket would not have been possible.

Things looked black inside the pocket. Hundreds upon hundreds of vehicles that had been put out of action by enemy fire, untended wounded, and innumerable dead characterized a battlefield in a manner rarely seen throughout the entire war.

Reconnaissance carried out by the Panzer division had shown that driving by night would be nearly impossible, on account of the many derelict vehicles. Therefore, XLVII Pz. Corps decided not to attack before daybreak, so that only 1 SS-Pz. Div. and 2 Pz. Div. left their concentration areas in the region of Bailleu[l] about 0400 hrs, driving toward Chambois.

II Para. Inf. Corps, on the other hand, had commenced the attack at 2230 hrs. On account of terrain difficulties, 353 Inf. Div., in setting out, was unable to detour around Tournai-sur-Dive. The village was afire, and the roads were jammed with derelict vehicles, dead horses, and tanks that had failed. The work necessary to clear the way delayed movement by three hours. A further factor that delayed all movement by the division was the heavy artillery fire laid down by the enemy. As a result, this division also only managed to reach its assault positions in the region west of the line Chambois – St-Lambert at dawn. The right assault wedge of the division, which came from what was actually the attack sector of II Para. Inf. Corps around Chambois, there met elements of 1 SS-Pz. Div.; tanks and infantry combined to form composite assault groups.

At 3 Para. Inf. Div., the Commander, Gen. Schimpf, was wounded immediately after the attack began in the vicinity of Hill 107. Thereupon, Gen. der Flieger Meindl assumed command of the division personally. The assault groups stole past the enemy tanks of the Polish 1 Armored Division, patrolling south and southwest of Magny, and reached the Dives without any major engagements. Meanwhile, the east bank of the Dives had also been blocked by numerous enemy tanks between St-Lambert and Magny. After careful reconnaissance and a long wait, Para. Inf., under cover of the dark, managed to work themselves through between the enemy tanks, and thus overcame the Dives obstacle in small groups. By avoiding major engagements, taking advantage of all cover afforded by the terrain, and detouring round each enemy strongpoint, the small combat groups crept along. In this manner, a considerable number of them succeeded in breaking through the enemy encirclement, and reached the attacking spearheads of II SS-Pz. Corps. During daylight, the majority of the groups remained under cover, only resuming their march after nightfall on 20 August. A large part of 3 Para. Inf. Div. was thus safely brought out of the pocket, but this by no means meant that a gap had been broken in the encircling ring.

The night of 19/20 August was pitch black, and in the dark Seventh Army Chief of Staff [the author] had lost contact with Panzer Group and lost his way. Toward dawn, about 0400 hrs on 20 August, he arrived at the southern entrance to St-Lambert, where he found a column of vehicles of all types without unified command. The Trun – St-Lambert – Chambois road was blocked by enemy tanks and antitank guns, and every vehicle using the road was shot at, without exception. Included among the various vehicles, the Army Chief of Staff found two Mark V Jagdpanzer of 2 Pz. Div., which he sent forward to fight the enemy antitank guns. Once this had been accomplished, he followed up the tanks along the road in his Kuebelwagen command car (a German jeep), and this was taken by a large number of hitherto hidden combat vehicles—Panzers, assault guns, armored personnel carriers, "Hornisse" 88 mm self-propelled antitank guns and others—to join in this thrust. A regular "hunt" (Parforcejagd) ensued, driving right across and over hedges, embankments, gardens and ditches, under heavy enemy machine-gun and antitank fire, but no artillery fire. The enemy, taken under fire by all guns, were so surprised that the majority surrendered, though, actually, the tanks were unable to take them prisoner. The breakthrough only came to a halt when the foremost tanks encountered an enemy tank or antitank front and were knocked out.

In one of the orchards so typical of Normandy, the Chief of Staff collected all those who had joined him. After securing the perimeter and reconnoitering, he formed a Panzer group consisting of six to eight tanks, four to six assault guns, 25–30 armored personnel carriers, a number of "Hornisse" 88 mm self-propelled anti-tank guns and 150 mm "Hummels" (self-propelled field howitzers) under the command of Maj. Bochnick, commander of the Pz. Jg. Bn of 116 Pz. Div., and rounded up all stragglers—roughly one thousand men. These were hastily formed into companies. Sturmbannfuehrer Brinkmann, of 12 or 17 SS-Pz. Div., assumed command of the infantry.

After brief preparations, the battle group thus formed set out at about 0600 hrs from the area approximately 1 km north of St-Lambert to attack in a drive northwestward. Again and again, enemy tanks attempted to obstruct the advance, or to attack the flanks of the assault group from the hills, but were effectively taken under fire by our own armor-piercing weapons, 10–15 enemy tanks being set afire. Without any delay worth mentioning, the attack reached the elevated terrain around Goudehard, so that a breach had been laid in the enemy encircling ring. Upon returning at about 0900 hrs in order, as far as circumstances permitted, to search for the Army Commander, and to arrange for protection of the flanks in the gap created, the Chief of Staff found that the entire region between Chambois and St-Lambert was now under terrible intense artillery fire. Nevertheless, the enemy, who was preoccupied with the attacks by other breakthrough groups which were taking effect at Chambois as well as at and northwest of St-Lambert, for the time being made no attempt to close up the gap again. An endless line of infantry and vehicles now flowed along the road through the gap.

Meanwhile, the energetic commander of 353 Inf. Div., with his right assault group, Gren. Regt 941, had succeeded in crossing the Dives at an unnamed locality between St-Lambert and Chambois. In the locality, though under heavy enemy artillery fire, he formed new battle groups. The tanks committed by him along with the battle groups were destroyed, but, nevertheless, the bulk of the infantry, which had been joined by innumerable stragglers from practically all formations in the pocket, were successfully conducted through the enemy tanks by a route reconnoitered personally by the Divisional Commander in the direction of Mont Ormel.

Elements of all divisions controlled by XLVII Pz. Corps had already fought in the breakthrough groups, and Corps itself now reached the Chambois – St-Lambert area, with the main body of 1 SS-Panzer and 2 Pz. Divs, between 0600 and 0700 hrs on 20 August. At about 0700 hrs, artillery fire of an intensity never experienced previously throughout the entire campaign started, obviously in reaction to the breakthrough effected by 353 Inf. Div. and the "Armeechef" (Commander-in-Chief) of the battle group. Owing to the Chambois – St Lambert zone being so crowded with men and material, this fire caused heavy losses.

As the St-Lambert area was again covered by antitank and infantry fire, as well as by fire from tanks, 2 Pz. Div. had to fight anew to break out. From noon on 20 August, enemy tanks also resumed their efforts to penetrate to St-Lambert. Reconnaissance revealed that the road passing through the unmanned locality between Chambois and St-Lambert northeastward was the best covered and the safest. One after the other, Commander 2 Pz. Div., Gen. Freiherr von Luettwitz, himself wounded, sent out separate breakthrough groups at this point, the majority of which managed to get through with comparatively light losses in personnel.

116 Pz. Div., protecting the rear of the XLVII Pz. Corps, had withdrawn during the forenoon on 20 August as far eastward as Hill 168 east of Bailleu[l], without any enemy following up in forces from the west and southwest. After clearing a way through roads in St-Lambert, which were chocked with all types of vehicles that had been destroyed, 116 Pz. Div. succeeded in breaking through with roughly 50 combat vehicles between 2300 and 0100 hrs in the night 20/21 August without serious losses. Artillery fire and bombings by the enemy had indicated which roads were apparently clear of the enemy. In spite of the radio order, the battle group of this division that had been committed in Argentan failed to make contact, and, after an unsuccessful attempt to effect a breakthrough at Trun, was captured with its main body.

LXXXIV Inf. Corps had escaped in part from the pocket on 20 August, together with the Corps Staff and the remnants of its battle groups. 363 Inf. Div. covered the rear in the line Bailleu[l] – Bon [?] – Ménil. At this point, enemy pressure was somewhat heavier, so the division slowly withdrew eastward in the course of the day. In three battle groups, this division also broke through via St-Lambert in the direction of Goudehard – Champosoult after dark during the night 20/21 August, beginning about 2200 hrs. One battle group ran up against a combat command of the Polish Armored Div. southwest of Goudehard, but was able to bypass it.

LXXXIV Inf. Corps had detached its forces—namely, 277 Inf. Div. and 12 SS-Pz. Div.—to II Para. Inf. Corps, and parts of these divisions had escaped the pocket together with 3 Para. Inf. Div. and the other breakthrough groups. Considerable portions, however, had been captured by the enemy, particularly parts of the infantry division. The entire Corps Headquarters Staff was also captured by the Polish 1 Armored Div. in the forenoon on 20 August, while trying to break through at St-Lambert. It was purely a matter of luck whether the moment chosen for the attempt to break through happened to be auspicious. The staffs of LXXXIV Inf. Corps and 84th Inf. Div. were the only two out of the 20 higher-level staffs that did not succeed in escaping from the pocket.

Meanwhile, II SS-Pz. Corps, with the Corps command post in a farm east of Vimoutiers, had started its diversionary attack at 0400 hrs on 20 August. The units employed were:

9 SS-Pz. Div., operating from the Vimoutiers region along the Champeaux road toward Trun. This division was weaker than 2 SS-Pz. Div., and, apart from other losses, had lost an entire battalion in the recent fighting against the Polish 1 Polish Armored Division.

2 SS-Pz. Div., operating from the zone south of Vimoutiers in two battle groups, with Pz. Regt Der Fuehrer on the right, the main body of which was to move in a thrust via Camembert toward Neauphe-sur-Dive, and Pz. Regt Deutschland on the left, in a thrust via Champosoult – Goudehard to St-Lambert.

On the Corps left flank, the Reconnaissance Battalion of 2 SS-Pz. Div. was to advance on Mont Ormel.

The attack by 9 SS-Pz. Div. did not get under way properly, as the tanks of the division had not been deployed yet, and the weak combat groups of the Panzer Grenadier regiments were unable to overcome the strong enemy resistance. For this reason, the attack was halted in the heights of Les Cosniers.

In the region north of Goudehard, at Hill 239, 2 SS-Pz. Div. ran into a counterattack launched by the enemy with 60 tanks. How far superior the enemy were is best shown by the fact that the entire 2 SS-Pz. Div. had less than one-quarter of its armor strength. A bitter tank battle developed, without the attack by Corps gaining any further ground toward the southwest. In the meantime, however, the first elements of the various breakthrough groups arrived at the spearheads of 2 SS-Pz. Div. Thus the success achieved by II SS-Pz. Corps lay in fact that their attack had contained the main body of the enemy encircling forces, and thus made it possible at 11 [?] to break out of the pocket.

While, along the front between the Seine and the pocket, the enemy on 19 and 20 August had only probed with reconnaissance detachments, in the course of which he had succeeded in penetrating our own security line at St-Georges-Motel, on 21 August he attacked with his entire US XV and XIX Corps in a northerly direction. As was to be expected, the thin German front was easily broken through. The enemy pushed forward, with his main concentration passing east of Verneuil toward Conches, thereby slicing LXXXI Inf. Corps in halves. 17 Lw Field Div. withdrew to the line Damville – St-André [-de-l'Eure?] – Epieds, attempting as rapidly as possible to reinforce its right wing (Jg. Regt 47) once more with elements of Jg. Regt 34 that had been brought forward. It was therefore possible to hold Damville and St-André, but Conches was lost. Once again, the enemy had struck precisely at the seam between two German units.

The battle group of 331 Inf. Div., which had been reinforced by the elements of Pz. Lehr Div., remained behind, but still held out along the Gacé–Vimoutiers road, north of Gacé. Ahead of the forces of Seventh Army, through which the enemy had broken, the tireless 353 Inf. Div. had again assembled its forces at Mont Ormel. From the countless stragglers, the Divisional Commander, who was slightly wounded, formed one battle group each of Army personnel, paratroopers and men of the SS. To begin with, the high massif of Mont Ormel was occupied. However, as reconnaissance showed that the enemy forces were north of Mont Ormel, the division withdrew behind the Vis [?] sector during the night 20 to 21 August.

II SS-Pz. Corps likewise withdrew behind this sector during the night 20/21 August. During the latter phase of the breakthrough operations, Commander Seventh Army had been seriously wounded while in the front lines. He passed on the command to the senior commanding general, Gen. der Pz. Tr. Freiherr von Funck. From its new command post at Le Sap, Army headquarters once more endeavored to regain control over the forces, but this proved impossible for the time being. Along all roads, the soldiers poured out of the pocket in small groups in a northeasterly direction toward the Seine, carrying only their small arms. The way these overtired, exhausted and starving soldiers persevered in carrying along their machine guns and their Panzerfausts was admirable.

Fifth Panzer Army now assumed control over the entire sector west of the Seine. Seventh Army, the Staff of which was no longer at full efficiency, was assigned the mission of collecting the infantry units east of the Seine. It is now no longer possible to give the exact numerical strength of the units broke out of the pocket, but, on average, the infantry divisions each mustered some 1,500–2,000 men east of the Seine. An average remaining strength of 3,000 men to each Panzer division can be assumed, as their rearward services, being motorized, had been able to escape the encirclement at greater speed, and as their fighting units were stronger on the whole. Hence, roughly 30,000–35,000 men escaped from the pocket. The bulk of the matériel, particularly the artillery, was destroyed.

The Allies gained a great victory at Falaise – Argentan, but it was not complete. It would have been complete had not the seam between the American and the British forces delayed the quick and full encirclement, and the thrust by the American XV and XIX Corps west of the Seine toward the north.

Chapter 12

13–18 August

by Generaloberst Paul Hausser
Translated by EWS (B-179)

13 August 1944

The movements into the new line were carried out during the night, according to plan. There were now leading:

Right: II Para. Corps, with 3 Para. Jg. Div.

Center: LXXXIV Corps, with 363, 353, and 84 Inf. Divs. At this time, there was one regiment from 331 Inf. Div. committed by 353 Inf. Div.

Left: LVIII Pz. Corps, with 2 SS-Pz. Div. and 10 SS-Pz. Div., and units from 708 Inf. Div.—only remnants—with Armored Reconnaissance Bn 9.

The combat style of fighting of the armed forces was now near to that of "prolonged resistance." In contradiction to "pure defense," by which a position is to be defended to the last man, an evading movement is arranged, during which absorption takes place into prearranged rear-area positions. Consequently, more fighting goes on in order to gain time. The enemy is supposed to be induced to reconnoiter, rally, march into position, and make all preparations for the attack. When these are completed, the defender retires, mostly during the night.

This day led to heavy battles in the LXXXIV Army Corps area. The enemy achieved penetrations at a point southeast of Vire, near Great Boursigny [?] – Truttemer-le-Petit, from east of St-Saveur to the forest near St-Christophe. Heavy enemy pressure in the south was directed against Loulay. No communication existed with Panzer Group Eberbach. It seemed that, out ahead of this group, the enemy was pushing ahead in the direction of La Ferté-Macé – Carrouges – Sées. Apparently, the stretch from east of Domfront to west of La Ferté-Macé seemed at this time not to be in danger.

The events which took place at the front and the relief of 2 SS-Pz. Div. made necessary a local withdrawal of the center and the left wing to a line at St-Quentin – 304 – St-Christophe – east bank of the Egrenne – Domfront.

14 August

The attacks were being continued, with their main points of effort from northwest and west, against Tinchebray, and from the south against Domfront. Penetrations had been made near St-Quentin, St-Christophe, and north of Domfront. Here, Hill 201 was also lost. It seemed that the point of main effort was now located here—as before.

Any idea as to the relief of 10 SS-Pz. Div. at this moment had to be rejected. The situation at this time called for a far-reaching decision, if we were to prevent the encirclement threatening. Any thought of launching a counterattack of our own to the coast had now finally to be dropped.

The reestablishment of communication with Panzer Group Eberbach showed that here, too, the plan for an offensive against the threat to the rear of Army Group had to be abandoned. Here it had been of importance only to hold the front to the south; this, too, would be a difficult task. Panzer Group was now standing on a wide front, north of Carrouges, in the line Rânes – Ecouché – Argentan and to the east; in this sequence were 1 SS-Pz. Div., 2 Pz. Div., and 116 Pz. Div.

The Army requested permission for a large-scale withdrawal to the east, to be completed over a period of several nights, with the intention of eliminating the threat (by protection of the flanks) of a breakthrough. To avoid a scattering of the center, and to secure a unified command, it was proposed to subordinate the units on the wings – in the north, to II SS-Pz. Corps, and in the south, to Panzer Group Eberbach. These considerations were based on the new danger arising in the vicinity of Fifth Panzer Army, where a British assault had been launched which had reached Gonde [Condé-sur-Noireau?], 12 km north of Flers.

An evading movement to the area west of the Noireau river, as at first ordered, was now no longer possible. In the night of 15 August, the troops had to be withdrawn behind this stream, into a line from Mont de Cerisi [Cerisé?] – Mont Crespin [?] – hills south of St-Omer—northeast of Domfront.

15 August

The withdrawal movement was carried out without incident; near Tinchebray, it was recognized by the enemy, but just too late. An attack from one of 10 SS-Pz. Div.'s combat groups, near Domfront, resulted in a temporary relief.

The pressure on the front decreased. Conditions at the flanks, however, appeared to have worsened. Despite the fact that a penetration had been made near Condé by the enemy, 9 SS-Pz. Div. had been withdrawn just at this very spot, bringing in its train a weakening of the Fifth Panzer Army's left wing.

In the south, the Panzer Group Eberbach was engaged in stiff defensive battles along a wide front, from north of Rânes to east of Argentan. The main point of effort was believed to be located in the region north of Rânes. Additional enemy forces pushed beyond La Ferté-Macé to La Sauvagère. These were an immediate threat to the rear of Seventh Army. Here, a gap existed which the Panzer Group was likewise unable to close.

This Group intended to rally its two recently assigned divisions (2 and 9 SS-Pz. Div.) for a counterattack in the woods northeast of Argentan. For this, Headquarters LVIII Pz. Corps and 10 SS-Pz. Div. were also supposed to be withdrawn from their former positions and brought up.

A further withdrawal of Seventh Army was approved, and orders were given in the night of 16 August to set up a line behind the Vere stream – Aubusson – east of Flers – La Ferrière and the northern edge of the Forêt d'Andaine. For this, 10 SS-Pz. Div. was to be assembled around Bellou. Leading in the front by this time were:

Right: Corps Headquarters II Para. Corps with three parachute divisions, and 363 Inf.
Div.

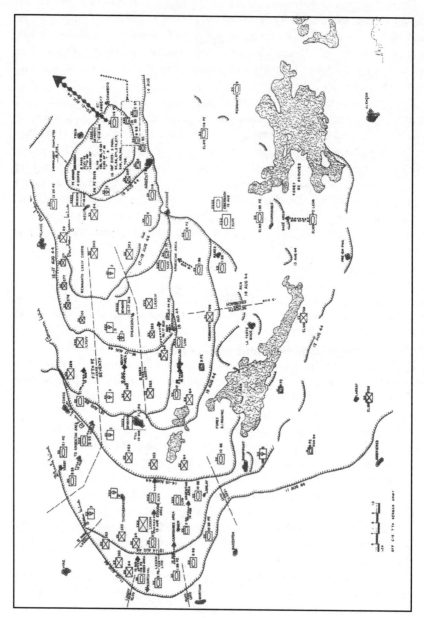

Seventh Army front, 11–21 August 1944.

Left: Corps Headquarters LXXXIV Corps, with 353 Inf. Div., including units from 331 Inf. Div. and 84 Inf. Div.

The Army's advanced CP was transferred to Chênedouit.

16 August

The days from 16 to 18 August were similar—long daily withdrawals, shortening of the front, decreased contact along it, but, in turn, increased pressure on both flanks. The junction with the north remained secure, but in the south gaps occurred which could be closed only at the Orne. Lack of fuel and ammunition remained a depressing daily phenomenon. According to orders, only vitally important combat vehicles were allowed to be taken along; all others had to be destroyed.

On 16 August, skirmishes took place at the front only near Flers, although they had no special significance. Conversely, the attack on both sides of the Forêt d'Andaine, against La Ferrière, and from the south in the direction of Bellou, forced the withdrawal of our southern wing to Saires [-la-Verrerie?] – Buisson [Villons-les-Buissons?], and the recommitment of the previously withdrawn 10 SS-Pz. Div. in an easterly direction, to preserve contact with Panzer Group Eberbach. The situation of both neighboring armies had taken a turn for the worse.

A deep enemy penetration was made in the north, near Falaise. Enemy pressure on Panzer Group Eberbach was especially strong at Argentan, east of Ecouché and Fromentel [?], where the threat of a breakthrough to the Orne appeared. This situation, as well as the developments between Alençon and Chartres, forced a decision on us.

Disengagement and Retreat Behind the Orne

This was executed during the night of 17 August. Strict control from above was particularly necessary for this. 363 and 84 Inf. Divs were to be transferred to Fifth Panzer Army, west of the Orne.

Orders issued now were as follows:

1. Next line of resistance behind the Rouvre in line Bréel—N.D. [-Notre-Dame-] du-Rocher – Ste-Opportune – Briouze – Faverolles.
2. Occupation of this line only with partial forces. 363 Inf. Div. ahead to Neuvy, 84 Inf. Div. to Rônai.
    The other divisions on the Orne with a bridgehead on the west bank.
3. Unified control and supervision of the river crossing by Corps Headquarters LVIII Pz. Corps. Use of bridges for retreat or bringing up of ammunition. etc., to be only one-way.
4. 10 SS-Pz. Div. assigned to Group Eberbach, on the Orne, southeast of Putanges [-Pont-Ecrepin?].

17 August

All movements ordered were carried out without incident. No enemy interference was experienced, until north of Briouze. Adjoining on the south and near Fromentel, the enemy started to launch strong attacks. The success of the latter was alarming. However, it was

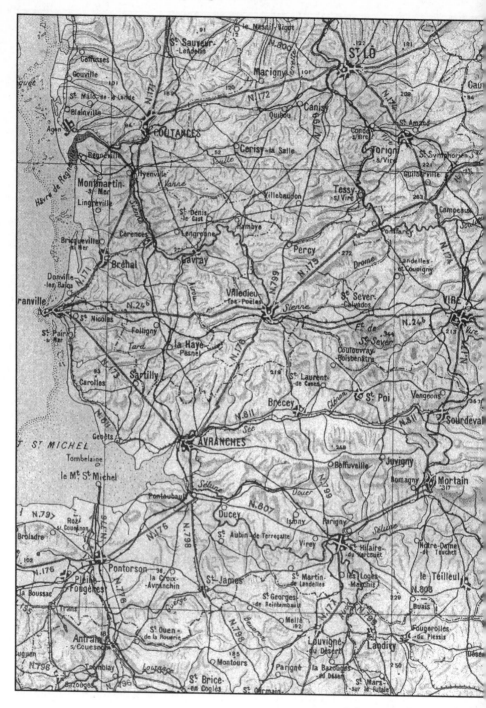

A German Army map of the area

of the breakout and the Falaise Gap.

possible to prevent any serious consequences therefrom, and this position could be held until nightfall.

Panzer Group Eberbach turned its western wing back, and crossed the Orne under the protection of 2 Pz. Div. and 10 SS-Pz. Div. Our resistance at Argentan was successful. Further to the east, the enemy attacks were increasing in intensity against Le Bourg-St-Léonard (116 Pz. Div.).

The Army's advanced CP was transferred to Nécy.

18 August

In spite of the very difficult local conditions (very steep river banks and very few bridges), enemy artillery fire, and fighter-bomber surveillance, our troops succeeded in crossing the Orne.

The bridgeheads had held out. Losses caused through fighter-bomber activity during our crossing were kept to a minimum. This was due to the loosening-up and wide dispersal of the formations, the distribution of the movement over two nights, and the strict regulation of the traffic over the bridges (bridge commanders, widely separated points of departure for the retreat, telephone contact between the commanders, start of any retreat only when signal given of a clear road, ruthless removal of broken-down vehicles).

East of the Orne, the bushy terrain of Normandy came to an end. Here, the terrain offered no cover at all. The number of disabled tanks and vehicles, knocked out by the enemy air force, increased to alarming proportions.

On 18 August, it because clear that the area of Falaise – Argentan would become a trap for units of the Fifth Panzer Army, Seventh Army, the Panzer Group Eberbach.

During the night, CinC Seventh Army and CinC Panzer Group Eberbach were ordered to report on 18 August to the new CinC Army Group, FM Model. Therewith, personal subordination on my part came to an end. FM von Kluge was of the same age and came from the same cadet corps as myself. In spite of this, I had to work with him for the first time as his subordinate. I admire him as a soldier of great ability. As a superior he was not easy-going; he realized the seriousness of the situation fully. In spite of occasional disagreements with him, my admiration for him did not decrease.

I saw it as my duty not to try to get out of the pocket in the tense situation prevailing, and ordered the Chief, Brig. Gen. Frhr von Gersdorff, to proceed to Army Group. 363 and 84 Inf. Divs were now allotted to Corps Headquarters Fifth Panzer Army (Gen. of the Inf. Straube), to whom the CinC Seventh Army subordinated himself during 19 August. The Corps' divisions consisted only of weak remnants.

The British now pushed ahead from the east to Trun; another attack along the Falaise – Argentan highway gained ground up to Nécy, so that the Army's CP had to be hurriedly moved to Villedieu. During this, we lost our radio posts. Severe battles raged for the narrow mountain ridges northwest of Nécy—262–255–245. The Orne could not be held against severe enemy pressure from the south: the superior enemy, with his fighter-bombers and artillery, worked his will in the open and uncovered terrain here. During the noon hours, 353 Inf. Div. carried out an evading movement to the line Neuvy – Courteilles – Vaux.

All divisions in the front were now commanded by Corps Headquarters II Para. Corps. Corps Headquarters LXXXIV was to be relieved.

The situation of Panzer Group Eberbach, too, had taken a turn for the worse. Ecouché had been lost, and in Argentan fighting still went on. The point of main effort was in the Forêt de Gouffern; Fougy [?], on the eastern edge, fell in the hands of the enemy. Chambois was in danger.

Corps Headquarters II Para. Corps, which had been brought up by Fifth Panzer Army to Panzer Group Eberbach, had been shifted into the Vimoutiers area by Army Group; Seventh Army's attempt to subordinate and send in the latter, and to have it to hold open the rear, failed.

Chapter 13

19–20 August

by Generaloberst Paul Hausser
Translated by Thomas Woltjer (B-179)

American forces were located further east, south of Gacé, the 3rd US Army, in the region of Dreux and Chartres, west of Paris.

More exact details regarding the Falaise – Argentan region are not known, owing to the transfer of the Army CP, and the loss of radio posts. This applies especially to parts of the 5 Panzer Army. It was impossible to establish contact with the LXXIV Corps Headquarters.

Gen. von Gersdorff returned unexpectedly that evening. He had detected a gap near Chambois, between the British and the Americans. He brought the following instructions from Field Marshal Model: "The Army is to withdraw behind the River Dives, which is to be held. II SS-Pz. Corps, gathered around Vimoutiers, is to launch an attack to the southwest, to relieve the situation along the approximate line of Trun. More news is not yet available."

It was obvious that it could no longer be a matter of systematic retreat, but, on the contrary, a breakout to the east. It remained a question as to how long the narrow pass between Trun and Chambois would remain usable; and we still lacked precise news, particularly of certain portions of Fifth Panzer Army. It seemed as though some of them were still located in the corner between the La Baise [Baïse?] stream and the Orne. The front had been pushed back approximately to the railroad, south of Rônai.

The night of 18 and day of 19 August had to be taken advantage of to clear details on the situation, and to issue the orders required for the breakout which was to take place during the night of 19 August.

The harassing fire at night—coming concentrically from every direction—became unusually fierce. This was judged to be a preparation for storming our positions. Over half of the officers of the CP in Villedieu were wounded, and consequently rendered *hors de combat*.

19 August

Many details remain unclarified in regard to 19, and particularly 20, August, and, more especially, concerning units under Fifth Panzer Army and the Eberbach Panzer Group, encircled at the time.

It was quickly clear that the pocket would soon be closed. Chambois was occupied. English and American troops had linked up with one another. The pressure from the south and southwest continued. A deep penetration occurred in the Forêt de Gouffern, east of the road from Argentan to Chambois. Troop columns and individual vehicles had endeavored to escape to the east during the night. These attempts continued during the course of the next day, especially for the sake of the wounded. The enemy artillery assaults continued through the entire day. Activity in the air was very lively, despite the fact that the fighter-bombers were apparently not engaged, for fear of injuring their own troops. The roads were blocked in many places by destroyed vehicles. Ammunition blew up frequently, and fuel supply trucks were burning.

The thought of deliverance was most likely uppermost in the minds of the rearward troops. They were, and remained, at the disposition of their COs, generally speaking.

LXXXIV Corps Headquarters, although superfluous on the west front, was again committed for the sake of control aims, to take command on the northeast front of 12 SS-Pz. Div., 84 Inf. Div., and the last few remnants of 89 and 277 Divs.

Preparatory orders for the breakout planned were given early.

Further news was still not available concerning the situation of LXXIV Corps Headquarters, 363 Inf. Div., and remnants of 326, 271, and 276 Inf. Divs, the main body of which still appeared to be west of the road from Falaise to Argentan. II Para Corps, with 3 Para. Jg Div., 353 Div. and a third of 331 Div., had withdrawn to the heights east of the railroad.

It transpired that the advanced CP of Seventh Army was the only higher-ranking headquarters to be restricted in the pocket. I succeeded in maintaining personal contact with all the Corps Headquarters, and in issuing orders for the night. This succeeded in the afternoon likewise with LXXIV Corps Headquarters. The gist of the verbal instructions given is as follows:

> A breakout from the pocket during the night of 19 August. II SS-Pz. Corps will thrust from the outside, from the direction of Vimoutiers, to absorb the units in and south of Trun. Further details not known.

Direction of thrust:

LXXXIV Corps HQ	on both sides of Trun	Leaving behind the rearguards, who would follow later, and who would stage a prolonged battle at Dives.
II Para. Corps	on both sides of St-Lambert	

> LXXIV Corps Headquarters will be in command of the of the west front and is to follow up as rearguard.
>
> Eberbach Panzer Group, whose Commander-in-Chief had not succeeded in breaking through the enemy barricading line, will forget about the left wing for the time being and will thrust with the right wing, under the protection of rearguards, over Chambois and northward. Both it and the left wing will join up.

Assembling areas:

> Panzer forces will immediately be pulled through the gap and will assemble in the Orville – Mardilly – Le Sap district.
>
> II Para Corps is to collect on the elevated terrain north of Caudehard – Mont Ormel.
>
> LXXXIV Corps will thrust towards Camembert.
>
> LXXIV Corps will be pulled through the gap in the Vic[ques?] district, south of Vimoutiers.

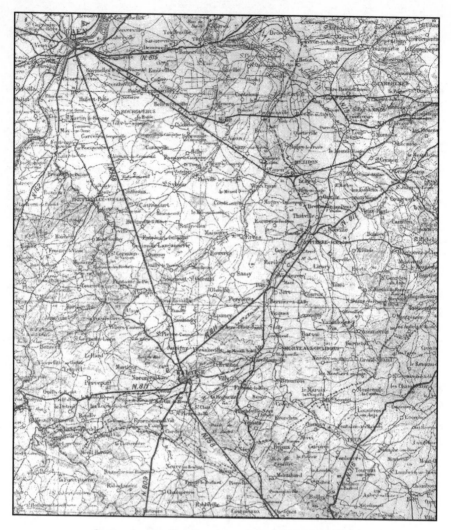

German Army tactical map of the area from Caen to Falaise
and the German escape routes to the west.

Scheduled time for the above operation: "At onset of darkness."

Commanding General LXXXIV Corps reported in the afternoon that a breakthrough in the direction of Trun would be impossible with his weak group against the strong enemy. He proposed a breakout in the area assigned to II Para Corps. This was authorized.

12 SS-Panzer Division behind Eberbach Panzer Group.

Foot-troops were to move off behind II Para Corps.

The enemy artillery fire diminished in fierceness towards evening. The night was very dark but the weather dry.

20 August

For further details of the breakout, see individual reports. The Army itself was not engaged here. (A man can only describe his own personal experiences!)

As more than half of the weakened command staff officers of the Army had been wounded (including, at last, the Chief of the General Staff), it became essential to assign those officers unable to march (i.e., to convey them by armored car) to the Staff of Eberbach Panzer Group. The Commander-in-Chief himself, with two or three others, joined the Staff of 3 Para. Div. and II Para Corps, who were marching on foot. The movement started at 2200 hrs, from the district northwest of Villedieu, with a precise compass reading to the east. The command was taken over after the loss of the Commander 3 Para Div., Maj. Gen. Schimpf, by Gen. of Paratroops Meindl.

Many delays supervened on the near side of the Dives, owing to delaying fire from Panzers and antitank guns. We had to cross the Dives without a bridge. On both sides of the stream, artillery fire, mainly from Panzers [enemy tanks], opened up fiercely. The group was consequently very quickly scattered.

After daybreak, when taking refuge in a farm building northeast of St-Lambert, I was able to confirm that a Polish armored unit had apparently been sent in here. The noise of battle increased, and arose gradually in a southern direction to unusual intensity.

After collecting a combat group from members of the Army, the Air Force and the SS, I committed it to an attack against the road from St-Lambert to Coudehard. Here, too, a penetration seemed to have succeeded, as a long column of motor vehicles of all sorts was moving in this direction (apparently, this was the thrust described by Gen. von Gersdorff). It stopped after reaching the road, accompanied by fire from easterly and southerly directions. Only after organizing further combat groups and carrying out reconnaissance could movement be resumed. It appears that Gen. von Gersdorff left us here. The road was soon blocked again. At the northern extension of Mont-Ormel, 1½ km north of Coudehard, enemy tanks barricaded the road and set fire to a row of vehicles. Consequently, the whole road was now blocked. At the same time, heavy artillery fire arose from a direction which was not ascertained.

We had to await the onset of darkness, when we succeeded in organizing a small Panzer combat group, which was supplied with fuel collected from abandoned vehicles, and in preparing for the breakout which was to take place during the night. I was then wounded by artillery fire.

A rally again took place in the open field at about 2100 hrs. The night was cloudy and wet. I cannot give the routes, but at all events we reached the Reconnaissance Battalion of 2 SS-Pz. Div. before break of day on the 21 August.

I immediately went via II SS-Pz. Corps Headquarters to the advanced CP of Seventh Army, to Le Sap. Gen. von Gersdorff had already found the opportunity to enlighten Army Group here about the prevailing situation.

The breakout had succeeded on the whole, with a comparatively large number of troops, especially in the case of Seventh Army; it was otherwise in the case of remnants of Fifth Panzer Army. The material loss was great. Of the higher staffs, only LXXXIV Corps was missing; it had been at the front since the beginning of the invasion.

See report of Gen. von Gersdorff for further measures. I did not take part in these, as I turned the command over at noon to Gen. der Pz. Tr. Frhr von Funk, XLVII Pz. Corps, as the senior officer.

Due to the fact that the Army Staff was no longer fit for combat, command was taken over of all units of Fifth Panzer and Seventh Armies by the first-named under Gen. der Pz. Tr. Eberbach.

Chapter 14

The Attack on Alençon
by 2nd Panzer Division

by General Heinrich Freiherr von Luettwitz (A-856)

The strength of 2 Pz. Div. on Aug. 13, 1944 was about: 3–4000 men, 25–30 tanks, 800–900 vehicles and some 40 guns. It was planned to assemble the XLVII Pz. Corps (Leibstandarte, 2 Pz. Div., 116 Pz. Div., and, later, SS-Reich), in the Forêt d'Ecouves and to attack through Alençon to the south and southwest, to clear the vicinity of Alençon and to destroy the enemy armored units (US 5 Armored Div. and French 2 Armored Div.), then to push the enemy back to Mayenne and further to the southwest.

LXXXI A. Corps was to participate with 708 Div, 9 Pz. Div. and Pz. Lehr Div. These LXXXI A. Corps units were practically nonexistent; only Pz. Lehr Div. consisted still of a small combat group. The enemy closed in on the assembly areas and forced the arriving units to take up immediate defensive measures, in order to keep their areas. The enemy thrust through Alençon and the north, and reached the vicinity south of Argentan. These circumstances made it impossible to carry out the attack as planned. Group Eberbach had been forced to go over to the defensive.

2 Pz. Div. was still on the way to its assembly area, when new orders were given to assemble in the vicinity east of Carrouges.

Nothing could be heard about the situation in which the LXXXI A. Corps was in, or the situation of Pz. Lehr Div. It was known that 116 Pz. Div. was on its way to a assembly point south of Argentan, but met strong enemy Panzer [armored] units and was then engaged in a bitter battle.

2 Pz. Div. was, on August 13, on the march with two columns. The northern column went through: Yorandes [Yvrandes?], St-Cerniere [St-Céneri?], Chanu, Bellou, Lignou, and Rânes, the southern column through Plaitre [?], Larchamp, L'Epine-d'Orbire [?], La Ferrière-aux-Etangs, St-Maurice, and La Ferté-Macé. Because of continued aerial attacks, these columns only reached the Domfront – Flers line by 13 August. The march was continued by 2300 hrs on 13 August, so that the main body reached Rânes by 14 August. Only the Reconnaissance Battalion arrived in St-Martin-des-Landes, south of Carrouges, on 13 August, at about 1000 hrs, and began to clear out the area to the south and east. Units from the Rcn Bn may have been in Ciral on 13 August. Connections with 9 Pz. Div. were nonexistent. Approximately 300 men of the division were captured in the pocket of Les Noës [?], and parts of other units. The line of departure had been ordered by the Army from Rânes – Ecouché to the northeast.

After 13 August, all contact with Gen. Eberbach was lost, and therefore 2 Pz. Div. was placed under the command of XLVII Pz. Corps.

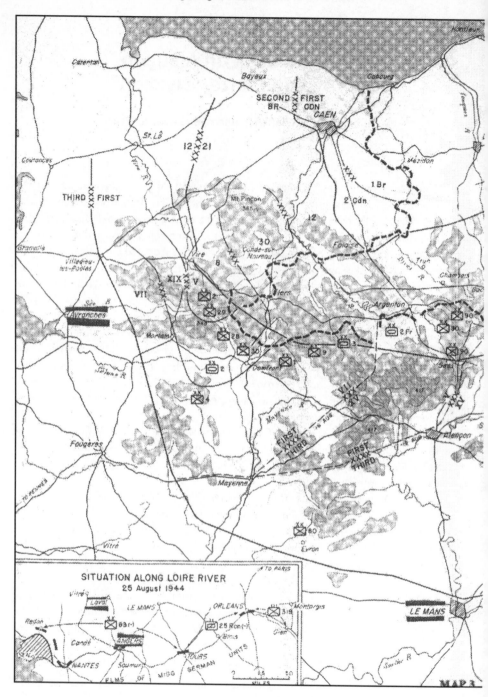

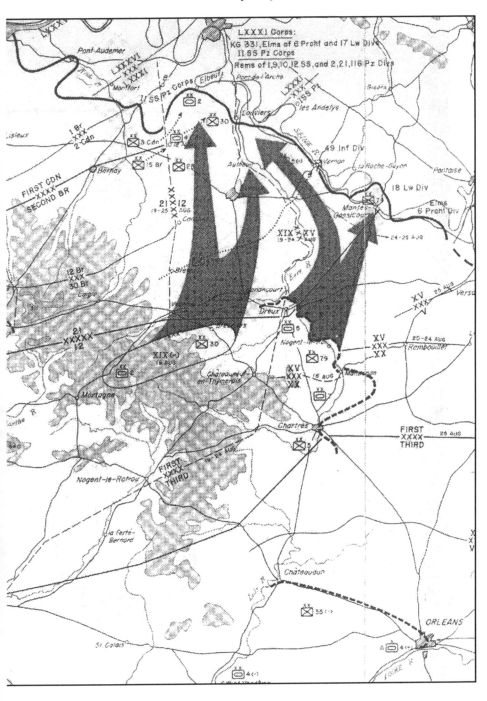

APPENDICES

Appendix 1:
Units of the Seventh Army, 24 July 1944 (B-722)

3 Fallsch. Jg. Div.	Fully qualified; about 80% of authorized strength
Fallsch. Jg. Regt 15	Limited combat-fitness; about 50% of authorized strength
352 Inf. Div.	Battle-weary; about 25% of authorized strength
Kampfgruppe, 266 Inf. Div.	Battle-weary; only remnants
Kampfgruppe, 353 Inf. Div.	Battle-weary
Pz. Lehr Div.	Still qualified; about 50–60% of authorized strength
Kampfgruppe Heinz, 275 Inf. Div.	About 50% of authorized strength
17 SS-Pz. Gren. Div.	Limited combat fitness; about 50% of authorized strength
5 Fallsch. Jg. Div.	Limited combat fitness; no combat experience
2 SS-Pz. Div.	Fully qualified; about 75% of authorized strength
Fallsch. Jg. Regt 6, 2 Fallsch. Jg. Div.	Battle-weary
9 Airborne Div.	Battle-weary; only a few hundred men combat strength
Kampfgruppe 343. Inf. Div.	Battle-weary; only remnants.
Kampfgruppe 265. Inf. Div.	Battle-weary; only remnants.
243. Inf. Div.	Battle-weary; about 25% of authorized strength
275 Inf. Div, without Kampfgruppe Heinz	About 40% of Div.; full (?), as yet not committed; no combat experience
353 Inf. Div., without Kampfgruppe at 352 Inf. Div.	Limited combat fitness, about 40% of authorized strength

Appendix 2:
Commanding Officers in Seventh Army, 24 July 1944 (B-722)

Panzer Group West: List of Commanding Officers, 24 July 1944
(Effective 1 August, Fifth Panzer Army)

Panzer Group West:	Commander-in-Chief	Gen. der Pz. Tr. Eberbach
	Chief of General Staff	Gen. Lt. Gause
	Ia	Oberstlt. i.G. von Rottberg

247

	OQ	Oberstlt. i.G. Colsmann
LXXXVI Army Corps	Commanding General	Gen der Inf. von Obstfelder
	Chief-of-Staff	Oberst i.G. von Wissmann
711 Inf. Div.	Commander	Gen. Reichardt
	Ia	Oberstlt. i.G. Vogt-Rueschewey
346 Inf. Div.	Commander	Gen. Diestel
	Ia	Oberstlt. i.G. Frank
21 Pz. Div.	Commander	Gen. Feuchtinger
	Ia	Oberstlt. i.G. von Berlichingen
16 Lw. F. Div.	Commander	Gen. Sievers
	Ia	
I SS-Pz Corps	Commanding General	SS-Obergruppenfuehrer Dietrich
	Chief-of-Staff	Brigadefuehrer Kraemer
12 SS-Pz Div	Commander	SS-Oberfuehrer Meyer
	Ia	
1 SS-Pz Div	Commander	SS-Oberfuehrer Wisch
	Ia	
II SS-Pz Corps	Commanding General	SS-Obergruppenfuehrer Bittrich
	Chief-of-Staff	SS-Standartenfuehrer Piepkorn
9 SS-Pz. Div.	Commander	SS-Oberfuehrer Stadler
	Ia	
10 SS-Pz. Div.	Commander	SS-Oberfuehrer Harmel
	Ia	
277 Inf. Div.	Commander	Gen Praun
	Ia	Oberstlt. i.G. Frhr von Wangenheim
XLVII Pz. Corps	Commanding General	Gen. der Pz. Tr. Frhr von Funck
	Chief-of-Staff	Oberst i.G. Reinhardt
276 Inf. Div.	Commander	Gen. Badinski
	Ia	
326 Inf. Div.	Commander	Gen von Brabich-Waechter
	Ia	Oberstlt. i.G. Marcks
2 Pz. Div.	Commander	Gen. Heinrich Frhr von Luettwitz
	Ia	Oberstlt i.G. Weiz
116 Pz. Div.	Commander	Gen. Gerhard Graf Schwerin
	Ia	Oberstlt. i.G. Guderian
Being brought up:		
272 Inf. Div.	Commander	Gen Schack
	Ia	
271 Inf. Div.	Commander	Gen Dannhauser
	Ia	
89 Inf. Div.	Commander	Gen. Heinrich
	Ia	Oberstlt i.G. Neitzel
LXXIV Army Corps	Commanding General	Gen. der Inf. Straube
	Chief-of-Staff	Oberst i.G. Zoeller

Commanding Officers of Units of Seventh Army
Committed in Brittany, 24 July 1944

XXV Army Corps	Commanding General	Gen. der Inf. Fahrenbacher
	Chief-of-Staff	Oberst i.G. Beder
77 Inf. Div.	Commander	Oberst Becherer
	Ia	
266 Inf. Div.	Commander	Gen. Spang
	Ia	
343 Inf. Div.	Commander	Gen. Rauch
	Ia	
2 Fallsch. Jg. Div.	Commander	Gen. Ramcke
	Ia	
265 Inf. Div.	Commander	Gen. Duewert
	Ia	
319 Inf. Div.	Commander	Gen. Graf Schmettow
	Ia	

(Excepting 319 Inf. Div., all the other divisions had transferred Kampfgruppen of regimental strength to the Normandy Front.)

Commanding Officers of Seventh Army, 24 July 1944

AOK 7	Commander-in-Chief	Gen. Ob. der Waffen SS-Hausser
	Chief of General Staff	Gen. Maj. P Pemsel
	Ia	Oberst i.G. Helmdach
	OQ	Oberst i.G. Wolff
II Fallsch. Jg. Korps	Commanding General	Gen. der Fallsch. Tr. Meindl
	Chief of General Staff	Oberst i.G. Blauensteiner
3 Fallsch. Jg. Div.	Commander	Gen. Schimpf
	Ia	Maj. i.G. Wagner
352 I Div	Commander	Gen. Kraiss
	Ia	Oberstlt. i.G. Liegelmann
LXXXIV A.K.	Commanding General	Gen von Coltitz
	Chief of General Staff	Oberstlt. i.G. Criegern
Pz. Lehr Div.	Commander	Gen. Bayerlein
	Ia	Maj. i.G. Kaufman
5 Fallsch Jg. Div.	Commander	Gen Wilke
	Ia	
17 SS-Pz. Gren. Div.	Commander	SS-Oberfuehrer Baum
	Ia	
2 SS-Pz. Div.	Commander	SS-Brigadefuehrer Lamerding
	Ia	
91 Airborne Div.	Commander	Oberst Koenig
	Ia	Oberstlt. i.G. Bickel
243 Inf. Div.	Commander	Oberst Klosterkaemper
	Ia	Maj. i.G. Gemmerich

Reserves:

275 Inf. Div.	Commander	Gen. Schmidt
	Ia	Oberstlt. i.G. Hass
353 Inf. Div.	Commander	Gen. Mahlmann
	Ia	Oberstlt. i.G. Witte

SOURCES FOR THE ORIGINAL DOCUMENTS

by Generalmajor Rudolf-Christoph Freiherr von Gersdorff

B-722

War Diary of Seventh Army

Report of First US Army

Daily situation maps of 12 Army Group

Reports written by:

Gen. Oberst Hausser, OB Seventh Army, Oberursel, Apr. 1946 (MS # B-179)

Gen. Bayerlein, Commander Pz. Lehr Div., Oberursel, 26 Jan. 1946 (MS # A-901, A-902, A-903)

Gen. Mahlmann, 353 Inf. Div., Oberursel, Mar. 1946 (MS # A-983, A-984)

Gen. Schmidt, 275 Inf. Div., Oberursel, Mar. 1946 (MS # A-975, A-973)

Gen. der Fl. Meindl, II Fallsch. Corps, England, 20 Apr. 1946 (MS # A-923)

Gen. Frhr von Luettwitz, 2 Pz. Div., St-Germain, Nov. 1945 (MS # A-904)

Gen. Graf Schwerin, 116 Pz. Div., Oberursel, 1945 (ETHINT 17)

Oral information received from:

Gen. Pemsel, Chief of Staff Seventh Army

Gen. Bittrich, II SS-Pz. Corps

Gen. Dannhauser, 271 Inf. Div.

Gen. Praun, 277 Inf. Div.

Gen. Sievers, 16 Lw. F. Div

Oberst i.G. Frank, Ia, 346 Inf. Div.

Oberst Neitzel, Ia, 89 Inf. Div.

Oberstlt. Ziegelmann, Ia, 352 Inf. Div.

B-723

War Diary of Seventh Army

Report of First US Army

Daily situation maps of 12 Army Group

MS # B-179: Written report of Genobst. Hausser, OB Seventh Army, Oberursel, Mar. 1946.

MS # A-901, A-902, A-903: Written report of Gen. Bayerlein, Pz. Lehr Div., Oberursel, 26 Jan. 1946.

MS # A-983–984: Written reports of Gen. Mahlmann, 353 Inf. Div., Oberursel, Mar. 1946.

MS # A-973: Written report of Gen.Schmidt, 275 Inf. Div., 1946.

MS # A-923: Written report of Gen. Meindl, II Fallsch. Jg. Corps, England, 20 Feb. 1946.

MS # A-904: Written report by Gen. Frhr. von Luettwitz, 2 Pz. Div., St-Germain, Nov. 1945.

ETHINt-17: Interrogation report of Gen. Graf von Schwerin, 116 Pz. Div., Oberursel, 1945.

Verbal information by:

Gen. Max Pemsel, Chief of Staff Seventh Army up to 28 July 1944.

Oberst i.G. Ziegelmann, Ia 352 Inf. Div.

B-725

War Dary of Seventh Army

Reports of First and Third US Armies

Daily situation maps of 12 US Army Group

MS # B-179: written report by Gen. Oberst Hausser, Oberursel, Apr. 1946

MS # A-922: written report by Gen. Eberbach, England. 1946

MS # A-968: written report by Gen. Elfeldt, England 31 Jul. 1946

MS # A-923: written report by Gen. der Fl. Meindl, II Fallsch. Jg. Corps, England, 20 Apr. 1946

MS # A-902: written report by Gen. Bayerlein, Pz. Lehr Div., Oberursel, 26 Jan. 1946

MS # A-984: written report by Gen. Mahlmann, 353 Inf. Div., Oberursel, Mar. 1946

MS # A-370: written report by Gen. Schmidt, 275 Inf. Div., Oberursel, 1946

ETHINT 17 and ETHINT 18: written report by Gen Graf Schwerin, 116 Pz. Div., Oberursel, 1945

MS # B-445: written report by Gen. Krueger, LVIII Pz. Corps, Oberursel, 1946

MS # A-956: written report by Gen. Heyking, 6 Fallsch. Jg. Div., Oberursel, 1 Jan. 1946

MS # A-904: written report by Gen. Frhr von Luettwitz, 2 Pz. Div., St-Germain, Nov. 1945

MS # A-921: written report by Gen. Frhr von Gersdorff, CinC Seventh Army, St-Germain, Nov./Dec. 1945

MS # B-358: written report by Brigadefuehrer Wisch, I SS-Pz. Div., 4 Jan. 1946

MS # B-163: written report by Gen. Dettling, 363 Inf. Div., Allendorf, 10 Jan. 1946

MS # A-911: written report by Oberst Emmerich, First Army, Allendorf, 3 May 1946

GLOSSARY

AA	antiaircraft
Abn.	airborne
Abt.	*Abteilung* . Battalion, unit.
a.D.	*ausser Dienst* . No longer in active service.
A Gp, A Gr	Army Group
A.K.	*Armee Korps*. Army Corps.
Am.	American
Art.	artillery
Aus.	*Ausbildung*. Training.
Brigf.	*Brigadefuhrer*. Waffen-SS-rank equivalent to Brigadier-General (US) or Brigadier (British).
Buhle	General Walter Buhle, Chief of Staff of OKW (q.v.).
Chef/Chief	Chief of Staff
Chief of WFSTB	Jodl
CofS	Chief of Staff
Div.	Division
Falkenhayn	General Erich von Falkenhayn, Chief of the General Staff 1914–16. Associated with the battle of attrition at Verdun and the concept of *Materialschalcht*, the battle of material.
Fallsch. JG	*Fallschirmjaeger* . Airborne *Luftwaffe* troops, nominally airdrop-capable.
Feld	Field
Felderstatz	Field replacement
FH	*Felbhaubitze*. Field (light) howitzer.
FHq	*Fuehrerhauptquartier*. Hitler's headquarters.
FHW	*Fremde Heere West*. Foreign Armies West (military intelligence).
Flak	*Flug(zeug)abwehrkanone*. Anti-aircraft artillery.
FS Jager	*Fallschirmjaeger* (q.v.)
Genfldm	*Generalfeldmarschall*. Equivalent to General of the Army (US) or Field Marshal (British)
Gen.	*General*. Usually of a branch (e.g., *Panzertruppen*). Equivalent to Lieutenant-General.
Genobst	*Generaloberst*. Colonel-General. Equivalent to General.
Gp	*Gruppe*. Group.

Hauptmann	Captain
Heeres Artillerie	Army-level artillery
Higher Command of German Forces in the West	OB West (q.v.)
HGr	*Heeresgruppe.* Army group.
Hornisse	Self-propelled 88 mm anti-ank gun on a tracked chassis.
Hummel	Self-propelled 150 mm howitzer on a tracked chassis.
I.D.	infantry division
i.G.	*im Generalstabdienst.* General Staff officer.
Jg. Pz.	*Jagdpanzer.* Turretless, tracked AFV with a tank-destroying gun.
Kfgr.	*Kampfgruppe.* Battle group.
Komm. Gen	Commanding General
Kp	*Kompanie.* Company.
KTB	*Kriegstagebuch.* War Diary.
Local defense	Defense of localities that may not make up a continuous defended front
Lw.	*Luftwaffe*
Maj.	*Major.* Major.
MLR	main line of resistance
ObdH	*Oberbefehlshaber der Heeres.* Commander-in-Chief of the Army.
ObdW	*Oberbefehlshaber der Wehrmacht.* Commander-in-Chief of the Armed Forces.
Oberf.	*Oberfuehrer.* Waffen-SS-rank between Colonel and Brigadier.
Oberst	Rank equivalent to Colonel.
Oblt	*Oberstleutnant.* Rank equivalent to Lieutenant-Colonel.
Obstgf.	*Obersturmmbanngruppenfuehrer.* Waffen-SS-rank equivalent to Lieutenant-Colonel.
OB	*Oberbefehlshaber.* Commander-in-Chief.
OB West	*Oberbefehlshaber West.* Commander-in-Chief West (von Kluge from 2 July until his death).
OKH	*Oberkommando des Heeres.* Army High Command.
OKL	*Oberkommando der Luftwaffe.* Air Force High Command.
OKW	*Oberkommando der Wehrmacht.* Armed Forces High Command.
Oqu	*Oberquartermeister.* Assistant Chief of Staff for supply.
Pak	anti-tank gun
Panzerfaust	"Tank fist." Single-shot, man-portable antitank weapon
Panzerjager	tank destroyer.
Panzerschreck	"Tank terror." Reloadable, man-portable antitank weapon
Pionier	combat engineer
PW	prisoner of war
Pz.	*Panzer.* Armor.
Pz IV	Mark/Type IV medium tank armed with 75 mm gun
Pz V	Mark/Type V Panther medium tank armed with long 75 mm gun

Pz VI	Mark/Type VI Tiger heavy tank armed with 88 mm gun
PzG., Pz. Gren.	*Panzergrenadier*. Mechanized infantry.
Qu	*Quartermeister*. Supply (broader than US Quartermaster).
SIGINT	signals intelligence
Stanf.	*Standartenfuhrer*. Waffen-SS-rank equivalent to Colonel.
Stellung	fortress, static
Sturm	storm, assault
Supreme Command	OKW (q.v.)
Von Kluge	Genfldm. Hans von Kluge. Commanded both OBWest and Army Group B (q.v.) for much of the Allied breakout. Holder of the Knight's Cross with Oakleaves and Swords.
Warlimont	Gen. Walter Warlimont. Deputy Chief of the Operations Section of OKW.
Werf.	*Werfer*. Multiple rocket launcher ("Nebelwerfer").
Werfebrigade	mortar brigade
WFA	*Wehrmachtfuehrungsamt*. Armed Forces Command Office (of OKW).
WFS/WFStab	*Wehrmachtfuehrungstab*. Armed Forces Command Staff (of OKW).
Ia	Operations Staff officer/section. Similar to US G-3, but with broader responsibilities and authority.
Ib	Supply Staff officer/section. Equivalent to US G-4.
Ic	Intelligence Staff officer/section. Equivalent to US G-2 (but could also have operational control of reconnaissance units).